10/98

D0844441

WITHDRAWN

IMAGINING THE EARTH

IMAGINING THE EARTH

Poetry and the Vision of Nature

John Elder

UNIVERSITY OF ILLINOIS PRESS

Urbana and Chicago

Publication of this work was supported in part
by a grant from the Andrew W. Mellon Foundation

This book is printed on acid-free paper.

Library of Congress Cataloging in Publication Data

Elder, John, 1947-
   Imagining the Earth.

   Includes bibliographical references and index.
   1. American poetry—20th century—History and
criticism. I. Title.
PS323.5.E46   1985   811'.54'0936   84-23987
ISBN 0-252-01177-5 (alk. paper)

For Rita

Contents

Acknowledgments

I would like to express my gratitude for the support I received during the writing of this book. Middlebury College assisted me in many ways—from grants covering the costs of research, typing, and permissions to the stimulating conversation of my colleagues and students. I want especially to acknowledge my indebtedness to the members of one class and to one faculty friend. The participants in my 1980 seminar on "The Poetry of Nature" provided an inspiring community in which to explore many of these ideas for the first time. Robert Pack has been my teacher as well as my colleague. Discussing Wordsworth with him deepened my understanding of the "feelings and emanations" through which poetry's landscape lives. This book was largely completed during 1981–82, when I held a fellowship from the National Endowment for the Humanities; I very much appreciate the generosity of that award.

Other friends around the country helped me a great deal. Lowell Turner, Hyatt Waggoner, and my father, James Lyn Elder, entered sympathetically into this book's design and, once inside, made numerous perceptive suggestions about how the structure might be tightened up or made more accessible. Jefferson Hunter, Bryan Wolf, and John Tallmadge have contributed so much to my work over the years that their assistance with this project is inextricable from a much longer history of kindness. Whatever faults this writing retains, it profited enormously from the discernment of all these lovers of poetry and nature. Finally, I want to thank my wife, Rita Lenore, for her discriminating and encouraging involvement with this book at every stage of its development. It is dedicated to her.

Introduction

THE ATTENTIVENESS to nature distinguishing today's American poetry often expresses itself as hostility toward Western civilization. Poets' vivid and informed response to the earth can also foster a revitalized sense of tradition, however, a vision of human culture in harmony with the rest of the natural order. Thus, poetry comes to resemble Hebrew prophecy in its quality of alienated authority. A solitary voice from the mountains calls upon the community to renew itself; a socially eccentric impulse makes possible a more balanced culture, concentric with the planet. In their imaginative passage from estrangement to transformation and reintegration, poets enact a circuit of healing. They move, in Coleridge's terms, beyond an art brilliant with the "hectic of disease" to one "grounded in cultivation" and offering "the bloom of health."[1] America's poetry of nature arises from the fever of cultural dividedness—man against nature, past against present, intellect against senses—but discovers grounds for reconciliation in the inextricable wholeness of the world.

My interest, then, is in that grounded cultivation which today's poetry manifests. With regard neither to poets' attitude toward tradition nor to culture's relation with the earth can there be a simple progression from estrangement to reconciliation; there must rather be a form of dialectic. I have not attempted to explore this process through any comprehensive survey of current American poetry. Instead I have chosen to focus on several writers who have been important to my own vision of nature and culture. By quoting extensively from these poets and by paying close attention to their complex and shifting responses to the natural world, I have tried to avoid the thematic linearity of a more inclusive study. Such concentration on just a few contemporary poets has also allowed for a fuller treatment of the specific tradition within which I read them, and which they make more vividly available to me.

The three sections of this book define my sense of the major dichotomies within American poetry's natural vision. The first section, "The Wasteland and the Wilderness," deals directly with the relation between attentiveness to nature and alienation from tradition. Robinson Jeffers is one of the most important precursors of contemporary nature poetry, especially in his radical critique of Western civilization. Through comparing the poetry of Jeffers first with that of Wordsworth and then with Eliot's *Waste Land*, the initial chapter of the section addresses the origin and instability of the poetry of cultural despair. To move on to the work of Gary Snyder, as the second chapter does, is to find a renewed effort at constructing a cultural wholeness that is also respectful of the larger balance of life on the earth. Snyder's social vision brings contemporary poetry of nature into a fruitful dialogue with such cultural critics as Arnold and Eliot; their premises, subject matter, and experience are obviously very different from Snyder's, but they ask many of the same questions, and with an urgency comparable to his. The first section concludes with a chapter discussing three current writers— Snyder, Wendell Berry, and Robert Pack—who are trying in their different ways to advance the process of cultivation and connectedness, through reverence for nature that is rooted in one chosen place.

"A Something Given," the second principal section, investigates the ways in which inner and outer landscapes inform and sustain one another. Wordsworth prepares for the synthesis of contemporary poetry in this regard. In his transfiguration of the ordinary, he anticipates the close, sustained attentiveness to nature in writers today, while at the same time establishing firm links with Milton and the epic tradition. He also displays a notable resemblance to the Japanese poet Bashō, and through him to the traditions of Zen and haiku which have contributed in such important ways to contemporary poetry of nature. If Wordsworth's gift to poetry is an actual earth, the extension of his vision in the poetry of Denise Levertov and William Everson is an awareness of the *body* as a world of experience. In the second chapter of the section I consider some of the ways in which those poets emphasize the body's immediacy. The third chapter focuses on the vision of A. R. Ammons, for whom the mental sphere expands to comprehend the swirls of body and earth. Ammons's poetry is a lyric of self-awareness, but, like Wordsworth, he is also taking a long walk through the world.

The book's concluding section, on "The Science of the Heart," treats one of the major contributions of poetry to contemporary culture. By assimilating scientific insights, poets carry out a crucial realignment of Western tradition. Whitehead's process-thought provides a framework for discussing the ecological and geological approach of these poets. In addition to its consideration of Whitehead, the initial chapter of the section treats Annie Dillard and Peter Matthiessen, as exemplars of the ecstatic science which Whitehead invokes. I return in the next chapter to Gary Snyder and A. R. Ammons, for both of whom science is a crucial ingredient of poetic vision. Their formal innovations reflect the earth's own vast cycles, while the incandescent particulars of their poetry reveal such processes as implicit in every aspect of the natural world. The final chapter draws the argument to its conclusion, first by relating the metaphors of reconciliation from each of the three main sections and then by connecting that larger metaphorical pattern back to the discussion of wilderness and poetry at the book's beginning.

There are two essays, separating the first section from the second and the second from the third, that I have called "Excursions." Although these two pieces are closely tied to the surrounding discussions, both thematically and as they advance the sequence of the argument, they are different in one important respect: in general I discuss attitudes toward nature within the context supplied by poetry, but the Excursions are framed instead by certain experiences I have had in the Vermont landscape where my family and I live. It seems important to acknowledge that natural scenes engender and inform meditations on literature as well as the other way around. I also hope through these two essays to convey something of the particular natural settings within which this book was conceived. In the Excursions, as well as in the character of my voice throughout the book, I have tried to emphasize that this consideration of poetry and the vision of nature is highly selective and personal.

Gary Snyder and A. R. Ammons are central to the development and unity of my argument. Snyder figures prominently in Section I, as Ammons does in Section II, and they both enter into Section III. Insofar as this book asserts the reinvention of tradition as a perennial cultural challenge, it is also not surprising that I have continually returned, in thinking about poetry's social function, to my own sense of tradition. Wordsworth, Whitehead, and Eliot are the writers who have particularly influenced my cultural perspective, and in linking them with current poets my intent has been, on either hand, one of grateful acknowledgment. The poems of Wordsworth, especially, underlie my sense of contemporary poetry's richness and enter as comparisons into a number of the readings here. Zen practice and literature, to which I was first attracted through Snyder's poetry, also help me, at various points in this book, to clarify my responses.

Finally, each section has a pair of concepts which focus it and tie it to the other parts of the volume. These initially opposed terms are represented in Section I by the words *culture* and *wilderness*; in II, by *imagination* and *landscape*; and in III, by *science* and *poetry*. The essentially circular nature of my argument reflects my sense that these terms, within an expanded context, become synonyms. New responses to nature may initially come into conflict with older expressions, but as Whitehead reminds us, "A clash of doctrines is not a disaster—it is an opportunity."[2] While insights into nature from Buddhism or from physics and ecology may at first seem foreign to the poetic tradition of the West, we must bear in mind, as *Science and the Modern World* states, that culture, like nature, is "a structure of evolving processes . . . [and] wisdom is the fruit of a balanced development."[3]

SECTION I

Wasteland and Wilderness

The Covenant of Loss

A horseman high alone as an eagle on the spur of the mountain over Mirmas Canyon draws rein, looks down
At the bridge-builders, men, trucks, and power-shovels, the
  teeming end of the new coast-road at the mountain's base.
He sees the loops of the road go northward, headland beyond
  headland, into gray mist over Fraser's Point,
He shakes his fist and makes the gesture of wringing a chick-
  en's neck, scowls and rides higher.
                    I too
Believe that the life of men who ride horses, herders of cattle
  on the mountain pasture, plowers of remote
Rock-narrowed farms in poverty and freedom, is a good life.
  At the far end of those loops of road
Is what will come and destroy it, a rich and vulgar and
  bewildered civilization dying at the core,
A world that is feverishly preparing new wars, peculiarly
  vicious ones, and heavier tyrannies, a strangely
Missionary world, road-builder, wind-rider, educator, printer
  and picture-maker and broadcaster,
So eager, like an old drunken whore, pathetically eager to
  impose the seduction of her fled charms
On all that through ignorance or isolation might have escaped
  them. I hope the weathered horseman up yonder
Will die before he knows what this eager world will do to his
  children. More tough-minded men
Can repulse an old whore, or cynically accept her drunken
  kindnesses for what they are worth,
But the innocent and credulous are soon corrupted.

Where is
our consolation? Beautiful beyond belief
The heights glimmer in the sliding cloud, the great bronze
    gorge-cut sides of the mountain tower up invincibly,
Not the least hurt by this ribbon of road carved on their
    sea-foot.[1]

Robinson Jeffers's poem "The Coast-Road" begins and ends in
the mountains' beautiful isolation. But between these two moments
the poet, looking out from his fasthold near Big Sur, turns his mind
to the rottenness of cities spreading toward him north and south
along the coast. This is a characteristic circuit in Jeffers's poetry: love
of the wilderness and hatred of civilization feeding on each other.
The polarization of his own feelings is further intensified for Jeffers
by his perception of a larger historical process of estrangement. At
the poem's beginning there is a man in nature, at one with the
mountains. By the end he is gone, and Jeffers has foreseen the
failure of his line; the heights remain, but diminished in extent, and
unpeopled.

Wordsworth's "Michael" provides an illuminating comparison
with "The Coast-Road." Like Jeffers's poem, it both depicts a landscape and relates it to a disrupted family and the end of a way of
life. In some regards the human defeat in Wordsworth's account is
even more final than that in Jeffers's. Not only has the shepherd's
son Luke gone, and with him the shared work that bound father
and son to each other and to the land, but their pastoral culture has
also been eradicated, by the beginnings of commercial agriculture.
The poem closes with Michael's death:

     There, by the Sheepfold, sometimes was he seen
Sitting alone, or with his faithful Dog,
Then old, beside him, lying at his feet.
The length of full seven years, from time to time,
He at the building of this Sheepfold wrought,
And left the work unfinished when he died.
Three years, or little more, did Isabel
Survive her Husband: at her death the estate
Was sold, and went into a stranger's hand.
The Cottage which was named The Evening Star
Is gone—the plowshare has been through the ground
On which it stood; great changes have been wrought
In all the neighborhood; yet the oak is left
That grew beside their door; and the remains

Of the unfinished Sheepfold may be seen
Beside the boisterous brook of Greenhead Ghyll.[2]

In "The Coast-Road," by contrast, the destruction following the
loops of highway is still in the future, to be registered most fully
only after the poet's own life, and after that of the lone horseman.
But the fact remains that Jeffers's poem manifests a bitterness,
directed at the coming human herd, which is notably foreign to
"Michael." In framing his poem's end, Wordsworth lingers sympathetically over the shepherd's visit to the unfinished sheepfold that
was to have symbolized his family's bond with the land.

There is a comfort in the strength of love;
'Twill make a thing endurable, which else
Would overset the brain, or break the heart;
. . . .
. . . 'Tis not forgotten yet
The pity which was then in every heart
For the old man.[3]

Human concern ties poet, reader, and long-dead shepherd together;
the whole poem also shows how the bond of human love strength-
ens each individual's love of the surrounding landscape, just as the
landscape itself has fostered the original growth of that love. Wordsworth's conclusion is the opposite of Jeffers's centrifugal reaction
and reveals the stark contrast between the two poets' worlds.

"Michael" reflects the exploitations, both human and natural, of
England in the industrial revolution. Factories and cities were filled
with a rural population displaced by the Acts of Enclosure; ancient
commons were turned over to large landlords' cultivation of grain.
In such a time, Wordsworth conceived his poem as a way of making
renewed connection between man and nature, of peopling an abandoned landscape. But Jeffers's California—with its tide of new settlement and its powerful technology for clearing timber, blasting
roads, irrigating deserts, and otherwise transforming the face of the
land—was one where continuity between man and nature was shattered, not by the people who went away, but by the droves who
came. The human capacity for subduing nature seemed to Jeffers, as
to many who have lived along his beautiful coast, to have a frighten-
ing momentum. He came to view humanity in the collective as an-
tagonistic to the wild beauty which he loved. In his poetry, as in the
wilderness ethic which he so influenced, Jeffers thus called for a
protective separation between man and nature, rather than striving

like Wordsworth for a balance. This desire for separation often translates, however, into a vision of mankind's obliteration, if it cannot otherwise be contained. Such is the fierce consolation proclaimed by Section V of Jeffers's poem "The Broken Balance":

> Mourning the broken balance, the hopeless prostration of the
>   earth
> Under men's hands and their minds,
> The beautiful places killed like rabbits to make a city,
> The spreading fungus, the slime-threads
> And spores; my own coast's obscene future: I remember the
>   farther
> Future, and the last man dying. . . . [4]

Wordsworth's ambition is for a fruitful reinhabitation of the landscape by human feelings, and a simultaneous possession of the feelings by the earth. Jeffers's hope, expressed at the end of "The Coast-Road" as at many other places in his poetry, rests in a world *devoid* of men, and in that way protected from them.

The drastic difference in Jeffers's and Wordsworth's views of humanity is reflected in the ways "Michael" defines and completes itself through sympathy. Being a lengthy narrative poem it is able to go beyond Jeffers's brief depiction of the horseman—silhouette and shaken fist. The heart of "Michael," over which Wordsworth pauses so long, is the celebration of a harmonious life, and of the process by which human love flows into the larger unity of nature:

> But soon as Luke, full ten years old, could stand
> Against the mountain blasts, and to the heights,
> Not fearing toil, nor length of weary ways,
> He with his Father daily went, and they
> Were as companions, why should I relate
> That objects which the Shepherd loved before
> Were dearer now? that from the Boy there came
> Feelings and emanations—things which were
> Light to the sun and music to the wind;
> And that the old Man's heart seemed born again? [5]

Since "Michael" is a story rather than a vignette, the reader may respond to the human loss, and to the landscape's alteration which registers it, in personal terms rather than in those of Jeffers's more abstract antagonism; compassion and longing become available, as well as rage. Poetry is thus for Wordsworth a landscape of memory, within which an individual may discover a circuit, not of estrangement but of reconciliation—between himself and the earth and, equally, between himself and his race. In the beginning of his poem, Wordsworth takes care to include the reader in such a circuit, sounding the note of sympathy that also reverberates at the end:

> Therefore, although it be a history
> Homely and rude, I will relate the same
> For the delight of a few natural hearts;
> And with yet fonder feeling, for the sake
> Of youthful Poets, who among these hills
> Will be my second self when I am gone.[6]

To turn back from "Michael" to "The Coast-Road" is to recognize the loss of a connection: attentiveness to nature expresses itself, for Jeffers, in a disavowal of civilization and a suspicion of humanity itself. But such alienation, as the Romantics showed, may come paradoxically to serve as the basis for its own countertradition. Robinson Jeffers, in his mountainous austerity, exerted a crucial influence on the naturalist tradition of disenchantment. Considering the tensions within his preference of nature over humanity is thus a way of understanding the conflicts—between animosity and celebration—in the poetry of nature that has followed him. In the way he inaugurates his own tradition by insisting on a central loss, Jeffers is also *akin* to Wordsworth; he too writes for the inspiration of "a few natural hearts." He cannot affirm with the same confidence as Wordsworth a human covenant grounded in the earth. But, in his poetic landscape's estrangement from humanity, he prepares for a new imagination of community, in which the earth and mankind are equally participants.

Jeffers's bond with Wordsworth is clarified by his contrasting affinities with poets of the early twentieth century. His misanthropic strain partakes of the general disillusionment of his generation; and within the context of such cultural despair, his fervid allegiance to the wild lands becomes especially moving. One of the most revealing of Jeffers's voyages beyond humanity is a poem entitled "Life from the Lifeless":

> Spirits and illusions have died,
> The naked mind lives
> In the beauty of inanimate things.
>
> Flowers wither, grass fades, trees wilt,
> The forest is burnt;
> The rock is not burnt.

> The deer starve, the winter birds
> Die on their twigs and lie
> In the blue dawns in the snow.
>
> Men suffer want and become
> Curiously ignoble; as prosperity
> Made them curiously vile.
>
> But look how noble the world is,
> The lonely-flowing waters, the secret-
> Keeping stones, the flowing sky.[7]

In moving beyond "ignoble," "vile" humanity, Jeffers continues to a place beyond all organic life. Revulsion from man and his works turns into rejection of all the mortal world of process and ambiguity. Flowers and grass, deer and birds must also be scoured away before one can come to the vast, elemental "beauty of inanimate things." Such a moment of nonhuman repose is inherently unstable, however: who, in the last stanza, is left to "look"?

This urge for purgation—so thorough that it removes all of life along with its diseased human manifestations—recalls other writers early in the century whose desire was to be washed clean of culture's pollutions. Rupert Brooke, in "Peace," which originally appeared in his volume entitled *1914*, had written of his generation's longing:

> To turn, as swimmers into cleanness leaping
> Glad from a world grown old and cold and weary,
>   Leave the sick hearts that honour could not move,
> And half-men, and their dirty songs and dreary,
>   And all the little emptiness of love![8]

Such a poem, and such an attempt at "cleanness," only makes sense for one who has embraced the prospect of annihilation. Brooke's sonnet concludes, "And the worst friend and enemy is but Death." Writers such as Robert Graves and Thomas Mann have written of the ardor with which young men on both sides of the conflict fled from the disappointments of peacetime into the prospective glory of the Great War. Submission to force does bring an explosive release from the world of irresolution, complexity, disappointment. But it also necessitates the surrender of ordinary happiness and of any prospect for nonviolent relationship. And often, Jeffers's poems of the mountains' austere truth have a resonance with the alienation and self-sacrifice of England's doomed subalterns. Here is the first stanza of "Birth-Dues" (published in 1927):

Joy is a trick in the air; pleasure is merely contemptible, the
    dangled
Carrot the ass follows to market or precipice;
But limitary pain—the rock under the tower and the hewn
    coping
That takes thunder at the head of a turret—
Terrible and real.[9]

Human affirmations of pain, death, and the inanimate are difficult
for the living to maintain for very long. To soldiers who do not die
in the first great burst of war are left the trenches, gangrene, mus-
tard gas, and sleeplessness. Isaac Rosenberg and Wilfred Owen survive Rupert Brooke, and evoke the stutter of lives pinned down by
death.

Repugnance for human life, if it is not stilled in war, must seek
other strategies for withdrawal from humanity. The hawk becomes
an emblem for Jeffers of nature's spirit, and of his own ambition for
a spirit beyond humanity. In the second half of the poem "Hurt
Hawks," though, the persistent deathly implications of such willed
loss of one's own humanity are evident. Jeffers makes it clear
enough that a kind of suicide is still involved, as he scorns his bond
with other men and identifies with the wounded bird.

I'd sooner, except the penalities, kill a man than a hawk; but
    the great redtail
Had nothing left but unable misery
From the bone too shattered for mending, the wing that trailed
    under his talons when he moved.
We fed him six weeks, I gave him freedom,
He wandered over the foreland hill and returned in the eve-
    ning, asking for death,
Not like a beggar, still eyed with the old
Implacable arrogance. I gave him the lead gift in the twilight.
    What fell was relaxed,
Owl-downy, soft feminine feathers; but what
Soared: the fierce rush: the night-herons by the flooded river
    cried fear at its rising
Before it was quite unsheathed from reality.[10]

Like Rupert Brooke and the shattered redtail, Jeffers disdains the
tawdriness of human society and craves the "lead gift" by which he
may be "unsheathed from reality."

T. S. Eliot is the poet who speaks most directly to Jeffers's disillusionment with his own humanity. As does Eliot, Jeffers considers
the "Unreal City" the overwhelming fact of human life.[11] The "Great

Wen" of Wordsworth's contemporary Cobbett has become for these two twentieth-century poets a cancer, and Eliot and Jeffers thus are driven to reject urban, technological culture. But even in their revulsion and anger, they become involved in the inevitable paradoxes of cultural despair. As human beings and as poets, they have nowhere to stand that is not encompassed by the humanity and the culture which they would reject.

Jeffers assumes the cultural decay which Eliot evokes so specifically in *The Waste Land*. An obvious but important point of contrast is that Eliot's lament for civilization is from within the city, by the banks of a weary, history-laden river, while Jeffers glares along the coast at San Francisco from his distant hawk's perch in Big Sur. Thus, while Wordsworth and Jeffers share a natural grounding, but differ in their evaluation of humanity's possibilities, Eliot and Jeffers write from sharply differing urban and mountain landscapes, but share the same view of man and history.

Contemporary American planners, following Ian MacHarg's lead in *Design With Nature*, work with transparent overlay maps, population centers darkened on one, natural resources on another, geological limiting factors on a third. When such maps are superimposed, a composite image emerges from which more meaningful planning can proceed; both the areas of critical congestion and those where thoughtful development remains possible become clearer. Superimposing the terrain of Jeffers's poetry on that of *The Waste Land* has a similar advantage. The problems of civilization, in such an aggregate view, are clearer than in Jeffers's poetry alone. And the impulse in Eliot for transcending the antinatural also registers more strongly. The urban wasteland is revealed as part, after all, of a larger world of mountains and ocean. Seeing the two landscapes on a single map restores the possibility both for a cultural passage into the wilderness and for a corresponding return to humanity. *The Prelude* establishes the precedent for such a poetic map, with its footpaths leading from Cumberland to London, Paris to the Alps, and with the routes Wordsworth discovers through present loss to a sustaining continuity with the past.[12]

The Waste Land's clearest depiction of culture's bankruptcy is in its second section, "A Game of Chess." The lady's dressing room is one in which history and art are manifest only as "withered stumps of time." Both in the passage's parallel with Pope's Belinda and in the extended opening allusion to Cleopatra on her barge, all of the elements for high literary irony are present. But instead of focusing the presence of this ornately framed woman, such associations only serve to emphasize her unsettled, isolated, disturbed state. Culture becomes a distorting hall of mirrors, a malign funhouse of noise and spectacle in which, finally, one is too bewildered to do more than watch. "Ivory and coloured glass," "the sylvan scene" and "the barbarous king" become alike impostures. Mythology is the reminder of an old rape; art, an overelaborate intimidation, serving neither to refresh nor to inspire.

This is, evidently, the dressing room of a wealthy and cosmopolitan woman. But it also exhibits an impoverished culture: "withered stumps of time" which, when they do occasionally become vital influences, are terrifying, "staring forms . . . hushing the room enclosed." In his contempt for modern, "civilized" humanity, Robinson Jeffers implies just such rooms, though he does not himself depict them. There are, further, two specific passages in this section with which Jeffers's own poetry might be connected. Like the nightingale, Jeffers takes recourse by filling "all the desert with inviolable voice"; his poetry, like Philomel's song, testifies to the ravishment of beauty. But though the singer may be isolated, and thus inviolable, "still the world pursues, / 'Jug Jug' to dirty ears."[13] The nightingale above the mantel centers Eliot's scene of desperation and ineffectuality. And Jeffers's song beyond man similarly evokes and focuses the human wasteland all around.

Another way of relating Jeffers to "A Game of Chess" is in "the air / That freshened from the window." Throughout this section of *The Waste Land* there are references to more basic, but avoided, elements of earthly experience. The air, like April at the beginning of Eliot's Section I, "The Burial of the Dead," is "stirring," but in a way cruelly troubling to individuals locked inside an antinatural culture. In such allusions Eliot acknowledges the same loss of natural harmony to which Jeffers's ongoing polemic is addressed. "The wind under the door" is a disturbing, threatening reminder of a world outside. Just as the man and woman in this section cannot communicate with each other, their response to the natural elements is one of isolation and avoidance: "And if it rains a closed car at four." The effect of this episode is one of frustration. A mounting, if still stifled, scream. Jeffers's poetry often reflects this same extreme irritability; the difference between him and the woman with bad nerves is that he *acts* on her momentary impulse of escape: "I shall rush out as I am, and walk the street / with my hair down, so." He follows the wind, rather than "waiting for a knock upon the door."[14] But even when he has left the streets and rooms behind, he carries the bitterness and jangle of the wasteland in his heart. The modern decay drives Jeffers to the mountains; in the beauty of rock and wind he experiences both a vindication and a reminder of his initial, and in some ways primary, emotion of revulsion.

The bitterness of Eliot's allusions also suggests, however, that something precious is being spoiled or overlooked, that much more might have been made of such cultural remains. Jeffers's cultural critique is much more radical. The most important flaw with culture is that it is *human* culture, and people are the disconcerting false note in nature. This proposition, embedded throughout Jeffers's poetry, is brought out most clearly in the final lines of "Shine, Perishing Republic":

> And boys, be in nothing so moderate as in love of man, a
>   clever servant, insufferable master.
> There is the trap that catches noblest spirits, that caught—they
>   say—God, when he walked on earth.[15]

Although Jeffers's critique is a more fundamental one, he and Eliot are nonetheless joined by their sense that modern culture is corrupt precisely because it is cut off from nature's regenerative power. In *The Waste Land*, the city's sterility afflicts the whole world and its pollutions deny the poet any vision of a landscape beyond his spirit's unforgiving desert rocks. Jeffers finds a *perfect* world in rock and ocean, but in order to preserve it must reject any possibility of human contact with it. At the meeting of man and nature there are hurt hawks and coast roads; the holiness of natural beauty is always beyond. Such images of isolation are central in the poetic universes of Eliot and Jeffers, and form a vision of human existence that is scarcely endurable. But in completing the long descent toward despair, a writer may also achieve a certain openness: when all possibilities of affirmation or forward motion seem to be exhausted, there is nothing left but to wait and watch. In such quiet moments, Jeffers experiences a unity beyond the human-natural antithesis, and he finds himself replenished by participation in it. These passages through despair, to a natural attentiveness beyond all isolating dualisms, are Jeffers's great achievement, and the gift he has offered to the poetry of nature following him.

Throughout his writing Jeffers proclaims his urgent desire to give up on humanity, to leave it behind. But occasionally he is able to give up his own bitter anger instead; surrendering himself to unpolemical nature, he conveys to his reader the gift which nature has for a man who can lay down his own assertiveness. In "Return," to me one of the loveliest of all Jeffers's poems, there is a tinge of quiet weariness. As Eliot also acknowledges in *The Waste Land*'s final section, men must come to the point of resignation before they can perceive a world beyond their own projects.

> A little abstract, a little too wise,
> It is time for us to kiss the earth again.
> It is time to let the leaves rain from the skies,
> Let the rich life run to the roots again.
> I will go down to the lovely Sur Rivers
> and dip my arms in them up to the shoulders.
> I will find my accounting where the alder leaf quivers
> In the ocean wind over the river boulders.
> I will touch things and things and no more thoughts,
> That breed like mouthless May-flies darkening the sky,
> The insect clouds that blind our passionate hawks
> So that they cannot strike hardly can fly.
> Things are the hawk's food and noble is the mountain, oh noble
> Pico Blanco, steep sea-wave of marble.[16]

Jeffers can neither tolerate the ugly trivialities of the city nor countenance civilization impinging in his mountainous realm. But he does discover a relation between the wilderness and the wasteland within the oscillation of his own feelings and experience. His need to come to the earth "again" shows that, in the larger pattern of a life, he has had to return to it before. The distracting insect thoughts will return, and even in this poem about his "kiss" he is turning from "things" to the thoughts and words that will express them. But the poem's composure derives from its pleasure in the moment of return for its own sake ("And dip my arms") and from its acceptance of *seasons*—"let the leaves rain from the skies"—that unify the round of life as of a year. Like Keats's "To Autumn," "Return" is a poem of reconciliation through participation; it includes poem and poet alike in nature, disclosing the field where life's beauty and its mortality may meet. The approximation to sonnet form is itself a quiet acquiescence to the value of poetic tradition. Like the marble cliff face, the poem's form has its own inner logic, and Jeffers gives himself to both without striving.

Jeffers finds it hard to allow other people, much less humanity in general, the same circuit of wholeness he occasionally discovers for himself. In this regard he reflects a larger difficulty of lovers of wilderness in our day: when hikers from different parties meet on a mountain's summit, their greeting, if any, often proves to be a wary or resentful one. Human beings spoil the status of wilderness as pristine, a sanctuary from civilization; yet who are *we* who find wilderness thus spoiled by all but ourselves? Jeffers confronts this problem in a wry, courageous poem entitled "People and a Heron," in which he both displays his resistance to other people enjoying his sacred landscape and reflects upon that response.

> A desert of weed and water-darkened stone under my western
>   windows
> The ebb lasted all afternoon
> And many pieces of humanity, men, women, and children
>   gathering shellfish,
> Swarmed with voices of gulls the sea-breach.
> At twilight they went off together, the verge was left vacant,
>   an evening heron
> Bent broad wings over the black ebb,
> And left me wondering why a lone bird was dearer to me than
>   many people.
> Well: rare is dear: but also I suppose
> Well reconciled with the world but not with our own nature
>   we grudge to see them
> Reflected in the world for a mirror.[17]

The final two lines of this poem represent a critical admission on Jeffers's part. The vision of human beings *in* the world troubles his sense of nature as *other*, it violates the blankness of nature which he so prizes. But his honesty here, in acknowledging a reflection of "our own nature" where he would have preferred to avoid it, is the culmination of indications throughout the poem that the people are truly a part of the scene. Even phrases ringing with contempt—"pieces of humanity," "swarmed with the voices of gulls"—also point to people's physical status: they have bodies, they feed, live, and move. To write people off because of the antinatural elements of modern civilization is thus impossible for one who would affirm nature: human beings, and human culture, find their existence in the natural world.

This need to acknowledge a basis for unity with other men, if one is to have open eyes for *all* reflections in the world mirror, answers to the thunder's second command in Eliot's poem: Sympathize.

> DA
> *Dayadhvam:* I have heard the key
> Turn in the door once and turn once only
> We think of the key, each in his prison
> Thinking of the key, each confirms a prison
> Only at nightfall, aethereal rumours
> Revive for a moment a broken Coriolanus.[18]

The principal incentive for sympathy in *The Waste Land* is our common woundedness, our painful loneliness, "each in his prison." The socialite in her art-nouveau dressing room and the toothless woman in the pub suffer alike from a life that has come to be fearful, from marriages that make them all the more isolated from themselves and from the world. In "The Fire Sermon," the narrative of the typist's listless amour is saved from disdainfulness by the poet-onlooker's recognition of kinship with such a state.

> (And I Tiresias have foresuffered all
> Enacted on this same divan or bed;
> I who have sat by Thebes below the wall
> And walked among the lowest of the dead.)[19]

In a poem like "People and a Heron," Jeffers discovers a similar sympathy. Seeing others, in their noisy, human individuality, reflected by the glistening sand-flat of the ebb, he can admit that his nature is as theirs, that in searching the world for an absolute he often descries the features of his own face.

Jeffers goes beyond such a basis for sympathy, though, and glimpses a human kinship with the heart of nature, as well as one that shines on the surface. In the last three stanzas of "Continent's End," Jeffers addresses the ocean, which he has previously envisioned watching the course of human history from its vast and ancient perspective. Besides addressing nature herself as a person—which is a shift from the abstracted voice of "Life from the Lifeless" or the isolated voice of "Autumn Evening"—he is able here to include himself, through the first-person plural form, as "a piece of humanity."

> The tides are in our veins, we still mirror the stars, life is your
>   child, but there is in me
> Older and harder than life and more impartial, the eye that
>   watched before there was ocean.
>
> That watched you fill your beds out of the condensation of thin
>   vapor and watched you change them.
> That saw you soft and violent wear your boundaries down, eat
>   rock, shift places with the continents.
>
> Mother, though my song's measure is like your surf-beat's
>   ancient rhythm I never learned it of you.
> Before there was any water there were tides of fire, both our
>   tones flow from the older fountain.[20]

"Continent's End," like "People and a Heron," struggles against what it affirms. Just as the wet flats mirror the human forms moving across them, people too reflect—in their chemical composition and shape—the ocean from which they emerged and the sky under which they have evolved. But in his final defiance of such a wholly derivative status, Jeffers makes an even more sweeping claim for human unity with nature. Just as the ocean had watched when life "crawled out of the womb and / Lay in the sun's eye on the tide-line," man contains in himself the older eye which watched the ocean's own birth. This is Jeffers's version of Wordsworth's concluding insight in the "Intimations" ode:

> The clouds do take a sober colouring from an eye
> That has kept watch o'er man's mortality.[21]

The imagination that creates man's self-conscious isolation also allows him to comprehend processes integrating his human lot in the turning of the world. Through imaginative investment in the beginning and the end of things, encountering the emptiness from which form arises and to which it perpetually returns, the poet can affirm himself as well as the world. When he can perceive the world from such a lofty perspective that man seems part of the ramifying system of control, then Jeffers can both be true to his revulsion against contemporary culture and affirm a countervision, within which man and nature may alike be valued. In a poem called "The Answer," he begins with a perspective of dreary human immediacy: civilizations always disintegrate, their dreams of good unrealized. But he closes with a cosmic view, characteristically austere, yet in its breadth comforting: man, despite the horrors of his history, may from a sufficient distance still be considered beautiful.

> Integrity is wholeness, the greatest beauty is
> Organic wholeness, the wholeness of life and things, the divine beauty of the universe. Love that, not man
> Apart from that, or else you will share man's pitiful confusions, or drown in despair when his days darken.[22]

Eliot and Jeffers glimpse reconciliations beyond the apparent logic of human history. But both poets find it hard to relate such visions to the present circumstances of civilization. The conclusion of *The Waste Land*, with its heap of fragments, testifies to the difficulty of resolving the thunder's voice with the poet's literary language and tradition. One suggestion as to a hopeful element in the final passage has been that the scraps of various languages represent a magical incantation: only through magic may such a world be healed.

Thus, to move into Sanskrit for the last two lines is an incantatory strategy near to despair: it is a spell in a language so distant, temporally and culturally, as to be practically out of our reach. But there is also another way to hear hope in the last two lines.

> Datta. Dayadhvam. Damyata.
> Shantih. Shantih. Shantih.[23]

The thunder speaks, and the long-awaited rain falls with a sibilant rush. On the level of sound, at least, the poet has found a way to bring rain: he has imported a thunderstorm into the poem, and has flooded the cracked earth of the wasteland with a torrent.

Jeffers, much more persistently than Eliot, tries to assimilate the integrity of nature into his language. Only through language—which in poetry's formal integrity attains the status of an object or event—may history, personality, and nature be one. Jeffers's clearest evocation of this poetic trinity appears in the following poem:

> Point Joe has teeth and has torn ships; it has fierce and solitary
>   beauty;
> Walk there all day you shall see nothing that will not make
>   part of a poem.
>
> I saw the spars and planks of shipwreck on the rocks and
>   beyond the desolate
> Sea-meadows rose the warped wind-bitten van of the pines, a
>   fog-bank vaulted
>
> Forest and all, the flat sea-meadows at that time of year were
>   plated
> Golden with the low flower called footsteps of the spring,
>   millions of flowerets,
>
> Whose light suffused upward into the fog flooded its vault, we
>   wandered
> Through a weird country where the light beat up from earth-
>   ward, and was golden.
>
> One other moved there, an old Chinaman gathering seaweed
>   from the sea-rocks,
> He brought it in his basket and spread it flat to dry on the
>   edge of the meadow.
>
> Permanent things are what is needful in a poem, things
>   temporally
> Of great dimension, things continually renewed or always
>   present.

Grass that is made each year equals the mountains in her past
   and future;
Fashionable and momentary things we need not see nor speak
   of.

Man gleaning food between the solemn presences of land and
   ocean,
On shores where better men have shipwrecked, under fog and
   among flowers,

Equals the mountains in his past and future; that glow from
   the earth was only
A trick of nature's, one must forgive nature a thousand grace-
   ful subtleties.[24]

In learning to find equivalence between mountains, grass, and man, we gain the composure of a larger design. It is not a fixed, symmetrical rose, like Dante's covering order, but rather a process of tidal exchange, of decay and renewal. Only as we learn to see it in a natural order beyond man's civilized system may the human wasteland be redeemed and the individual made whole. Conversely, unless the city is restored and human life brought back into physical and spiritual balance, the wilderness beloved of fierce solitaries like Jeffers will inevitably be destroyed. The circuit of mutual dependence between nature and civilization defines my understanding of the word *culture*: it is a process rather than a product, something that grows rather than being manufactured. And only in poetry is culture fully realized.

The ending of "Michael" illustrates poetry's necessary project of reconciliation. On the last day before Luke must leave him, Michael takes his son into the fields where they have found their common life. Luke lays the cornerstone for a sheepfold, which is to represent the bond between them and which the father is to work at in his absence. But Michael's words both anticipate the failure of that bond and foresee the terms in which it may ultimately be once more achieved:

>   Now, fare thee well—
> When thou return'st, thou in this place wilt see
> A work which is not here: a covenant
> 'Twill be between us; but, whatever fate
> Befall thee, I shall love thee to the last
> And bear thy memory with me to the grave.[25]

A work which is not there, seen by a young man who will never return, defines the center of loss around which the poem's own covenant of sympathy turns.

In Robinson Jeffers's world, harmony with nature has been shattered by human agency rather than abandonment, so that a first response is rage. Jeffers wants, in effect, to reduce the coast road to the "straggling heap" of stones which Michael's sheepfold always remained. But such passion for obliteration also establishes, and begins to redress, the loss from which new community may grow. American poets today continue with this effort to clear the ground. But in the next chapter I want to focus on the paradoxical continuities of this poetic field, and on the ways writers like Gary Snyder also help us to cultivate anew the tradition we have always had.

CHAPTER

2

Culture as Decay

FLIGHT from the wasteland brings no release from cultural stress and disillusionment. In the wilderness Jeffers hears, as Eliot does in the city, the voice of thunder—commanding a human effort of connection and reconciliation. The breadth of the chasm between Jeffers's isolated consciousness and the rest of humanity finally contributes to the force of the imperative. As Leo Marx has shown, there is a central place in America's literature for "the redemptive journey away from society in the direction of nature. As in *Walden, Moby-Dick*, or *Huckleberry Finn*, the journey begins with a renunciation. The hero gives up his place in society and withdraws toward nature."[1] In Marx's reading, though, these American classics and their heroes must ultimately renounce their own renunciations, those "primitive ideals" which he likens to Gonzalo's plantation speech in *The Tempest*. They must return to society, in the ironic modulation of pastoral: "What finally enables us to take the idea of a successful 'return to nature' seriously is its temporariness. It is a journey into the desert and back again—'a momentary stay against confusion.' "[2]

This century's poetry of cultural despair finds such a cycle of escape and return rather more problematic, I believe. Society, rather than seeming a relatively stable, ongoing reality to which individuals may return in their own fashion and at their own time, has itself become increasingly centrifugal. And for Jeffers and his inheritors it is not at all clear that society offers anything to go back to. *Moby-Dick* is the nineteenth-century work most prophetic of this loss of implicit social confidence in those who turn their backs on society. The ship

of all nations, driven toward a destructive collision with a monumental embodiment of nature, goes down with all hands but one.
Ishmael, bobbing along like flotsam on his coffin-lifeboat, survives
only because of his saving distance from the downward pull of the
ship's mass. As a parable of social collapse, framed in terms of
ecological admonishment,[3] such a scene has the most direct bearing
on the modern world's prospects. Ishmael has no mother-ship to
swim back to. His own survival as a solitary witness, as well as that
of an audience for his account, are at such a moment highly doubt-
ful. Contemporary poets of cultural despair are, like Ishmael, at sea.
Their integrity and fortitude come in their ability to watch as the
wreck goes down. The wreck they have, thus far, escaped from is
society's. But to survive they must still find a way to reach the shore
of reconciliation with their time and place.

The terms of sea and land, escape and return, are inevitably con-
fused when it is society itself that is foundering, and when nature
becomes a part of its disastrous wreck. Balanced dualities break
down under such bewilderment and dissolution. Marx suggests a
pattern of night and day within the American design of retreat and
return. But against the cities' artificial lights and falling towers,
night's sleep is banished and day's purposeful clarity falls into a
disturbing haze. Retreat into the wilderness and cultural integration
serve beneficial purposes when they represent smoothly revolving
sides of a balanced process of health and wholeness. But when such
terms grow rigidly antithetical, each focused on the other's destruction, the larger principle of complementary relation has been
broken. The only hope then lies not in identification with either pole
of opposition, but in discovering a more inclusive, sustaining
reality—some larger grammar in which the words *culture* and *wilderness* may both be spoken.

The hateful contraries in *The Waste Land* are the tradition versus
the present moment, the barrenness of urban civilization versus the
individual. Jeffers's view of these oppositions is even more bitter:
the poet against mankind, the wilderness against the city. To accept
a position on either side of such a cultural war is necessarily to do
battle against oneself. An individual can no more renounce his cultural heritage than he can deny his genotype; a poet through his use
of language gives the lie to his rejection of humanity; to turn from
the cities ignores the fact that they rise from the same earth and are
composed of the same elements as the unpeopled mountains. These
divisions between man and nature, man and himself, must be
healed by the construction of a new frame of mind and a new way

of life. In the contemporary poetry of nature we see both a depiction
of how far we have gone wrong and an attempt to find a healthier,
more inclusive understanding of culture—one that can value the city
and the wilderness alike, but without denigrating one or domesticating the other. Poetry's task is to ground human culture once more
on a planet rich in nonhuman life and beauty.

I believe that behind America's flourishing poetry of nature lies a
reinterpretation of culture, and that through the work of numerous
poets this new culture is now being further developed and exemplified. By way of introducing the major elements of this vision, I
would like to juxtapose passages of prose from T. S. Eliot and Gary
Snyder. Their similarities indicate a significant continuity between
contemporary poetry and the cultural and poetic ambitions of
writers at the beginning of the century. The points of divergence are
equally important, however, revealing characteristic values held
both by Snyder and by others among today's outstanding poets of
nature.

The passage from Eliot is a well-known one from his essay on
"Tradition and the Individual Talent":

> Tradition . . . cannot be inherited, and if you want it you must
> obtain it by great labour. It involves, in the first place, the his-
> torical sense, which we may call nearly indispensable to anyone
> who would continue to be a poet beyond his twenty-fifth year;
> and the historical sense involves a perception, not only of the
> pastness of the past, but of its presence; the historical sense
> compels a man to write not merely with his own generation in
> his bones, but with a feeling that the whole of the literature of
> Europe from Homer and within it the whole of the literature of
> his own country has a simultaneous existence and composes a
> simultaneous order. This historical sense, which is a sense of
> the timeless as well as of the temporal and of the timeless and
> temporal together, is what makes a writer traditional. And it is
> at the same time what makes a writer most acutely conscious of
> his place in time, of his contemporaneity.
>
> No poet, no artist of any art, has his complete meaning alone.
> His significance, his appreciation is the appreciation of his rela-
> tion to the dead poets and artists. You cannot value him alone;
> you must set him, for contrast and comparison, among the
> dead. I mean this as a principle of aesthetic, not merely histori-
> cal, criticism. The necessity that he shall conform, that he shall
> cohere, is not one-sided; what happens when a new work of art
> is created is something that happens simultaneously to all the
> works of art which preceded it. The existing monuments form

an ideal order among themselves, which is modified by the introduction of the new (the really new) work of art among them. The existing order is complete before the new work arrives; for order to persist after the supervention of novelty, the *whole* existing order must be, if ever so slightly, altered; and so the relations, proportions, values of each work of art toward the whole are readjusted; and this is conformity between the old and the new.[4]

Snyder's statement, corresponding in its broad cultural perspective, though differing significantly in its terms, was originally part of a talk at Brown University:

The communities of creatures in forests, ponds, oceans, or grasslands seem to tend toward a condition called climax, "virgin forest"—many species, old bones, lots of rotten leaves, complex energy pathways, woodpeckers living in snags, and conies harvesting tiny piles of grass. This condition has considerable stability and holds much energy in its web—energy that in simpler systems (a field of weeds just after a bulldozer) is lost back into the sky or down the drain. All of evolution may have been as much shaped by this pull toward climax as it has by simple competition between individuals or species. If human beings have any place in this scheme it might well have to do with their most striking characteristic—a large brain, and language. And a consciousness of a peculiarly self-conscious order. Our human awareness and eager poking, probing, and studying is our beginning contribution to planet-system energy-conserving; another level of climax.

In a climax situation a high percentage of the energy is derived not from grazing off the annual production of biomass, but from recycling dead biomass, the duff of the forest floor, the trees that have fallen, the bodies of dead animals. Recycled. Detritus cycle energy is liberated by fungi and lots of insects. I would then suggest: as climax forest is to biome, and fungus is to the recycling of energy, so "enlightened mind" is to the daily ego mind, and art to the recycling of neglected inner potential. When we deepen or enrich ourselves, looking within, understanding ourselves, we come closer to being like a climax system. Turning away from grazing on the "immediate biomass" of perception, sensation, and thrill; and re-viewing memory, internalized perception, blocks of inner energies, dreams, the leaf-fall of day-to-day consciousness, liberates the energy of our own sense-detritus. Art is an assimilator of unfelt experience, perception, sensation, and memory for the whole society. When all that compost of feeling and thinking comes back to us then, it

comes not as a flower, but—to complete the metaphor—as a
mushroom; the fruiting body of the buried threads of mycelia
that run widely through the soil, and are intricately married to
the root hairs of all the trees. "Fruiting"—at that point—is the
completion of the work of the poet, and the point where the
artist or mystic reenters the cycle: gives what she or he has done
as nourishment, and as spore or seed spreads the "thought of
enlightenment," reaching into personal depths for nutrients
hidden there, back to the community. The community and its
poetry are not two.[5]

The crucial principle affirmed by each of these extended statements is that culture must be understood in terms of dynamic continuity. The thunder's three commands at the end of *The Waste Land*—
give, sympathize, control—were likewise all verbs of process rather
than of possession, definitive action, or perception. Both of these
quotations also define culture as something one does, within which
one lives, rather than as a good that one simply receives or holds.
One enters into continuity with the past precisely through the relation of one's *efforts* to those of his ancestors. A crucial point to note
here is that Eliot's and Snyder's emphasis is itself in continuity with
an older, English tradition of writing about culture. Matthew Arnold, no less than Eliot and Snyder, sought to distinguish between
true, life-giving culture and the fastidiousness of connoisseurship:

> Culture has got its name touched, in the fancies of men, with a
> sort of air of bookishness and pedantry, cast upon it from the
> follies of the many bookmen who forget the end in the means,
> and use their books with no real aim at perfection. . . . But what
> we are concerned for is the thing, not the name; and the thing,
> call it by what name we will, is simply the enabling ourselves,
> whether by reading, observing, or thinking, to come as near as
> we can to the firm intelligible law of things, and thus to get a
> basis for a less confused action and a more complete perfection
> than we have at present.[6]

Arnold's concern for perfection is, like Eliot's and Snyder's cultural
thought, a social value rather than one directed primarily toward the
cultivation of the individual:

> Not a having and a resting, but a growing and a becoming, is
> the character of perfection as culture conceives it; and here, too,
> it coincides with religion.
>   And because men are all members of one great whole, and the
> sympathy which is in human nature will not allow one member
> to be indifferent to the rest or to have a perfect welfare indepen-

dent of the rest, the expansion of our humanity, to suit the idea
of perfection which culture forms, must be a *general* expansion.
Perfection, as culture conceives it, is not possible while the individual remains isolated.[7]

A recognition of Arnold's connection with modern cultural
thought is important, because other elements of his writing have
led him, and the literary tradition he represents, to be discounted
by many twentieth-century authors. Unfortunately, Arnold's emphasis on the "sweetness and light" of Hellenism can suggest a
static value as the goal of cultural striving. Raymond Williams has
written, "Perfection is a 'becoming,' culture is a process, but part
of the effect of Arnold's argument is to create around them a suggestion that they are known absolutes".[8] And Arnold's assumption
of cultural *standards* frequently leads him, just where his intention
seems most playful, to reveal a fearful snobbery. He discourses
pleasantly on the necessary cultural impoverishment of Noncon-
formists, as opposed to those nurtured, like Arnold himself, in the
Church of England. His complacency also bubbles out characteristically when he asks, of the Phillistines, "consider these people,
then . . . would any amount of wealth be worth having with the
condition that one was to become just like these people?"[9]
In their common divergence from Arnold's particular values, Eliot
and Snyder perpetuate his *central* contribution—the understanding
of culture as a dynamic continuity. Where Arnold sees the individual and the group striving back toward a classical ideal, Eliot and
Snyder point to the tradition itself as a working, continually re-form-
ing mass. An individual does not need to move *toward* culture, but
rather to find a way of participating *in* culture. Such a shift of emphasis makes it harder to be ensnared in the assumption that one's
own caste, as defined by classical education or inherited wealth, is at
the apex of a cultural hierarchy. It also leads automatically to a more
inclusive sense of culture and history. While for Arnold history is
implicitly the attenuation and retreat of true culture, Snyder, in particular, understands it as a widening circle, an enrichment analogous to the work of yeast in dough, or of microorganisms in the soil.
Such a dynamic sense of continuity accords more fully with the
experience of a century that has seen the dissolution of empire, the
collapse of culture's proudest towers. It also harmonizes with a shift
in scientific understanding, as we have moved from the precision of
Newton's mechanism to a world comprehensible only in terms of
relativity, of uncertainty, of progressive variation. Culture, in an era

like ours, makes sense only as a medium through which the past and the present mutually absorb and inform one another. Instead of Arnold's ironic distinction between the past and the present, Eliot emphasizes the present's perpetual groundedness in the past. At one point in "Tradition and the Individual Talent," Eliot writes, "Some one has said: 'The dead writers are remote from us because we *know* so much more than they did.' Precisely, and they are that which we know."[10]

Snyder has, in turn, remarked, "What's really fun about Eliot is his intelligence and his highly selective and charming use of Occidental symbols which point you in a certain direction. . . . He had the sense of roots."[11] Both poets are alert to a living tradition beyond that of Christian Europe. Whatever coherence the conclusion of *The Waste Land* achieves may be related to Eliot's use of ancient Sanskrit mythology and language. Even in *Four Quartets,* with its Dantesque vision of the mystic rose, the wisdom and symbolism of Buddhism are essential to Eliot's design. Snyder's debt to Buddhist insight, in particular, is even more pervasive than Eliot's. In the initial long quotation from Snyder, his reference to "the thought of enlightenment" and his final anti-dualistic admonishment both reveal the harmony between his understanding and that of traditional Zen Buddhism.

Gary Snyder's governing metaphor of the growth of soil clarifies an important implication also present in *The Waste Land*: the past and the dead only become accessible for recombination in the present because of their decay. "Poets are more like mushrooms or fungus," as Snyder says in a related statement from *The Real Work*. "They can digest the symbol-detritus."[12] The fact that he and Eliot, living in the Western cultural sphere, bring Eastern elements into their syntheses reflects decay in this positive sense. Separate cultures, as they break down, create new life in a composting, fermentive pattern. The extreme fragmentation of society in *The Waste Land* thus offers simultaneously the grounds for despair and the basis for hope. A bacteriological sense of culture allows Snyder to value decay as a crucial part of life's nutrient cycle. "That's really what we mean by being cultured—that the time process really does enrich and deepen what you have at hand at any time."[13]

Such an engagement with culture as a process of decay is simultaneously empowering and humbling, even annihilating. Artistic memory thus becomes a means to self-transcendence—becoming a part of larger realities by giving up one's own hermetic integrity, in what Thomas Mann has called "the warmth of decay." Eliot addresses this process when he writes, "The emotion of art is impersonal. And the poet cannot reach this impersonality without surrendering himself wholly to the work to be done. And he is not likely to know what is to be done unless he lives in what is not merely the present, but the present moment of the past, unless he is conscious, not of what is dead, but of what is already living."[14] A sense of impersonal surrender to a process comprehending present and past also underlies Snyder's affirmation that "poetry is a social and traditional art that is linked to its past and particularly its language, that *loops* and draws on its past and that serves as a vehicle for contact with the depths of our own unconscious—and that it gets better by practicing. And that the expression of self, although it's a nice kind of energy to start with, would not make any expression of poetry per se."[15]

This understanding that human beings may be nourished by tapping the nutrients of the past speaks to the resentment against culture discussed in the Introduction. From Snyder's perspective, the problem is not so much that of a present tyrannized by an overbearing past as it is an improverishment, a lack of significant *connectedness* with our legacy from "the dead." He would agree with Jung that "the 'newness' in the individual psyche is an endlessly varied recombination of age-old components . . . it is precisely the loss of connection with the past, our uprootedness, which has given rise to the 'discontents' of civilization. . . . We rush impetuously into novelty, driven by a mounting sense of insufficiency, dissatisfaction, and restlessness. We no longer live on what we have, but on promises."[16] The alternative to perpetually forging a new cultural continuity is to give in to the entropic drift of our throwaway society. Only with the detritus of the past can soil be made to sustain the cycle of life into a new present.

The main way in which Snyder extends Eliot's sense of culture is by his attentiveness to an even wider range of elements than were comprehended in *The Waste Land*. Eliot looks to the East for wisdom to address Western culture's decay. But his synthesis of European and Western symbolism still depends largely on the traditions of "high" culture and on the formal expressions of religion. Though equally respectful of the *sutras* and of traditional Oriental practices, Snyder places them within a continuum of cultural values which also includes "primitive," non-book-centered cultures. *Turtle Island*, in particular, explores Native American life and practice as a fulfillment of many Eastern values, and one which is especially suited to the topography and history of this continent. In his lengthy quotation at the beginning of this chapter, Snyder speaks of the natural world's tendency "toward a condition called climax, 'virgin forest.' " Only through the fulfillment of its cycles of growth and decay may a forest be *renewed*. Snyder finds the same principle of wholeness in traditional Native American cultures: because of their harmonious adjustment to particular regions, "the only societies that are mature are primitive societies."[17]

His ability to integrate values of primitive maturity into his poetry derives from Snyder's anthropological perspective on culture. He studied ethnography at Reed College and at Indiana University, and has consistently pursued this interest in his writing. In a recent interview, he states, "If I were recommending anybody to study anything in the university over anything else, I would either recommend biology or anthropology. Anthropology is probably the most intellectually exciting field in the universities. The most *intellectually* exciting, the one where something's happening in *humanistic terms*. If you want exciting science, you go into biochemistry or something like that. But if you want to get interesting ideas you go into anthropology."[18] Such an emphasis on the part of a poet is significant, since there has been a persistent tension over the past century, even a combativeness, between the literary and anthropological perspectives on culture. Throughout Kroeber and Kluckhohn's comprehensive survey of the social-scientific view—*Culture: A Critical Review of Concepts and Definitions*—disdainful reference is made to the hermetic literary tradition. As the following quotation suggests, there is a good deal of residual anger among anthropologists at the way humanists have defined culture:

The Arnold-Powys-Jaeger concept of culture is not only ethnocentric, often avowedly Hellenocentric; it is absolutistic. It knows perfection, or at least what is most perfect in human achievement, and resolutely directs its "obligatory gaze" thereto, disdainful of what is "lower." The anthropological attitude is relativistic, in that in place of beginning with an inherited hierarchy of values, it assumes that every society through its culture seeks and in some measure finds values, and that the business of anthropology includes the determination of the range, variety, constancy, and interrelations of these innumerable values.

Incidentally, we believe that when the ultramontane among the humanists renounce the claim that their subject is superior or privileged, and adopt the more catholic and humble human attitude—that from that day the humanities will cease being on the defensive in the modern world.[19]

Evidently, the defensiveness is not entirely on either side of this division between the "absolutist" literary view of culture and the "relativist" understanding of the social sciences. All the more reason, though, to celebrate the comprehensive view of culture in the writing of Gary Snyder. Poetry is the perfect medium for such a reconciliation. It belongs, on one hand, to the culture of the book, achieving formal and thematic resonance with the West's tradition of "high" poetic expression. But poetry also makes possible, especially for a writer as alert to its incantatory powers as Snyder, a connection with oral traditions of mythology and ritual. Snyder has been associated with the revival of poetry readings as an American cultural form, and such readings have made poetry's reverberation both with European and with Native American models more audible. University teachers and scholars of literature also need, in Snyder's view, a more "*tribal* sense of their own work." "Looping backward" to establish the tradition, they would benefit from "an anthropological or prehistoric perspective."[20]

As Snyder says, quoting Lévi-Strauss, arts do have a special cultural status: they are the "national parks of the mind."[21] But they therefore only make sense within a larger awareness of culture's landscape. To understand the geology or ecology of the largest park, one must still understand something of the region in which it is located, and of the earth on whose surface it rests. To protect such a wild preserve one must be concerned with the world beyond its boundaries, with the legislation keeping it out of private hands, and with the factors influencing the quality of air, groundwater, and rain which it must share with the cities and farms of a continent. Conversely, the broader culture depends upon the high definition of art just as our store of natural diversity and standards of environmental purity depend upon the reservoir of remaining wilderness. Art, human community, and the all-embracing physical cycles of the earth must be understood as mutually expressive and sustaining. To live in an urban world, cut off from tradition and nature alike, is to experience a life-threatening wasteland. But the inward withdrawal of a distanced tradition, without regard for current necessities of the tribe, becomes absurd; flight into the wilderness, accompanied by a denunciation of all human civilization, arrives finally at the utterance of self-cancellation. Art and the earth are poles around which culture must raise the double arc of its gravitational field.

The initial quotations from Eliot and Snyder differ most obviously in Snyder's scientific terminology and perspective. Anthropology approaches culture as a universal human phenomenon, and one which operates by a genetic principle rather than a mechanical absolute. But it still maintains the limits of a *human* sphere. Kroeber and Kluckhohn, in their most concise definition, state that "culture is the special and exclusive product of men, and is their distinctive quality in the cosmos."[22] Snyder goes beyond this aspect of the anthropological view, asserting that the cycles of human life only achieve health and wholeness in a community which also includes the earth's nonhuman processes and entities. One immediate advantage of such inclusiveness is that it amplifies an organic metaphor implicit throughout modern cultural thought. Snyder's biochemical analogy extends Eliot's definition of poetry as "a more finely perfected medium in which special, or very varied, feelings are at liberty to enter into new combinations."[23] Even "sweetness and light," Arnold's most ridiculed phrase, becomes more meaningful within this understanding of poetry as breaking down an anaerobic mass, making available to oxygen and sunshine the materials for new growth. Such a parallel holds up surprisingly well as one reads over Arnold's interpretation of Hellenism's function in a densely compacted "Hebraic" culture like that of the Anglo-Saxons.

Modern science has illuminated nature's creative cycles in ways that make the organic metaphor of culture even more helpful. Genetic information is retained and exchanged with a precision worthy of comparison with human memory, both that of the individual and that—which we call culture—of the species. In his essay on "The Wilderness," from *Turtle Island*, Gary Snyder writes, "If we can tentatively accommodate the possibility that nature has a degree of authenticity and intelligence that requires that we look at it more sensitively, then we can move to the next step. 'Intelligence' is not really the right word. The ecologist Eugene Odum suggests the term 'biomass' . . . stored information in the cells and in the genes."[24] An understanding that nonhuman life transmits precise information without recourse to human languages allows human culture, paradoxically, to reassert its own necessary connection with nature. Because nature is demonstrably *there* in its own terms, it becomes available once more for integration with the human cycle of life. It is neither inert nor a fabric of poetic conventions: earth's culture and human culture include and nourish one another.

Just as anthropology serves to admonish humanists against a narrowly construed cultural ideal, science provides objective leverage against a humanizing tendency that would finally blind us to nature, and to our human part in its processes. Robert Bly, in criticizing post-Enlightment culture of the West, has written that "Descartes' ideas act so as to withdraw consciousness from the non-human area, isolating the human being in his house, until, seen from the window, rocks, sky, trees, crows seem empty of energy, but especially of divine energy."[25] But the natural sciences, as Snyder has shown, may help people to reacknowledge the energy of the nonhuman; they show a doorway out of the empty house. Nature, within science's vivid apprehension, offers a vision of creativity and memory both analogous to human experience and distinct from it. A revitalized perception of nature counters the entropic drift of culture toward a rigid formulation of the past—through making available a dynamic present beyond the reach of *merely* human continuity. John Fowles has written, in his strange, beautiful book *The Tree*, that "Nature is unlike art in terms of its product—what we in general know it by. The difference is that it is not only created, an external object with a history, and so belonging to a past; but also creating in the present, as we experience it. As we watch it is so to speak rewriting, reformulating, rephotographing itself."[26] Nature fills the wasteland's need for a wider world by avoiding dissolution into human terms. Such a world elsewhere is the only hope for redemption in the face of radical cultural despair. When the exclusively human—even as elaborated in the overarching historical vision of an Ezra Pound—has failed to reinvigorate culture, there is a need for larger realities. Such is the situation recognized in the poignant simplicity of the final canto, CXX:

> I have tried to write Paradise.
>
> Do not move
>   Let the wind speak
>   that is paradise
>
> Let the Gods forgive what I
>   have made
> Let those I love try to forgive
>   what I have made.[27]

The bonded elements of a compound lens allow at once for a higher degree of optical precision and a greater focal range. Gary Snyder's perspective as a poet is a similarly compound one, with similar advantages for the quality of his attentiveness. While expressing the particular truths of his time, place, and personal vision, he attempts simultaneously to acknowledge the large processes of human culture and of the earth in which he is included. Like other contemporary poets of process, Snyder fulfills the cultural vision explored by Alfred North Whitehead in *Science and the Modern World*. Whitehead's goal was to combine the insights of advanced science with the wisdom of art and the feelings: "We want concrete fact with a high light thrown on what is relevant to its preciousness."[28] "Preciousness" is an attribute we discover by surrendering our assent to something for the sake of its beauty, by investing sympathy so intense as to be a form of deep identification. Give, sympathize, control—and gain both the sustenance of an independent outer realm and the composure of inward harmony. To invest oneself in a broader comprehension of culture and, through it, in the earth is to gain the double gift of intimate connectedness and a wider context within which freedom and adventure may be found. Culture and the individual are vivified by understanding with Whitehead that "nature is a structure of evolving processes."[29]

It is important, while exploring this widening conception of culture, also to heed Snyder's advice to "loop back." For there are significant ways in which he and other contemporary poets of nature are pursuing values asserted by the Romantics in Germany and England. Snyder's impulse toward cultural revaluation and inclusiveness represents one such loop back to the Romantic era. From the Brothers Grimm to the *Lyrical Ballads*, there was in fact an explicit intention to exalt undervalued artistic forms. Going along with this interest in *Märchen* and in ballads was a fascination with origins, as reflected both in the experience of childhood and in the legacy of "primitive" peoples. The artistic cult of "northern enchantment" has a particular affinity with Snyder's emphasis on Native American culture and art. Both aesthetics attempt to break down formulaic, hierarchical cultural systems and return to a more elemental relation with the earth and with one's own basic humanity. The "Gothic" and the "Indian" alike are examples of cultural perspectives which had come to seem exotic by virtue of their distance from prevailing norms. To reassert such values is to turn against that process of cultural universalization which might be interpreted also as entropy: the smooth interchangeability of symbols generalized for mass circulation.

Giving up "high" or "classical" cultural values to invest oneself in "primitive" tradition is often related to a process of localization. A characteristically Romantic version of "the genius of the place" involved the phenomenon of *haunting*, as Geoffrey Hartman has pointed out. Fascination with demonic energy and supernatural experience is of course something the Germans could draw directly from their folktales and the English from their ballads. Goethe's "Erlkönig" draws on folk tradition's connection of childhood, night, and the demonic, and on the sense that all three realities are elusive for adult rationality. But in Wordsworth's "The Danish Boy," a tale of haunting also expresses the poet's own emotional and artistic response to a particular spot.[30] Ghosts of the past and the work of art empower and perpetuate each other, and the medium of their interfusion is a given natural terrain. In response to the general displacement of native peoples and culture on this continent, Snyder advocates a new experience of transformative haunting. Where San Francisco has spread its net of streets, the Ohlone peoples once practiced their very different way of life—more finely attuned to the cycles of water and sky and, as of yet, a good deal longer in possession of this soil. Though the Ohlone, like so many peoples in the West, are now largely gone, artists like Snyder remind us of their stories and offer to the urban wasteland a haunting memory. Even when a place's ancient tale, as this one does, reminds the hearer of despoliation and loss, the ache of sympathy is a valuable bond, and the "loop" is experienced as a pang. Wordsworth, in poems such as "Nutting" and "The Thorn," explores this negative avenue to oneness with a place and with its vanished inhabitants. In *Turtle Island,* Snyder performs the same mediation for North Americans in our day.

Recognition of a local muse, by acknowledging *spirit* in a particular natural scene, also allows a more concrete attentiveness in a writer. Snyder, with his anthropological and ecological awareness, pursues what Gilbert White, in the late eighteenth century, called "the idea of *parochial history.*" In his delightful volume of anecdotal and autobiographical nature study, *The Natural History of Selborne,* White makes a couple of comments that bear on Snyder's concerns. There is, White finds, an *economy* in restricting study to small areas: "It is, I find, in zoology as it is in botany: all nature is so full, that the district produces the greatest variety which is most examined."[31] White argues that a comprehension of nature's large processes, such as the migration of birds, also benefits from a resolutely localized effort: "Men that undertake only one district are much more likely to advance natural knowledge that those that grasp at more than they can possibly be acquainted with: every kingdom, every province, should have its own monographer."[32] Snyder's version of parochial history is the study of what he calls *drainages*—those geologically determined water systems that in turn regulate climate, animal, and plant life, and, ideally, human culture as well. His point is that a culture harmonious with the cycles of nature must be attuned to the various characters of the regions in which people live. A natural culture is thus a localized culture, in which art and tradition develop from a deep familiarity with the beings and cycles of a given place.

To define culture with reference to "drainages" also sustains the antihierarchical understanding so central to Snyder's anthropological and scientific perspectives. Raymond Williams, in *Culture and Society*, summarizes the various ways in which English humanistic tradition too has affirmed the *minority* status of true culture. For Coleridge, culture was the vocation of a particular class, which he called the "clerisy." Arnold spoke of a *"remnant"* in each of his three classes—individuals who had attained an understanding beyond the smug rigidity of habitual class feeling. Leavis opposed his "literary minority" to the prevailing "mass civilization."[33] But Snyder's local concern is counter to such a conception of a single embattled elite upholding true culture. Rather than envisioning a map of culture with a capital and provinces, Snyder sees each community and each region as forming its own center. The true culture of place is both an ecologically harmonious one and one which is inherently egalitarian. If every place has its culture, all places have equal status within the larger ecosystem of ecosystems. The apparent fragmentation of numerous local cultures offers, in fact, the most hopeful approach to a community beyond the dualism of Eliot's urban humanity and Jeffers's antihuman wilderness. In contrast with Arnold's classical ideal, diffusing downward through society, a naturalized, localized culture, emanating from diverse communities, would attain the ecological intricacy of broadening, concentric transfer.

The local, organic understanding of culture circles back to this chapter's earlier discussion of cultural decay and the soil's cycle of health. Although culture, on some level, always persists wherever there are people, it can grow sterile, as Eliot takes such pains to show in *The Waste Land*. And when such breakdowns occur in the continuous cycle we call fertility, the only recourse is to undertake an intensive process of cultivation in a particular place. Even where one's own relation with place does not include farming or gardening, the cultivation of self and nature involves a process of composting and deep digging. As Snyder says in the initial extract, "we deepen or enrich ourselves, looking within." Thus, although culture does not disappear, there is a balance that can be tipped from abundance to impoverishment. In the earth and in human culture alike, the present task is to achieve "the retreat of virus before soil fertility."

In Kroeber and Kluckhohn's etymological survey, two primary derivations for culture are suggested. The first is from the Latin verb *colere*, meaning to tend or to cultivate. Christian authors grafted onto this root a sense of *cultura* as worship.[34] Contemporary poets of nature, who so often focus on a chosen landscape, illustrate both of these meanings. Cultivating their lives and their art, they dig at once more deeply into the soil and into themselves. And finding their lives sustained as they grow out of the earth, they attain a reverence for nature informed by the most precise observation and familiarity. The contemporary evolutionist Ernst Mayr has coined the term "allopatric speciation"[35] to indicate the way in which a given landscape's character has evolutionary influence fully equal to that of intra- or interspecies competition; the development of species must therefore always be understood in localized terms. Poetry, too, becomes a manifestation of landscape and climate, just as the ecosystem's flora and fauna are. A human voice becomes the voice of a place.

The next chapter is an attempt to ground the discussion more deeply in the terrain which this one has explored, by considering three poets of attentiveness to place. There are a number of fine poets today whose work would be appropriate to discuss in such a context; the three whom I have chosen represent an especially wide range of interest and approach. One obvious difference among them is regional: Gary Snyder's drainage is, in its larger compass, all of Northern California and the Northwest, and in its specific definition, the western slope of the Sierra; Wendell Berry writes from his reclaimed farm in Kentucky; Robert Pack's home is in central Vermont's landscape of orchards, dairy farms, and villages. The three poets' relations with the land in their life and art also take in a broad spectrum, from Snyder's hunter/gatherer ideal, to Berry's farming on a human scale, to Pack's circle of gardening and pruning. Finally, their verse forms, too, represent important variations in contemporary poetic practice. Snyder often moves toward the unelaborated or elliptical expression characteristic of Eastern or Native American literature, while Pack, by contrast, is often drawn to traditional verse forms of the West. In their divergent expressions of both groundedness and artistic concentration, these three writers exemplify the richness of contemporary poetry's ecosystem.

Reinhabitation

To START from the soil again is the task, when human culture has become impoverished. A poetry that draws its nourishment from rootedness in a chosen spot defines the interchange of past and present through that spot's own cycle of renewing surrender and inheritance. And tradition thus comes to be measured against the most pragmatic of criteria: will it grow here, will it enrich this field? A broad awareness of culture and poetry is useful to a person in the same way that his or her natural responsiveness is enhanced by knowing the basic principles of ecology. But creatures live, and grounded poems emerge, within the discrete interchanges of a particular ecosystem. Gary Snyder, Wendell Berry, and Robert Pack, the poets on whose work this chapter focuses, are writers with important differences in the manner of their imaginative grounding. Regionally (California, Kentucky, Vermont), in the ways each experiences the wholeness of nature in his place, and in the poetic forms through which their respective experiences and visions are expressed, they illustrate the cultural divergence attendant on localized engagement with the earth. However, there are also common principles which begin to emerge, just as there are when one compares several ecosystems; and these principles of groundedness are sometimes most clearly revealed precisely at the points of divergence. A poem's form must find some way of responding to its terrain; a poet must determine the sacrament through which his relation to place is best expressed, and must acknowledge with reverence the deaths through which he lives; the rooted relation with nature must also comprehend the larger world, including the realities of the human wasteland.

Gary Snyder has explored in many ways the insights and life of pre-agricultural humanity. And the hunter/gatherer culture in which he has expressed such interest may also be related to important strains in his poetry. Section 6 of "Hunting," one of the three divisions of *Myths and Texts,* is a poem which reveals many of Snyder's characteristic themes and evokes as well his poetry's wide range of emotions:

this poem is for bear

"As for me I am a child of the god of the mountains."

A bear down under the cliff.
She is eating huckleberries.
They are ripe now
Soon it will snow, and she
Or maybe he, will crawl into a hole
And sleep. You can see
Huckleberries in bearshit if you
Look, this time of year
If I sneak up on the bear
It will grunt and run

The others had all gone down
From the blackberry brambles, but one girl
Spilled her basket, and was picking up her
Berries in the dark.
A tall man stood in the shadow, took her arm,
Led her to his home. He was a bear.

In a house under the mountain
She gave birth to slick dark children
With sharp teeth, and lived in the hollow
Mountain many years.
         snare a bear: call him out:
honey-eater
forest apple
light-foot
Old man in the fur coat, Bear! come out!
Die of your own choice!
Grandfather black-foot!
         this girl married a bear
Who rules in the mountains, Bear!
         you have eaten many berries
         you have caught many fish
         you have frightened many people

Twelve species north of Mexico
Sucking their paws in the long winter

Tearing the high-strung caches down
Whining, crying, jacking off
(Odysseus was a bear)

Bear-cubs gnawing the soft tits
Teeth gritted, eyes screwed shut
                    but she let them.
Till her brothers found the place
Chased her husband up the gorge
Cornered him in the rocks.
Song of the snared bear:
          "Give me my belt.
          "I am near death.
          "I came from the mountain caves
          "At the headwaters,
          "The small streams there
          "Are all dried up.

—I think I'll go hunt bears.
          "hunt bears?

Why shit Snyder,
You couldn't hit a bear in the ass
          with a handful of rice!"[1]

Snyder's poetic relation with nature is—to use a word he has himself adopted—primitive. Right relation with the earth involves a *return* for him, to ways people understood their world before the development of technological civilization. In the introduction to *Myths and Texts,* Snyder writes, "As a poet I hold the most archaic values on earth. They go back to the upper Palaeolithic: the fertility of the soil, the magic of animals, the power-vision in solitude, the terrifying initiation and rebirth, the love and ecstasy of the dance, the common work of the tribe."[2] Allegiance to the archaic is foremost an act of sympathetic imagination. At the heart of *"this poem is for bear"* is a Native American tale, told with the swiftness and simplicity which give such tales their atmosphere of dreamy magic. To enter into the life of Indian song and myth is to run against the current of American history. It is an antidote to the greedy compulsiveness in our use of the land, which may itself reflect a deeper, guilty conviction that we do not belong here. Snyder has written in *Earth House Hold,* "Something is always eating at the American heart like acid: it is the knowledge of what we have done to our continent, and to the American Indian."[3] To approach an Indian relation with animals and the earth is to grow back toward nature, to surrender to a spiritual change from which many other changes in our practice may also flow. In *"this poem is for bear,"* as in a poem like "Anasazi" from *Turtle Island,* Snyder evokes a wholeness of life greater than our American culture has achieved since the colonial origins of the nation. Participation, kinship, magical transformations, all work in the interest of a lively and coherent sympathy.

Native American models also serve as an avenue to enhanced sympathy and identification with animals. Chants and prayers from tribes across North America make reference to four-legged and two-legged people, crawling people and flying people. Other life forms are thus accorded full recognition as persons, rather than being lumped into a soulless mass with the rest of the nonhuman world. Such enlarged sympathy with the prey seems at first contradictory within the framework of a hunting culture. In *"this poem is for bear,"* the bear is both husband to the woman, by whom children at once humans and bears are born, and victims to her brothers; he is both a beast trapped and destroyed in the mountains and a hero who gathers himself into a farewell song at the moment of his death. The poem is a confusion of identities, and a confusion of emotions, unless we can break down the boundary between humans and other animals, between hunting and loving. It was the custom of numerous native people in the western states to put on the hide and antlers of a stag when hunting deer, both to allow themselves to approach the herd unobserved and to enter reverently into the lives of the animals which they wished to kill and eat. In *Earth House Hold,* Snyder writes,

> Almost all animals are beautiful and paleolithic hunters were deeply moved by it. To hunt means to use your body and senses to the fullest: to strain your consciousness to feel what the deer are thinking today, this moment; to sit still and let your self go into the birds and wind while waiting by the game trail. Hunting magic is designed to bring the game to you—the creature who has heard your song, witnessed your sincerity, and out of compassion comes within your range. Hunting magic is not only aimed at bringing beasts to their death, but to assist in their birth—to promote their fertility.[4]

Hunting, within such an understanding, is a sacrament; it brings men closer to nature, rather than estranging them from it. Gratitude and admiration binds the hunter's life to the lives of animals he has killed.

One of the works which most profoundly depicts the shifting

balance between man and nature in our American history is
Faulkner's *Go Down, Moses*. It also provides a very pointed and
useful comparison with *"this poem is for bear."* In "The Old People,"
from that volume, Sam Fathers, the son of a slave and of a Chickasaw chief, instructs Ike McCaslin in the ritual and meaning of the
hunt. Faulkner tells how, after Ike shot his first stag, "Sam stooped
and dipped his hands in the hot smoking blood and wiped them
back and forth across the boy's face."[5] The old man's action
"marked him forever one with the wilderness which had accepted
him."[6] The traditional sign of unity with the slain animal also serves
to bind *people* together, both with each other in the present and with
all of their ancestors in the reverence of the hunt.

Despite these important similarities between Faulkner's depiction
and Snyder's presentation of hunting, however, there is also a crucial difference between the two writers. For Faulkner, such sacrificial
unity is itself sacrificed to the imperatives of modern history:

> They were the white boy, marked forever, and the old dark
> man sired on both sides by savage kings, who had marked him,
> whose bloody hands had merely formally consecrated him to
> that which, under the man's tutelage, he had already accepted,
> humbly and joyfully, with abnegation and with pride too; the
> hands, the touch, the first worthy blood which he had been
> found at last worthy to draw, joining him and the man forever,
> so that the man would continue to live past the boy's seventy
> years and then eighty years, long after the man himself had
> entered the earth as chiefs and kings entered it;—the child, not
> yet a man, whose grandfather had lived in the same country
> and in almost the same manner as the boy himself would grow
> up to live, leaving his descendants in the land in his turn as his
> grandfather had done, and the old man past seventy whose
> grandfathers had owned the land long before the white man
> ever saw it and who had vanished from it now with all their
> kind, what of blood they left behind them running now in
> another race and for a while even in bondage and now drawing
> toward the end of its alien and irrevocable course, barren, since
> Sam Fathers had no children.[7]

When Sam Fathers dies, the original Chickasaw people of that place
die. He passes his understanding on to the boy, but Ike will also
produce no progeny himself and will live to see the wilderness
logged over and destroyed. The blood-bond in the forest is thus
doubly marked by death, for it is inevitably a doomed connection

with a past world and vanished lives. Snyder's appreciation of the old ways is not characterized by this same sense of lyrical nostalgia. He states in an interview, "Although it's clear we cannot again have seamless primitive cultures, or the purity of the archaic, we can have neighborhood and community."[8] Standing in the present, Snyder is able both to affirm the archaic values and to forecast a reassertion of them after the follies of this age have passed. As a poem like "For the Children," from *Turtle Island*, indicates, he recognizes the disasters potential in mankind's immediate future. But still, in the very broad view, he can state with confidence, "I'm in line with the big flow."[9]

The humorous ending of *"this poem is for bear"* is an admission, I feel, of the distance separating Snyder and his society from the sacramental unity of Native American culture. But the fact remains, in contrast with Faulkner's writing, that Snyder expects his archaic values to prevail eventually in the social and political realms, as well as in the present pattern of his art. He continues, in several different sorts of forest, to hunt bear. The strong affinity between his interest in Indian culture and his practice of Zen Buddhism may be one factor saving him from Faulkner's fatalism. The synthesis in his own life and art between the two ancient cultures is itself a basis for hope: Native American vision, like the Dharma, may be transmitted and developed in cultural contexts different from its origins. Furthermore, as Snyder has asserted on several occasions, Zen arises from the same emptying of self as hunting does. For this reason, at one point in *The Real Work*, he describes himself as a "Buddhist-shamanist." An important point with respect to the contrasting historical visions of Faulkner and Snyder is that Buddhist thought has always attributed a far greater age to the world than was generally allowed within the Judeo-Christian tradition; Western science is just beginning to catch up with the vastness of Buddhist history and cosmology. Zen's "big mind" is thus open to the interfolding unity of the eons, beyond the present's strife. And within such a scope the *pastness* of archaic values is not a matter of disappearance. Like culture and like soil, man's relation with nature cannot be understood either as a thing or as a series of discrete phases: it is a cyclical process within which death and life are not a duality but an organism, always changing and always the same.

The Zen discipline of emptying the mind, so that reality may be perceived unclouded by plans and desires, confirms the identification with nature found within Native American traditions. In Snyder's poem "Piute Creek," the place itself is thus encountered,

with all its particularity of terrain, after the poet's surrender of his
own exclusive humanity:

> One granite ridge
> A tree, would be enough
> Or even a rock, a small creek,
> A bark shred in a pool.
> Hill beyond hill, folded and twisted
> Tough trees crammed
> In thin stone fractures
> A huge moon on it all, is too much.
> The mind wanders. A million
> Summers, night air still and the rocks
> Warm. Sky over endless mountains.
> All the junk that goes with being human
> Drops away, hard rock wavers
> Even the heavy present seems to fail
> This bubble of a heart.
> Words and books
> Like a small creek off a high ledge
> Gone in the dry air.
>
> A clear, attentive mind
> Has no meaning but that
> Which sees is truly seen.
> No one loves rock, yet we are here.
> Night chills. A flick
> In the moonlight
> Slips into Juniper shadow:
> Back there unseen
> Cold proud eyes
> Of Cougar or Coyote
> Watch me rise and go.[10]

"The mind wanders" and loses itself in clear attentiveness. In this
regard, too, Snyder's understanding of Zen has an important affinity with Native American practice. Most of the Indian peoples
moved back and forth across the land with the alteration of seasons.
In avoiding permanent settlements and a rigid sense of private
ownership, they were also able to gain a deeper familiarity with the
face of nature and with fellow creatures; living without permanent
walls helped them to keep open to the world. In contrast, as Snyder
says of America's modern civilization, " . . . we haven't discovered
America yet. People live on it without knowing what it is or where
they are. They live on it literally as invaders. You know whether or

not a person knows where he is by whether or not he knows the plants. By whether or not he knows what the soils and water do."[11] Wandering through the wilderness involves a continual disassembly, of assumptions as well as tents. It allows for experience beyond the concepts of abstract conventions: "No one loves rock, yet we are here." Details that would have seemed barren within an aesthetic or religious hierarchy emerge as richly connected with each other and with all of life.

Holding on to such clarity in the daily experience of life is not always so easy. "All the junk" comes back and needs to be let go again. Poetry is one access to such openness, providing a way for a person to wander back to the liberation of "dry air" and to share the gift of it with others. Since poetry presents itself through fixed language, however, preventing its freshness from lapsing into mere convention is an especially pressing need. Snyder's humor in *"this poem is for bear"* springs the trap of words, and his unexpected movement from one syntactic stream to another serves a related purpose. These are ways he keeps his poem from subsiding into an idea or a single, familiar experience. But, in a more specific way, there still remains a problem with *names* we give to things in nature, and the way such terms can mislead people as to the firmness with which they really perceive other entities. "Foxtail Pine," from *The Back Country*, reflects poetry's need to break down nomenclature, as well as tone and grammar, if wandering in the wilderness is to remain an experience of kinship and enlightenment:

FOXTAIL PINE

bark smells like pineapple: Jeffries
cones prick your hand: Ponderosa

nobody knows what they are, saying
"needles three to a bunch."

    turpentine tin can hangers
    high lead riggers

"the true fir cone stands straight,
the doug fir cone hangs down."

—wild pigs eat acorns in those hills
cascara cutters
tanbark oak bark gatherers
myrtlewood burl bowl-makers
little cedar dolls,

> baby girl born from the split crotch
> of a plum
> daughter of the moon—
>
> foxtail pine with a
> clipped curve-back cluster of tight
> five-needle bunches
>   the rough red bark scale
> and jigsaw pieces sloughed off
>   scattered on the ground.
> —what am I doing saying "foxtail pine"?
>
> these conifers whose home was ice
> age tundra, taiga, they of the
>   naked sperm
> do whitebark pine and white pine seem the same?
>
>   a sort of tree
>   its leaves are needles
>   like a fox's brush
> (I call him fox because he looks that way)
>   and call this other thing, a
>   foxtail pine.[12]

Snyder's poetic practice and language find a number of ways for expressing his sympathies with the wild and the primitive. His general avoidance of a regular, fixed rhythm expresses a desire for openness to the ever-changing forms in which the world embodies itself. The frequent spaces between lines and groups of lines also expresses such an openness, as does the simple, direct language which he usually chooses. A verbal surface that was highly wrought in too obvious a way might seem to be self-referential and complete; if words retain a suggestive looseness in their arrangement, they may point to the stillness beyond themselves. When asked in an interview how he composed, Snyder indicated to what extent the origins and meanings of his poems were preverbal: " . . . before I write I do it in my head many times. Almost the whole thing. The first step is the rhythmic measure, the second step is a set of preverbal visual images which move to the rhythmic measure, and the third step is embodying it in words—and I have learned as a discipline over the years to avoid writing until I have to. I don't put it on the page until it's ripe."[13]

A problem which the localizing imagination must face is that of isolation. This is finally an issue not of geography but of conception and outlook. The speaker in Jeffers's "Coast-Road," like Lear saying

"Let us away to prison" or like the weary Prometheus at the end of
Shelley's verse-drama, seeks the enclosure of a place of *refuge*. But
attachment to such a region of retreat can also be an abandonment,
both of the larger world and of the other human beings who continue to inhabit it. Art, like religion, has traditionally offered its adher-
ents a vision through which they might gather their lives into a
larger unity. For a poet to wall the world out is to be guilty of a
betrayal of trust and a lack of compassion. A poem in which Snyder
draws the modern world into his spirit-vision is this one from *Turtle
Island*, "The Dead by the Side of the Road":

> How did a great Red-tailed Hawk
>   come to lie—all stiff and dry—
>   on the shoulder of
>   Interstate 5?
>
> Her wings for dance fans
>
> Zac skinned a skunk with a crushed head
>   washed the pelt in gas; it hangs,
>   tanned, in his tent
>
> Fawn stew on Hallowe'en
>   hit by a truck on highway forty-nine
>   offer cornmeal by the mouth;
>   skin it out.
>
> Log trucks run on fossil fuel
>
> I never saw a Ringtail til I found one in the road:
>   case-skinned it with the toenails
>   footpads, nose, and whiskers on:
>   it soaks in salt and water
>   sulphuric acid pickle;
>
> she will be a pouch for magic tools.
>
> The Doe was apparently shot
>   lengthwise and through the side—
>   shoulder and out the flank
>   belly full of blood
>
> Can save the other shoulder maybe,
>   if she didn't lie too long—
> Pray to their spirits. Ask them to bless us:
>   our ancient sisters' trails
>   the roads were laid across and kill them:
>   night-shining eyes
>
> The dead by the side of the road.[14]

Interstate highways, slicing through the wild country, represent a mode of contact with nature which is the opposite of wandering. Blinded by headlights where the asphalted roads transect game-trails and gullies, animals become the victims of blind force—far more destructive of creatures than Native American hunters, and with no allowance for human reverence in the rapid and unmedi-tated taking of lives. The people in the poem who gather up the bodies of the dead animals—hit by trucks, shot by careless hun-ters—are engaged in an effort of preservation. In saving the skins and feathers, they bring them into relation with their own lives. Recognizing in them dancing fans and pouches for magic tools, they perpetuate as well values of the native peoples struck down by the same force of speed and technology that killed the doe and the skunk. This is a poem in which the circle of vision is redemptively widened to include the dead by the side of the road. From a local-ized basis, and with a highly meditated style of relation with nature, the poet undertakes the task of Whitehead's God of process—a tender redemption, from this world's wreckage, of everything that can possibly be saved. Magic, prayer, and blessing are all necessary for the success of such a task. In the sterile realm of the fisher-king, where Eliot situates his *Waste Land*, there is no hope if not through religious quest and incantation. In Snyder's poem, the rituals and values of primitive cultures also become an alternative to those of the modern world, through which we may once more approach health and understanding. To strive for an archaic perception of the problems of our age is to undertake the long process of healing the community and the earth.

"Sours of the Hills," from *Regarding Wave*, is a good poem with which to round off this discussion of natural rootedness in Snyder's poetry. Walking across the seed-and-berry-wild world, Snyder expe-riences a rich and comic interpenetration with nature. He eats the berries, bears the burrs, and serves as a body of soil in which seeds plant themselves. His is the song of a juice-smeared face:

> barbed seeds in double ranks
> sprung for sending off;
>
> half-moon hairy seeds in the hair of the wrist
>
> majestic fluff
> sails . . . rayed and spined . . . up hill at eye level
>   hardly a breeze;

amber fruit with veins
on a bending stem,
size of an infant pea.

plumes wave,
seeds spill.

Blueblack berry on a bush turned leaf-purple

deep sour, dark tart, sharp
   in the back of the mouth.

in the hair and from head to foot
stuck with seeds—burrs—
   next summer's mountain weeds—

a strolling through vines and grasses:

into the wild sour.[15]

If Gary Snyder's identity in relation to his chosen region is that of
a hunter/gatherer, with wandering as the metaphor for his life and
poetry, Wendell Berry's self-definition is as a farmer; in his daily life,
as in his writing, he commits himself to labor in the soil. "The Man
Born to Farming," opening poem of Berry's volume *Farming: A Hand
Book*, is a poem of ecstatic declaration, indicating several of the principal elements of Berry's poetry:

The grower of trees, the gardener, the man born to farming,
whose hands reach into the ground and sprout,
to him the soil is a divine drug. He enters into death
yearly, and comes back rejoicing. He has seen the light lie
  down
in the dung heap, and rise again in the corn.
His thought passes along the row ends like a mole.
What miraculous seed has he swallowed
that the unending sentence of his love flows out of his mouth
like a vine clinging in the sunlight, and like water
descending in the dark?[16]

The back-breaking work is also for Berry a dance. Seed-time and
harvest, the farmer and the earth are partners who take turns in the
dance's lead, and the ongoing rhythm helps the man in such a
round to achieve forgetfulness of his separate self. The drug is divine because it offers a *fruitful* oblivion: the sprouting and falling
and rising again of life from the earth mark time in the farmer's
entranced, creative labor. An aspect of such a life to which Berry
comes back often in his poetry is that of surrender. To take part in

the rhythms of earth, one must be prepared to enter into death, to lie down like light in the dung heap, to descend like water into the dark. One must become, as Berry suggests in the title to his most recent book of poems, *A Part* of the earth, not a calculating consciousness held *apart* in its own individuality.

Berry identifies his life as a farmer and a poet with the cycle of decay and renewal in the soil. This is an analogy for the process of health in art and human life to which Gary Snyder also returns. In *The Real Work*, Snyder affirms Berry's writing in such terms: " . . . maybe we can discriminate between poets who have fed on a certain kind of destructiveness for their creative glow (and some of those are no longer with us, consequently) as against those who have 'composted' themselves to become richer and stronger, like Wendell Berry, whose poetry lacks glamor but is really full of nutrients."[17] Snyder's distinction is like Coleridge's opposition between the two forms of civilization: the one brilliant in "the hectic of disease" and the other flourishing with "the bloom of health." A poem, like a body, must always burn, but the difference between fever and health is one of a balance, in which life's present provides for a future as well as feeding on the past. The healthy equilibrium of soil is assured when the nutrients for an ongoing, vital interchange are abundant.

The farmer-poet assures his own fertility through continually composting the elements of his earlier seasons of life, and of the lives of his ancestors, into the cleared ground of fall. After each harvest he surrenders to the earth and arches his mind across the winter. In "Enriching the Earth," Berry describes his provision of green manure for the soil, which, tilled in and decaying, will nourish in its death the new life of spring:

> To enrich the earth I have sowed clover and grass
> to grow and die. I have plowed in the seeds
> of winter grains and of various legumes,
> their growth to be plowed in to enrich the earth.
> I have stirred into the ground the offal
> and the decay of the growth of past seasons
> and so mended the earth and made its yield increase.
> All this serves the dark. Against the shadow
> of veiled possibility my workdays stand
> in a most asking light. I am slowly falling
> into the fund of things. And yet to serve the earth,
> not knowing what I serve, gives a wideness
> and a delight to the air, and my days

do not wholly pass. It is the mind's service,
for when the will fails so do the hands
and one lives at the expense of life.
After death, willing or not, the body serves,
entering the earth. And so what was heaviest
and most mute is at last raised up into song.[18]

Through allegiance to the fertility of the soil, one gains a heightened respect for "offal" and for the process of decay: Berry is as intent upon elevating the status of these words in his poetry as Snyder is on asserting the claims of the primitive and the archaic. As a poet and a farmer, he too might be characterized by the phrase Hazlitt applied to Wordsworth: "proud humility." In healing the "skinned" fields of his Kentucky farm, Berry also enriches his art and unifies the world. To love a chosen place truly is to learn that earth and mankind are one.

The closely knit quality of Berry's language and rhythms in "Enriching the Earth" registers the composting wholeness of his world. Important words, such as "growth" and "earth," are repeated. The regenerative cycle of language is further amplified by the strong use of half-rhymes ("sowed," "grow," and "plowed" in the first two lines) and consonance ("grass," "grow," "grains," "growth," "ground" in the first five lines). Such echoes are often in the middle of lines, and thus suggest a resonant continuity beyond the little seasons or distinctions of a human life. Lines four, seven, and sixteen are end-stopped, and emphasize Berry's central values in that way: they conclude "to enrich the earth," "and made its yield increase," "at the expense of life." But in general there is a strong tug across line-breaks, created both by the stretching of tight phrases, such as "the seeds / of winter grains," and the many verbs, such as "stirred" and "falling," whose action is only completed in a subsequent line.

In discussing *"this poem is for bear"* and "Piute Creek" by Gary Snyder, I touch on two of the lines of ancestry Snyder affirms for himself: the culture of Native American peoples and the practice and literature derived from Zen Buddhism in China and Japan. In his various essays, Berry also acknowledges a sense of tradition which, composted in the circumstances of his life and work, informs his writing. Sometimes the relation is implicit, as in Berry's connection with Ezra Pound through his respect for Adams, Jefferson, and the principle of "usufruct." Sometimes, as in *The Unsettling of America*, the construction of a literary tradition takes the form of appreciative criticism; in his lovely discussions of *King Lear* and of the ending of

The Odyssey, Berry provides a background for his own concerns for humility and for marital fidelity as a model for human relation with earth. And then there is the procession of figures, in what he calls a "secular pilgrimage" to nature, whom he picks out by name as especially important to him: Marvell, Wordsworth, and Thoreau, the poetry of William Carlos Williams, and "Kenneth Rexroth's *100 Poems from the Chinese,* which immediately influenced my work and introduced me to Oriental poetry. . . ."[19]

The many kinds of organic matter composted into soil act together to produce several general characteristics: soil that drains well, is accessible to human labor and the seeding of plants alike, and sustains beneficial bacterial action. Berry's sources, too, combine for him in several principles of continuity between his work and the earth; he expresses these principles most directly in the essay entitled "A Secular Pilgrimage," from *A Continuous Harmony.* First is the need for humble participation in the natural process. The artists he most admires reveal " . . . an implicit and essential humility, a reluctance to impose on things as they are, a willingness to relate to the world as student and servant, a wish to be included in the natural order rather than to 'conquer nature,' a wish to discover the natural form rather than to create new forms that would be exclusively human."[20] For Berry, as for Snyder, such humility has formal implications. It is no coincidence that Berry should draw inspiration both from the efforts of Williams to open his art to the "unartistic" elements of Paterson and from the unelaborated impressions of Chinese poetry. In both cases the language and meter move away from what Robert Bly has called the rhetorical tradition in English poetry. In a comment on the writing of A. R. Ammons, Berry speaks to values underlying the qualities of simplicity and transparency in his own poetry: "It is one of the obligations of [Ammons's] religious vision to refuse the presumptions of the closed forms of a humanistic art. Form, he believes, is in all things, but the forms comprehended in nature or achieved in art are necessarily partial forms, fragments, inferior to the form of the whole creation, which can neither be comprehended nor imagined."[21]

As the statement about Ammons indicates, above all Berry's is a world of implications. He would agree with John Muir's observation that if you try to pick out one "fact" about nature you find that it is hooked to everything else in the world. Berry's poetry equally derives from and determines the rest of the poet's work in the world; and only in the union of life and poetry may the fullness of his "continuous harmony" be perceived. In his essay on "A Secular

Pilgrimage," Berry quotes R. H. Blyth: "Poetry is not the words written in a book, but the mode of activity in the mind of the poet." Poetry may no more be separated from the natural world for a writer like Berry than sensibility and activity may be isolated from one another. In the resonance of writers like Berry and Snyder there is a determination to imply and affirm more than they can say, to erase the boundary between the work of art and the world from which it grows. I am reminded of these lines by the eighteenth-century Zen monk Ryokan:

> Who says my poems are poems?
> My poems are not poems,
> After you know my poems are not poems,
> Then we can discuss poetry.[22]

For a poet who, in cultivating a rooted life and art, begins to achieve a beauty of balanced process, the pressing imbalances of the world beyond his locale are a harsh challenge. The present reliance of our nation on the nuclear balance of terror seems to cast our individual efforts at health and wholeness into a coldly satirical light. In his poem "The Morning's News," Wendell Berry tries, by relating his work as a writer and farmer in Kentucky to the atrocities of the Vietnam War, to face the word "complicity":

> To moralize the state, they drag out a man,
> and bind his hands, and darken his eyes
> with a black rag to be free of the light in them,
> and tie him to a post, and kill him.
> And I am sickened by complicity in my race.[23]

Human evil, prevailing against nature and against humanity itself, seems to give the lie to humble, local efforts at reconciliation. Berry's ecstatic labor in the fields is doubly threatened by the "sullen labor that perfects hell": the spreading political storm endangers the balanced life he has begun to make for his family while also making it harder to see humanity, his own included, as an ingredient of harmonious natural process. Humility, then, appears either as too weak to survive or, in fact, as a sham. In the course of Berry's poem it becomes clear that the only way out of such a conflict is through it.

> What must I do
> to go free? I think I must put on
> A deathlier knowledge and prepare to die
> rather than enter into the design of man's hate.

I will purge my mind of the airy claims
of church and state, and observe the ancient wisdom
of tribesman and peasant, who understood
they labored on the earth only to lie down in it
in peace, and were content. I will serve the earth
and not pretend my life could be better served.
My life is only the earth risen up
a little way into the light, among the leaves,
Another morning with its strange cure.
The earth is news. Though the river floods
and the spring is cold, my heart goes on,
faithful to a mystery in a cloud,
and the summer's garden continues its descent
through me, toward the ground.[24]

As Robinson Jeffers does, Berry finds that his movement "to ground" which made human abuses so hateful in the first place can only be persisted in if bitterness is to resolve into a more luminous and powerful response. Humility finally means to value something for its own sake, not for the way it reflects oneself or one's values. To serve the earth for its own sake means to reject, equally, "the airy claims of church and state" and the anguish of history. If a man is not to give up he must use the morning's news to make himself "lie down," to "descend" beneath his abstract problems into the strengthening order of nature; joining with the earth may finally be our best avenue back to human unity as well, to the "ancient wisdom / of tribesman and peasant" which Snyder too affirms. To continue reading the human news with energy and determination we must also remember, and so console ourselves, that "the earth is news."

Berry finds that his fields are not on the periphery but at the center of the human world; standing by the plowed ground, he is most keenly aware of the need for reconciliation between humanity's isolation and its naturalness. In *The Long-Legged House* he writes, "Sometimes I can no longer think in the house or in the garden or in the cleared fields. They bear too much resemblance to our failed human history—failed, because it has led to this human present that is such a bitterness and a trial. And so I go to the woods."[25] The fields, like the house, are not a retreat from the problem of humanity in this age of the world: they *represent* the problem. However, because they are bounded by the woods and lie across the earth, they do at least provide a focus for human attempts to reconcile nature and man. The fields at dawn are lovely, but, no less than

the urban wasteland, they express the worst depradations of human
history. Reading them right, one sees that the Vietnam War did
begin at home. As Berry writes, "I am forever being crept up on and
newly startled by the realization that my people established themselves here by killing or driving out the original possessors, by the
awareness that people were once bought and sold here by my
people, by the sense of the violence they have done to their own
kind and to each other and to the earth, by the persistent failure to
serve either the place or their community in it."[26]

In the fields one sees both the earth's wound and its healing, the
angry loss of love and its renewal. Because Berry understands the
human suffering and injustice of his place, he loves all the more
keenly the enduring possibilities for human relation with nature. All
love, it may be, has in it an edge of nostalgia, an elegiac strain.
Death gives birth to love, as well as to beauty. Berry has explored
such a paradoxical genesis in this meditation on the continual loss of
Kentucky's topsoil, as acres of abused fields wash away in the heavy
seasonal rains.

The Slip

for Donald Davie

The river takes the land, and leaves nothing.
Where the great slip gave way in the bank
and an acre disappeared, all human plans
dissolve. An aweful clarification occurs
where a place was. Its memory breaks
from what is known now, begins to drift.
Where cattle grazed and trees stood,
emptiness
widens the air for birdflight, wind, and rain.
As before the beginning, nothing is there.
Human wrong is in the cause, human
ruin in the effect—but no matter;
all will be lost, no matter the reason.
Nothing, having arrived, will stay.
The earth, even, is like a flower, so soon
passeth it away. And yet this nothing
is the seed of all—the clear eye
of Heaven, where all the worlds appear.
Where the imperfect has departed, the perfect
begins its struggle to return. The good gift
begins again its descent. The maker moves
in the unmade, stirring the water until

> stirring and darkening the soul until pain
> perceives new possibility. There is nothing
> to do but learn and wait, return to work
> on what remains. Seed will sprout in the scar.
> Though death is in the healing, it will heal.[27]

The river, leaving nothing, leaves a gift. The pain of losing ground drives us back to the earth for healing, or we too will be lost. This is Berry's insight everywhere in his poetry: because of the wounds to nature in our time, we must learn, for the first time or not at all, to become true servants of the earth. Fear and trembling alone, Kierkegaard taught, can drive us to necessary truth. And watching the land in which his life found root literally falling out of view, Berry experiences the paradox that "emptiness / widens the air for bird-flight, wind, and rain." To perceive in the contemporary abuse of natural cycles the end of processes on which our life has depended is also to experience the precious wholeness at every point of the process, beginning and end alike. Anger grounded in love is, to use Ian MacHarg's word, a negentropic response. A poem moves into the emptiness, perceiving that "this nothing / is the seed of all." It is for planting such a seed that Berry's poetry exists: in the mind and in the earth, he labors so that seed "will sprout in the scar."

Berry's understanding in "The Slip" has an affinity with Wordsworth's in the poem "Nutting." As the youth in that poem lolls in the still-unviolated hazel-grove, his pleasure in nature is of a listless sort: the earth seems but a store, ample but inert, of matter for a person's purposes:

>   . . . of its joy secure,
> The heart luxuriates with indifferent things,
> Wasting its kindliness on stocks and stones,
> And on the vacant air.

But when the idler has arisen to break down the boughs and disperse their shade, the wrecked grove suddenly becomes a living entity, to which a personal response is possible:

> Ere from the mutilated bower I turned
> Exulting, rich beyond the wealth of kings,
> I felt a sense of pain when I beheld
> The silent trees and saw the intruding sky.—
> Then dearest Maiden, move along these shades
> In gentleness of heart; with gentle hand
> Touch—for there is a spirit in the woods.[28]

Like the boat-stealing scene in Book I of *The Prelude*, "Nutting" is
presented in sexually charged terms. The "virgin scene" is "merci-
lessly ravaged" and "sullied." And it is left to the "dearest Maiden"
to return to the woods with a gentler touch. For Berry, too, the
transaction between humanity and nature may usefully be understood in the terms of human sexuality. But Berry moves beyond the
passive ache of violation and regret to the more reciprocal and inclusive relation of marriage. In this regard he is closer to Wordsworth's
predecessor Milton. At the end of Book X of *Paradise Lost*, Milton
makes a crucial pun on the word "repair." Adam and Eve must
"repair" to the place of their sin, in order to begin "repairing" the
breach they opened between themselves and God; thus joined in
intentions, they may also be "re-paired," moving past the divisions
and recriminations which blighted their own marriage just after the
Fall.[29]

Milton's theme of the fortunate fall may be expressed in the idea
that true marriage is only possible after a divorce. The Adam and
Eve departing hand in hand from the garden at the end of Book XII
have been joined on levels inaccessible to the happy pair in the
rose-bower of Book IV. Their eventual relation to God, through
Christ, also promises them a role of more dignity and satisfaction
than would otherwise have been theirs. The loveliness of the lost
garden is no less real for such consolation, and Berry in Kentucky
feels it no less than Adam and Eve, and Milton, looking back at the
gates of Paradise. Berry writes, "The pristine America that the first
white man saw is a lost continent, sunk like Atlantis in the sea. The
thought of what was here once and is gone forever will not leave me
as long as I live. It is as though I walk knee-deep in its absence."[30]
His response to such loss is one of chastened resolution. Section 9 of
"Reverdure" reflects his determination to repair the disruptions of
his place:

> Though I came here
> by history's ruin, reverdure
> is my calling:
> to make these scars grow grass.[31]

Berry reads the earth as well as works in it, and the lesson he draws
from his reading is expressed in lines from the *I Ching* which he uses
as the epigraph for his volume *Clearing*: "What has been spoiled
through man's fault can be made good again through man's work."

One of the corollaries of Berry's insistence on marriage as a model

for right human relation with the earth is the high value he places
on fidelity. In "The Body and the Earth," a particularly rich chapter
in Berry's *The Unsettling of America*, he writes, "The modern failure
of marriage that has so estranged the sexes from each other seems
analogous to the 'social mobility' that has estranged us from our
land, and the two are historically parallel."[32] In his essay "Discipline
and Hope," from *A Continuous Harmony*, Berry develops his sense of
marriage in Miltonic language of atonement, which he breaks down
to its component words, at-one-ment. The exercise of fidelity in one
sphere enhances its possibility in another.

> Thus, if the metaphor of atonement is alive in his consciousness
> a man will see that he should love and care for his land as for
> his wife, that his relation to his place in the world is as solemn
> and demanding, and as blessed, as marriage; and he will see
> that he should respect his marriage as he respects the mysteries
> and transcendent powers—that is, as a sacrament. Or—to move
> in the opposite direction through the changes of the metaphor—
> in order to care properly for his land he will see that he must
> emulate the Creator: to learn to use and preserve the open
> fields, as Sir Albert Howard said, he must look into the woods;
> he must study and follow natural process; he must understand
> the *husbanding* that, in nature, always accompanies providing.[33]

A heartless relation with nature is possible only for one distracted
from its immediate reality. When the mind is opened and clear, a
whole world flows in. Such is the advantage of a marriage to the
earth, consummated in intimate familiarity with a single chosen
place.

> It is only in a country that is well-known, full of familiar names
> and places, full of life that is always changing, that the mind
> goes free of abstractions, and renews itself in the presence of the
> creation, that so persistently eludes human comprehension and
> human law. It is only in the place that one belongs to, intimate
> and familiar, long watched over, that the details rise up out of
> the whole and become visible: the hawk stoops into the clearing
> before one's own eyes; the wood drake, aloof and serene in his
> glorious plumage, swims out of his hiding place.[34]

Familiarity is the long enactment of surrender to a place. Through
marriage a person may come to human singleness beyond distraction. In Berry's words, "We thus come again to the paradox that one
can become whole only by the responsible acceptance of one's
partiality."[35] To be partial is the opposite of inertness, in the chemical sense of that term: an element that will not enter into combina-

tion. Partialness, living rooted in one's own perpetual decay, allows for connection, for the cross-pollination that lets flowers bear their message from the earth. As Berry's poem "The Current" shows, marriage with a place is a wedding, too, with every vital interchange between humanity and the earth, past and present. History is comprehended, one's own personality lifted into a larger light, in the act of stooping to bear seed back to the earth.

> Having once put his hand into the ground,
> seeding there what he hopes will outlast him,
> a man has made a marriage with his place,
> and if he leaves it his flesh will ache to go back.
> . . . .
> The current flowing to him through the earth
> flows past him, and he sees one descended from him,
> a young man who has reached into the ground,
> his hand held in the dark as by a hand.[36]

Hunting and gathering are the words with which I have described Gary Snyder's relation, as a poet, with nature, just as cultivation described the plowman-poet Berry's responses to the land. For Robert Pack, pruning is the corresponding verb of interaction with the physical world. Pack's more stationary form of groundedness may be contrasted with Snyder's wandering encounters and with Berry's active, engendering life in the soil; but his quiet shaping vision may also be connected with their art, as another attempt to participate in an order larger than the merely human. Like Wendell Berry's, Robert Pack's life and poetry have a rural setting, yet Pack's self-definition in his writing is as a householder rather than as a farmer. The value he places on his home's nurturing enclosure in turn reflects and influences both the formal dimensions of his poetry and the fundamentally conservative view he takes of history and the human prospect. The self which Pack develops in his poetry is outwardly conventional in comparison with Snyder's or Berry's. Like theirs, however, his is also a deeply meditated and chosen world, one in which tradition is carefully fitted to a certain landscape and time. A poem representative in important ways of Pack's art is "The Stone Wall Circling the Garden," from his volume *Keeping Watch*.

> Instantly my fingers know surely
>   where the stone will fit.
> Its curved weight surges up my arms,
>   humming in my blood:
> *I have waited now a hundred years, knowing*
>   *I belong here.*

A twist, a nudge, and there it is
          in its fixed place
in a destined design, balanced in the sun
          which says: *So be it,*
I adore all circles, I commend your work.
          I hear the bees arrive
and the earth revolve, tightening the grip
          of each stone, one
to the other, to the other, to the other,
          in the bronze heat,
ore of my bones, which says: *Breathe in*
          the bees' dark rose
and the dust of the air. And so I do
          as the circle grows
more still, gathering the garden in,
          while bees follow
the odor the wind-lanes waft away
          beyond my sight.
And there another circle tightens, made
          of the shape of stones
as bees revolve and the dust follows
          in the wind-lanes,
each speck shaped like a star, where a circle
          tightens and holds
like a single stone, like the stone
          in the clutch
of my hands which says: *There is nothing further*
          for you to desire.[37]

An obvious element of this poem is its strong, regular cadence, as the alternation of shorter and longer lines keeps the beat to which the poem revolves. In its formal regularity the poem draws a circle around itself, focused on the single stone in the poet's hand. To this extent Pack's poem may be opposed to a piece like Snyder's *"this poem is for bear,"* with its sudden shifts of rhythm, syntax, and voice. But though Pack's poem may have a more marked centripetal impulse, it is like Snyder's and Berry's writing in its attempts to achieve a circularity harmonious with that of the earth. Wandering away from cities, into the wilderness, is a way for Snyder to gain a wider compass, and a greater possibility for wholeness in his poetry: it is an arc of inclusiveness. Digging compost back into the earth is also an exercise in rotation, enriching Berry's identification with the cycle through which soil retains its health.

Pack's dynamic circularity is paradoxically characterized by an essential motionlessness. Lodging the stone in its place in the wall, he

centers the concentric world. Star-shaped specks of pollen hang, like
the bees and like the sun, over the gripped stone. Each object is the
center of a solar system; each is the satellite for a garden of suns.
There is no need for anything, in the fulfillment of such a configuration, to move, for to stand still is also to circle with the dancers of
the Great Wheel. These seem to me the resonances of Pack's last
line: *"There is nothing further / for you to desire."* His poems occupy a
smaller plot of land than Snyder's and Berry's do, and they are often
characterized by stillness or by relatively undramatic action. I think,
though, that this muted, modest quality is yet another version of
"proud humility." Pack does not need to leave his garden, because
the world is there. His poetry reveals the expansiveness which follows from affirmation of one's enclosure; isolation only comes when
a person feels that the vital center of life is *separated* from him by a
wall. In the opening lines of "Michael," Wordsworth wrote of the
remnant of another stone wall that "to that simple object appertains
a story." In lifting a stone, Pack gains the objective point to which a
world may appertain. The things in a physical world both focus and
expand a mind that would otherwise be a planetless sun, an orbit-
less erratic.

"Rondo of the Familiar," from *Waking to My Name,* is a poem
which further develops this understanding of domestic enclosure as
the basis for life's expansive wholeness.

> Beside the waterfall,
> by the lichen face of rock,
> you pause in pine shade to remember blue
> for drawing back, and green
> for trust, replenishing yourself
> among familiar leaves
> with scattered sunlight.
> And beyond those trees in time not ours,
> you see our children search
> for what we gave them, only to find
> our love again
> in other hands and faces
> where our bodies cannot go.
> And I step forth
> into the scattered light
> where you elude me,
> though my hands reach out
> to share these daily losses,
> each beloved breath rounded to a pause,
> that still compose our lives.

And the waterfall spills on;
and lichen holds to the rock-face
in the slowness
of its quiet life, deliberate
as the dividing of a cell;
and you remember blue
for each round pause you made
freshening a bed,
washing a window with even strokes.
And I step forth
into quickening light
that restores you and
takes you away, telling my hands
to be true to their green truth—
as our children, preparing faithfully to depart
beyond those trees,
hold for an instant in the pause
you have composed for them.
And I enter that pause,
though the waterfall spills on,
and pollen dust stains
our windows, and the familiar bed
deepens its repeated sigh,
as you wait for me,
each loss fragrant in your arms,
blue as the early crocus
our children soon will stoop to,
pausing by a waterfall
in familiar time beyond us
in pine shade
by the lichen face of rock.[38]

A word to which the poem repeatedly turns is "pause"; Pack affirms the possibility in each *moment* for a pause, within which the patterns of life must find their fulfillment or not at all. A pause thus represents the achievement of a personally significant order, a respite from the waterfall of temporality. In this sense, marriage is also a pause. And the house within which a family gathers is a similar enclosure in time, all the more meaningful because it is momentary. Pack is like Berry in finding the union of man and woman a microcosm for the marriage of humanity with the physical world. But he is also reminiscent, in his sense of the married pair's bedroom as a windowed enclosure centering and comprehending the whole world, of Donne. In the grave wit of his final lines in "The Sunne Rising," Donne writes,

Thine age askes ease, and since thy duties bee
To warme the world, that's done in warming us.
Shine here to us, and thou art every where;
This bed thy center is, these walls thy spheare.[39]

The world achieves its order, finally, within the inclusive act of perception fostered by love.

The human problem with such order is the transience of each pause; to perceive a momentary meaning is also to perceive its passing. The consolation offered by the poet's house, with its walled garden amid the fields, is that in it moments may "be / bound each to each / in mutual piety"; familiar elements cycle through the family's life like the repeated patterns of a rondo. Only a deeply known landscape in which one has invested his life can offer such reassurance of continuous identity. Chosen place thus becomes the bowl in which experience gathers and brims. But even beloved places vanish at last, as "Michael" shows us, and the beauty of a landscape is only a moment. There are many levels on which this fact may be understood, but in "Rondo" it is expressed through the poet's imagination of his children, as they pass into a world without him and find their own new homes. Knowing that they will move "beyond those trees in time not ours," the poet feels a challenge to his familiar order. It seems, in anticipation, the breaking of the circle.

There are, I believe, two ways in which the poem deals with the anxiety of transience. One is that, just as the poet's children raise the problem in its most pressing form, they provide the medium of its resolution. A meditation that begins with a mother "beside a waterfall" closes with her children "pausing by a waterfall," too. The principle of continuity here is genetic, sameness within difference, like "the dividing of a cell." It is important that, although it may be the same waterfall from the poet's beginning, the indefinite article holds the connection on a more general plane. The ordering pause is counter in the poem to the water's spilling rush: the waterfall has a relentless quality, like that Frost ascribes to his "west-running brook," "the universal cataract of death / That spends to nothingness." It is the world's flux, beside which all momentary human meanings must arise. But in this way the world's unceasing change itself becomes an element of stability in people's lives. Because their time and place grow different from those of their childhood, the poet's children are eventually bound even more closely to the lives of their parents, who also came to pause beside a waterfall of change. Upon hearing of Parmenides's saying that a man cannot step into the same river twice, Anaxagoras remarked that a man cannot step into the same river *once*: our present moments are in continuity with the past because they, like it, exist in the midst of flux. The precarious separations of such a world make possible a deeper bond of sympathetic identification than would otherwise have been possible. It is noticeable, in fact, that even husband and wife in the poem's beginning appear in sequence, as if searching for each other in the bewilderment of sun and shade. Their unity is expressed most fully in the future of their children, a future in which they themselves cannot directly participate—the "familiar time beyond us."

The second level of resolution relates to an image appearing at the poem's beginning, its middle, and its end: "the lichen face of rock." Lichen relates Pack's poem in an interesting way to Gary Snyder and the understanding of poetry as "the fungus of mind." Fungus digests, and makes more widely available, the elements of decay, and it is one of the two types of organism contributing to the symbiosis we call lichen. Like Snyder's, Pack's poetry expresses the possibility for human meaning in the terms of decay and collapse. However, where Snyder's woodland fungus is part of the leaf-rich fermentation of the forest floor, and thus of a more broadly conceived ecosystem, Pack's exists on the inert granite surface of a boulder, and embodies a much smaller, more direct circle of interaction. Fungus provides the structural support and protection for the alga which is a lichen's other constituent. The alga, in turn, is able to photosynthesize new nourishment and, in its process of decay, provides the fungus with food. The lichen is thus a microcosm, both of the surrounding cycles of life and of the circle of human meaning. Its isolation reflects a world of fewer possibilities than are available in Snyder's forest, but it also allows, in its very marginality, for a forceful connection between the local and the general.

Lichen and rock evoke New England's terrain, where meager soil is often unable to hide the bones of the landscape's history. A certain bleak courage has emerged in the New England character and is typified in the frigidity and compactness of Frost's work. It is hard to make a crop where the soil is so thin and the summer so short; the waves of emigration from Vermont in the nineteenth and twentieth centuries washed the early settlers' optimism back down out of the hills. The regional mood that has since developed is one of guardedness and caution; satisfaction has come in the achievement of modest goals against bad odds. As all three of these grounded

poets acknowledge, there is an important connection between local
history and ecology and the kind of poetry arising in a given place.
Pack's dramatic monologue "Trying to Separate," from *Faces in a
Single Tree*, speaks to such a connection.

> Please give me room, Howard! I've tried before
> to tell you this—I have to leave you, oh
> that came out wrong, there's no way I can find
> the words that sound as if I'm making sense.
> Not *you*, Howard, it isn't *you* I'm leaving,
> it's Vermont, the starving deer, the spring
> that never comes, the gloomy ice and clay.
> Even when late sun lingers in the birches,
> darkness fills my mind. I need more light,
> more red—not just a pair of cardinals,
> but flocks of them. There's no red in the earth;
> purple spreads in the mountains when the sun
> descends behind the hemlock trees as if
> the animals were grieving there. And fall
> comes much too soon, the yellows are too brief;
> I don't have time here to forget myself.
> I want to go to Tucson where I lived
> before my mother died, where stones are red,
> the desert light *feels* red—a gradual
> slow, steady red. I need more time to dwell
> on images I want to paint. Don't joke
> again about my always *seeing red*!
> You once said that my painting is the cause,
> but that's not first; I need a different light
> than you to *see*, and then the paintings come.
> You need Vermont, you need an inward light;
> you need the feeling that each day is hard.
> Love cannot feed itself with love. We've tried.
> Love needs something outside itself—children—
> and we've delayed deciding that too long.
> You said one only chooses children after
> one has had them; then they become like *place*,
> then they're the *given* like the landscape is.
> You think there's got to be some deeper cause
> for breaking up—I fear you may be right,
> but I can't find that cause; Howard, believe me,
> I've really looked. All that I know is red,
> and you desire grey—punishing winter
> is your season, white birches are your light.
> You need Vermont to be yourself. You do!
> Don't try to comfort me; don't touch me now—

that makes me angry when I want to talk—
for then you'll have a reason I should stay.
You'll say: admit it's *me* you want to leave,
admit you're angry, that it's not because
you love the goddamn red; you'll say we have our sunsets
blazing on the snow, we have our fire at night,
as if I'll give in like I always do.[40]

"Trying to Separate" creates a counterpoint to "Rondo of the Familiar." "Rondo" shows how marriage borrows its wholeness from a chosen landscape, while this monologue brings out a corollary truth: without the ability to agree upon an enclosing space, a marriage falls apart. Though the domestic circle is, from one perspective, a narrow achievement, it is also a demanding one. Without the steady relinquishment attending choice, there is no center and the marriage will not hold. The interdependent relation of marriage, children, and place in this poem also amplifies the meaning of "Rondo." Wife and husband, from their different standpoints, both perceive the place of children in the equation, she in saying "Love needs something outside itself," he in the sense that children, "after one has had them," "become like *place*, / then they're the *given* like the landscape is." In the resolution of "Rondo of the Familiar" is an understanding that children carry a couple into a "familiar time beyond us," and thus allow an overtone of intimacy above the dissonances of the present. But to have children with such a capacity for finding their own pauses in the world assumes that they have themselves been grounded in a family with *its* footing in a chosen place. To marry is to choose a place; to belong to that place is to have it remembered and reenacted by your children. The wife who is this monologue's speaker moves, like one baffled by an elusive need, from one reason to another to explain why she must leave Vermont: hard winters, darkness, the absence of children. But all of her reasons finally seem real, bound together by their disconnectedness, and by its contrast with the circle that would have allowed a married life.

The woman in the monologue is a painter, and her comparison of New England with the Southwest is primarily in visual terms—the gloom of a grey-white world versus "a gradual / slow, steady red." But this scenic, closely observed quality is also typical of many of Pack's other landscapes; it is particularly noticeable in the painterly way he registers and balances his colors: bronze and green, yellow and blue. Windows are often important, too, as the mind's passage between a world of natural process and the specific enclosures of human order. Whereas Snyder and Berry show themselves moving through the natural world, Pack's self-presentation in his poems is frequently one of quiet attentiveness to a world moving around him. This characteristic of his vision is brought out clearly in the opening lines of "Looking at a Mountain-Range While Listening to a Mozart Piano Concerto":

> Looking eastward through my picture window
> over the snow, the sun just down, I see
> the mountain-range hazing to one shade of blue. . . . [41]

It is understandable, given the rapidly changing, and often inhospitable, climate of New England, that meditations standing or sitting by a window should play a prominent part in his poetry. In addition, though, the way in which a window *frames* the landscape is appropriate to Pack's New England grounding in tradition and history. There are, for him, limitations of human possibility, just as there are certain conventional forms with a proven usefulness.

This monologue, like so much of the poetry of Frost—and before him, of course, Wordsworth, Milton, Shakespeare—is in blank verse. The verse form, like the window, frames and focuses the poet's regard for the flowing forms of nature. It represents one kind of traditional relationship with the physical world. But just as the man and woman in the monologue need different landscapes and different lights, poets grounded in disparate terrains must also each find the particular forms and themes suited to their places. So often there is a partisan, even polemical, quality in our poetry of nature's response to tradition. It is vital, though, as the localized process of reinhabitation continues, to recognize the worth of more than one kind of poetic order, as we do of many distinctive landscapes. On a round, circling earth, inclusiveness rather than a dualistic discrimination should guide our aesthetic. Through such a comprehensive effort Robert Pack's location of New England within the Western tradition may be juxtaposed, and in some measure connected, with Gary Snyder's ancient Native American and Asian values and with Wendell Berry's deeply rooted agricultural perspective.

The waste and despoliation of our present-day civilization has provided one of the principal reasons for *questioning* the worth of any tradition underlying it. In a lengthy poem from *Keeping Watch* entitled "Jeremiah," Pack raises the question of complicity between himself, with his domestic order and happiness, and the ravagers of the world beyond his garden's stone wall. It is similar to Snyder's "The Dead by the Side of the Road" and Berry's "The Morning's

News," in that all three poems are attempts to confront and, if possible, to integrate elements of the world which would otherwise undermine the reality or worth of the poets' achieved order. "Jeremiah" opens with a stark image of prophetic nature, shattering the concentric order of the poet's life and art.

> In that jagged maple tree,
>   its torn leaves streaming
>   with October wind,
>   furious Jeremiah
> shakes his hair, his mouth
>   circles to a groan,
>   his eyes see all that strains
>   against his will to sleep:
> rubble of cities,
>   scorched apple orchards,
>   the bloated belly
>   of the bone-legged child,
> gazing at nothing.
>   Why has it come
>   to this? What laws
>   have we broken
> And break? I cannot find
>   the cause in my heart
>   that has brought us down.[42]

How may a man making his life in a settled rural landscape connect his good fortune with the fate of America's cities or with the devastation by warfare or greed of other landscapes? An even more fundamental problem, in view of the importance of children to the generational order of Pack's poetry, is what to do with the image, brought into the family's home by television or a magazine photograph, of a child dying of starvation?

The poet's first response is to deny any real connection between such horror and his own life. He seeks to exorcise these images which he can neither accept responsibility for nor forget, assigning any blame for gross violations of "the law" to his "brothers." The crisis, and the achievement, of "Jeremiah" is in its gradual recognition that the poet, just as he is damaged by his brothers' crimes, is implicated in them. The poem's emphasis shifts from a third-person account, to accusation's second-person form, to the confession of first person—both in the inclusive acknowledgment of "we" and in the responsible voice that can finally say, "I seek a cure in my own life." For, after all, even in rural Vermont's serene remoteness from

so many of the modern world's evils, those abuses the poet first
ascribed to his fallen and distant brothers enact themselves constantly in his presence and in his person:

> We go to the stream
> and return, confounded,
>   for the water is sludge;
>   we go to the field
>   where the huge-headed calf
> drags his tongue;
>   and the rotting city
>   plunders the light.
>   Is it you,
> my brother,
>   who goes there, disguised
>   in my rejected face,
>   wearing my shoes?[43]

The small circle of garden and house cannot hold out the chaos of
the age; in one sense, to cultivate a *personal* order is to *permit* the
surrounding ruin. At this point in the poem Pack comes very close
to Berry's position early in "The Morning's News"—he is heartsick
about a painstakingly cultivated order that suddenly seems either
hopelessly vulnerable or, in fact, fraudulent. The acknowledgment
of such hateful entanglement is hard to bear, but it is also accompanied in the poem by a sudden cessation of the wind agitating the
Jeremiah-tree. In the terms of the poem's subsiding resolution, there
is a final attempt at relating the wind's prophecy to the protective
enclosure of the house, at understanding the connectedness of suffering and happiness.

> From my chair,
>   I see the maple tree
>   suddenly go still,
>   returning to itself,
> obeying its season,
>   the law of its kind.
>   Its red leaves shimmer
>   in the late, slant rays.
> How beautifully it glows,
>   possessing its time!
>   Oncoming winter
>   kindles my house,
> making the wooden walls
>   intimate about me.

I cling to what I have
keeper of myself.
Cause of the law within me,
just power to accuse
and to atone—sleep now,
Jeremiah, furious wind!
And how would I live, brother,
as our parched roots
shrivel and withdraw,
if I cannot
trust you?[44]

Human meaning, like the "pause" of "Rondo," is always evanescent, rendered precious by the overwhelming disorders of the surrounding world. Winter kindles a house both with the colored angles of its long-drawn dusk and with the seasonal hearth-fires of those living within. Finally, though, there is a *dependence* of order upon disorder for its definition, a sense in which the human seasons, like those of nature, find their fulfillment, rather than their competition, in one another. The face of nature provides one model of such wholeness within variation: the sudden stillness of the tree resolves the poem on a level beneath that of the poet's questioning. The speaking tree suddenly returns to itself, yet when wind comes it is ready to speak again. Human contradictions must be accepted lest the seasons of happiness too turn bitter. In such an awareness the poet writes, "I cling to what I have." Nature both serves as a redemptive model of wholeness and acts to make the human disorder more evident. Pack's is a world with walls and windows, but at times one also sees a *natural* order kindled by the long onset of *human* winter. Pack is a traditional poet but, by that very token, not a complacent one. In the face of nature's beauty he finds, as Virgil does, the mortal tears of things, and the basis for human sympathy. Nature, in its order and its flux alike, leads the attentive individual toward self-forgiveness and a renewed impulse of reconciliation. It discloses a humanity familial in its perpetual struggle for harmony.

In concluding this discussion of Pack I want to look briefly at a poem which synthesizes the largest terms of his affirmation: through loss and the acceptance of it we gain the possibility for oneness with the physical earth and with other people. "Pruning Fruit Trees," from *Keeping Watch*, also exemplifies the way in which nature and tradition are able to serve Pack as vehicles for one another.

Begin by cutting
all branches away
that are now dead.
It is March. One surely feels
in the air a softness
that has not yet arrived.
The cut must be made close
to the parent limb,
following the angle
of its growth.
Used snow inches deep shows
yesterday's boot prints,
my son's and mine, circling
each other, circling each tree.
Where equal branches
now divide, choose one and cut—
it is not good that they contend
for vital sap.
The cut must be made close
to the parent limb,
soon it will heal.
The chickadees scold us;
by their feeder they have their rights.
Don't be afraid to cut—that's it,
cut more, it's good for the tree,
lengthening life,
making its fruit full.
A farmer told me to talk
to the trees. Tell them
"this is good for you."
Speak softly, thank them.
It is June. Our footprints faintly
circle the trees in the moist grass.
Like little berries, the fruit is hard.
They will make it, they will hold on.
See, they will hold on, they will ripen,
they will do well.
It is June. I have learned
to ask for nothing more.
I have never
been happier than this.
Tell them they will do well.
As wind flutters their leaves,
praise them.
It is March. The cut

Must be made close
to the parent limb.[45]

This poem unifies the themes of the previous four. The seasons, March and June, bear testimony to each other in the wholeness of the year and help to prepare the father for giving assent to his son's eventual growth and separation from him. Footprints, circling the tree, circle each other; on a turning earth such cycles of separation and return seem fitting, and bring quietness to the heart. Talking to the trees he prunes, the father counsels himself, in a therapeutic identification with nonhuman life. And as his words recur in season—"the cut / must be made close / to the parent limb"—there is a corroboration of the natural harmony of relinquishment. When Pack writes, "A farmer told me to talk / to the trees," he brings in an element also important in the natural vision of Snyder and Berry. Traditional *lore* reminds us of a necessary intimacy with the world; the seasonal growth brings back the words of those who have found the effectiveness of healing and sacrifice. Such memories teach us to be at home both in the world and in our own humanity.

Excursion:
Hitching a Ride
with the Cumberland Beggar

Route 116

I stood at the intersection of Quarry Road and Route 116 in an hour transfigured by fall, by sunset, and by Wordsworth's poetry. The air of central Vermont begins in September to hone its edge against the sugar maples, but warm gusts still rise from the low ground and summer can glide up Lake Champlain for the space of an afternoon. At six o'clock the sun balanced about forty minutes above the line of Wood Brothers' Orchard, and the sky as I looked west was flooded with cumulostratus clouds—a close-packed mass, tinged yellow and pink, rushing north to signal a change in the weather.

After teaching a late seminar on the *Lyrical Ballads*, I was hitchhiking from Middlebury College to Bristol. My carpool had evaporated, and a ride from town had dropped me off here at Route 116, nine miles south of home. Not having done much hitching in the twelve years since graduating from college, and standing under such a sky, I found that my mood was one of exhilaration, release. I looked around, in the conviction that I had somehow passed into Wordsworth's Lake District, where narrow bands of human settlement lie cut off from one another by the unpeopled ridges. The *Ballads'* landscape frames a world of humanity at the edge. It is a margin where poverty abounds: beggars, returning soldiers, infirm laborers, young mothers crazed by adversity. But within Wordsworth's bleak mountains people also live in the closest of relations with nature, involved in the cycles of the land, and with the landscape's features supplying the mind's terrain. It was easy, standing on Route 116, to feel

myself in just such a tenuous niche. The ridge of the Green Mountains rose steeply at my back, while Bristol Cliffs loomed over the
highway to my north. Middlebury was blocked from sight, and
mind, by the orchard's densely planted slope. Between the darkening trees and the clouds, blue ridge beyond blue ridge, hung the
distant high-peak region of the Adirondacks. On this strip of
houses, trailers, chicken coops, following a path beneath the crests,
I smiled, stuck out my thumb, and thought complacently of the Old
Cumberland Beggar.

As in so many of our encounters with Wordsworth's rural poor, we
come upon the Beggar "by the highway side." These ballad highways
are not merely routes from one village to another, but public places in
themselves, avenues along which the dislocated find each other and
discover a basis for community. Unfortunates take to the road so that it
will be easier for others to help them; the Old Cumberland Beggar
makes his way down a highway of benevolence:

> He travels on, a solitary Man,
> So helpless in appearance, that for him
> The sauntering horseman throws not with a slack
> And careless hand his alms upon the ground,
> But stops,—that he may safely lodge the coin
> Within the old Man's hat; nor quits him so,
> But still, when he has given his horse the rein,
> Watches the aged Beggar with a look
> Sidelong and half-reverted. She who tends
> The toll-gate, when in summer at her door
> She turns her wheel, if on the road she sees
> The aged Beggar coming, quits her work,
> And lifts the latch for him that he may pass.
> The post-boy, when his rattling wheels o'ertake
> The aged Beggar in the woody lane,
> Shouts to him from behind; and if thus warned
> The old man does not change his course, the boy
> Turns with less noisy wheels to the roadside,
> And passes gently by, without a curse
> Upon his lips, or anger at his heart.[1]

With these images of kindness in my mind, I happily offered myself
as the human object for any who might, as Wordsworth's dwellers
in the Lake District did,

> Long for some moments in a weary life
> When they can know and feel that they have been,
> Themselves, the fathers and the dealers-out
> Of some small blessings.[2]

After three quarters of an hour, when the sun had rolled behind the apple trees and the clouds had subsided to gray, I began to reconsider my situation. A cold wind was whipping up. Although I was not yet angry at the twenty or so drivers who had sped past me, I could feel my disappointment starting to fizz. When I first planted my briefcase conspicuously in front of my feet and began to hitch, I had registered with pleasure the fact that I was wearing my nicest tweed jacket; recognizing that I was a teacher at Middlebury College, stranded on the way home after a long day, someone would be especially likely to offer me a ride. As this prim reflection slowly blurred, I was possessed by non-Vermonter's paranoia, and decided that my briefcase and jacket were probably *keeping* me from getting a ride. I shifted my Chester A. Reilly–style lunchbox in front of the briefcase to show that, although temporarily overdressed, I was a man of the people. Then I held the lunchbox up under my arm and put the briefcase behind me. After I had tried my most wholesome smile on seven more cars (for luck), I hung it up and started walking up the road, disgruntled in my stiff new cowboy boots. With the temperature and my blood-sugar level dropping off at about the same rate, I had slipped from disillusionment to self-pity. The question that I asked myself as I creaked along, feeling aged and abandoned, was why so many people were kind to the Old Cumberland Beggar and not one would do a good turn for me.

There is a problem with having too much time to ponder the inquiries of self-pity, namely, that there are usually good answers, which end up making it hard to sustain a proper self-respecting inwardness. In fact, Wordsworth's poem offered an obvious answer to my question about unequal treatment. His neighbors were *used* to seeing the Old Cumberland Beggar and were used to granting him alms. My initial sense of adventure testified to the fact that I had never attempted to hitch on this road before; nor, as I thought back, was it common to find anyone else thumbing a ride on Route 116. Whereas the country people of the Lake District associated the Beggar with their own pleasure at past kindnesses to him, I had no such place in the lives of people passing me. If I had any associations at all for these drivers, it may have been with the anonymous murderers of headlines and prime-time melodrama; several people whose eyes met mine glared, as if I had threatened them.

But Wordsworth's insight in the poem finally has to do with something subtler than this fact of social familiarity: he also recognizes the powerful force of habitual response in lending wholeness to one's emotional universe and, ultimately, to the landscape itself.

> While from door to door,
> This old Man creeps, the villagers in him
> Behold a record which together binds
> Past deeds and offices of charity . . .
> . . . .
>
> Where'er the aged Beggar takes his rounds,
> The mild necessity of use compels
> To acts of love; and habit does the work
> Of reason; yet prepares that after-joy
> Which reason cherishes. And thus the soul,
> By that sweet taste of pleasure unpursued,
> Doth find herself insensibly disposed
> To virtue and true goodness.[3]

Like the old man of "Resolution and Independence," the Cumberland Beggar possesses the quality of humble endurance. But, in contrast to the leech-gatherer's "lofty utterance," he never speaks, nor does he even appear to notice another person. His is a consistency almost to the point of inertness; as the narrator states near the beginning of his account,

> Him from my childhood have I known; and then
> He was so old, he seems not older now.[4]

For Wordsworth the shifting experiences and emotions of a life can only achieve form when tied to some stable entity outside the self. Unlike Eliot's "objective correlative," which offers a metaphorical focus for the field of thought, Wordsworth's ideal is for a poetry of fully comprehended *external* reference. The Beggar becomes for his neighbors "a silent monitor." Like nature, "the anchor" of the poet's "purest thoughts" in "Tintern Abbey," the old man comes to serve as a touchstone of thought precisely because "that vast solitude to which / The Tide of things has borne him" has given to him the dignity of a thing. He embodies Wordsworth's distinctive sensitivity to the human landmark: the individual who is so closely associated with a natural scene that he catalyzes the union between a world of objects and the emotional universe. In "Michael," the landscape of the shepherd's life is similarly enhanced by the associations of terrain with Luke, the son of his old age:

> Why should I relate
> That objects which the shepherd loved before
> Were dearer now? that from the Boy there came
> Feelings and emanations—things which were
> Light to the sun and music to the wind. . . . [5]

The Old Cumberland Beggar, by virtue of his extreme infirmity, takes on a special mediating power. By the end of the poem it becomes clear that he is not just in nature, but of it. He is midway between the aged leech-gatherer, whose head and feet are "coming together in life's pilgrimage," and the dead girl of "A Slumber Did My Spirit Seal":

> No motion has she now, no force;
> She neither hears nor sees;
> Rolled round in earth's diurnal course,
> With rocks, and stones, and trees.[6]

He is still moving *through* the world, at the far edge of his life, but his oblivion gives the Cumberland Beggar a oneness with nature that is deeper than the senses' communication. As the concluding benediction affirms, only a creature beyond particular response can give himself fully to the weather, can attain the consummation of gravity:

> Let him be free of mountain solitudes;
> And have around him, whether heard or not,
> The pleasant melody of woodland birds.
> Few are his pleasures: if his eyes have now
> Been doomed so long to settle upon earth
> That not without some effort they behold
> The countenance of the horizontal sun,
> Rising or setting, let the light at least
> Find a free entrance to their languid orbs.
> And let him, *where* and *when* he will, sit down
> Beneath the trees, or on a grassy bank
> Of highway side, and with the little birds
> Share his chance-gathered meal; and, finally,
> As in the eye of Nature he has lived,
> So in the eye of Nature let him die![7]

At this point in my lengthening afternoon, Vermont had effectively detached itself from my Lake District of the mind. As I pondered the stillness and gravity of the Beggar, I was walking along the highway's graveled shoulder. Each time a car passed I was buffeted by the wall of air traveling at fifty miles per hour, insulted by the exhaust fumes swirling up at the rear bumper like a Bronx cheer. This highway, for reasons beyond its asphalt surface and its yellow line, seemed to offer few of the possibilities for meditation and community found along our routes through the *Lyrical Ballads*. I was by now just a couple of miles from a friend's house, on the

Bristol Flats, which was in turn just a few miles south of the Bristol village; from there I could call home for a ride. As I continued to walk, my thoughts turned from the discredited analogy between me and the Old Cumberland Beggar to the more general question of how far a contemporary landscape *can* match the Lake District's capacity to inform a universe of thought and feeling. What had begun as a reverie was gradually taking on a momentum born of curiosity fused with escapism.

Following such an avenue of thought, I was reminded of E. M. Forster's novel *Howards End* (1910), which is on one important level a meditation about the relation between his beloved English landscape and the dawning era of the motorcar. The Wilcoxes, who are associated with automobiles throughout the novel, are oblivious to the beauty of England. Even the sensitive Margaret Schlegel, when she takes a ride in the Wilcoxes' sedan, feels her grasp of natural form and harmony blur, as her speeding vehicle makes the hills hump and bubble like porridge in a vast boiling vat. In New England, automobile tourism exposes thousands to the fall colors and to the broad vistas of mountain and lake, but the particular and familiar features of terrain are whirled up in a passing cloud, like the dust sucked along in the wake of Charles Wilcox's car. No time is allowed for the slow weaving of association's web, tying the mysteries of our human life to a certain tree along the road, a half-fallen stone wall.

The speed of automobiles is only the most obvious way in which mobility has eroded the Wordsworthian possibility for a oneness with nature through long familiarity. Another theme of *Howards End* is what happens when a family must give up the house which has contained its whole life together and move into a London of "bricks and mortar rising and falling with the restlessness of water in a fountain." Even if one can stay still long enough to cultivate deep familiarity with a place, many locales in our society have themselves lost the physical stability which the heart requires. When Wordsworth returns to the hills above Tintern Abbey after "five years have passed," he finds that nothing has changed in the outward scene. The ruined abbey is, to be sure, a reminder of historical process; but having already been a ruin for centuries, it has come to function as an architectural equivalent of the Cumberland Beggar—an indication of the way in which human process can subside into a sort of fossil, a landmark outside of time. In the California county where I grew up there were also hills, all around our town, for walks, picnics, kite-flying. They are now mostly covered with gaudy luxury homes,

fenced off from walkers and vagrants of all sorts. The stable landscape supplied Wordsworth with a gauge to measure the centrifugal
course of his own mind, and to provide it with a sort of focus. But
when subdivisions revise the hills of childhood, the task of reconciliation with oneself becomes harder to carry out; outward disorientation mirrors but does not clarify the inward process.

For Wordsworth, as Book VII of *The Prelude* makes evident, the
problem of cities and of ceaseless construction goes even beyond
this matter of land consumed and obscured; it is most importantly a
question of disproportion, relative to the human mind's own powers
of receptivity. To a boy nursed by quiet and mountain solitude, the
hubbub of the city was a distraction from life's depths and from the
mind's settled dignity amid natural cycles. London for him was "a
storm," intensely absorbing but unable to pass "beyond the suburbs
of the mind"; the frenzied celebration of the city's street-poor at
Bartholomew Fair presented him with his central example of London's spiritual disaster—"A work completed to our hands, that lays/
If any spectacle of earth can do, / The whole creative powers of man
asleep!"[8] Wordsworth finds the mind paralyzed by the busyness of
society:

> Oh, blank confusion! true epitome
> Of what the mighty city is herself,
> To thousands upon thousands of her sons,
> Living amid the same perpetual whirl
> Of trivial objects, melted and reduced
> To one identity, by differences
> That have no law, no meaning, and no end—[9]

The speed of an automobile and the density and constant change of
a great city are alike in being leveling agencies. The mind, presented
with an incessant flood of stimuli, grows passive. Discriminations as
to the personal value of objects or events fade, for want of that still
moment which preserves them in existence.

From the perspective of his disappointment in London, we can
reflect back, as Wordsworth did, on the world of the *Lyrical Ballads*.
Wordsworth's country people have a bond with nature that is both
imaginative and emotional. A poem such as "The Two April Morn-
ings" reveals that this bond is also characteristically *progressive*—
with the emotional responses of later life building upon those of
youth—and thus able to integrate experiences of suffering and loss
within a larger affirmative response to the world. The poem is a
simple progression of moments: a certain sky recalls to the character

Matthew his earlier grief for a dead daughter; a similar scene makes the poet recall Matthew, himself since dead, as he was on that first occasion "with a bough / Of wilding in his hand." "The will of God be done," says Matthew, and the musing poet quietly joins his own voice to such an affirmation, within the delicate simplicity of his verse.[10] There is a redemption offered to human cycles within the order of natural cycles, an equilibrium as precise and comprehensive as an ecosystem.

These Wordsworthian turnings finally led me home. My wife and children fetched me from our friends' house in the Bristol Flats, and our warm car whisked us through the rising wind to our warmer house. Sitting on our living-room sofa that evening, absorbing the exhalations of our wood-burning stove, I realized how hard it was to gather together my hike along Route 116. In view of my first expectations, and of my subsequent emotions, the human landscape had seemed absurd, too disorderly even to serve as an ironic context for my thoughts. Until coming to the long-awaited way station—the First Homely House—and being rescued there by my family, my relations with other people along the road had felt equally estranged: staring faces glimpsed for a second, silent people and roaring machines. Around the order of home there seemed a world in disarray, resistant to Wordsworth's unifying power.

Gary Snyder, Wendell Berry, and Robert Pack are writers who have labored at reinhabitation, at cultivating a place to live in the wasteland of the modern world. They are pioneers, edging like white pines into abandoned fields, enriching and aerating the soil, striking their roots through eroded slopes. Through grounded poets like these, it becomes possible to draw our landscapes closer to the composted richness of a tradition which includes Wordsworth and his Lake District. Just as with the juxtaposition of Eliot and Jeffers, when the terrains of Wordsworth and our contemporaries are finally pieced together on one map, our possibilities for cultural and personal wholeness are enhanced. The enlarged map can depict a natural geography—with a network of human destinations as well as a system of asphalted highways.

Club Moss

I have been told that the club mosses in which central Vermont abounds—the common variety called running ground pine and the other sorts looking like everything from palm trees to hemlocks to fallen stars—have maintained their basic shapes longer than any other multicellular organism. They persist despite having shrunk from the towering canopy which they formed during the Triassic period to their present domain three inches above the forest floor. The botanist who told me of club mosses' longevity as a life form also commented that they colonize disturbed terrain by preference, frequently growing along the edges of trails and other clearings. They have thus survived, though diminished, by a mode of existence that could be expressed in human terms equally well as opportunism or as humility. Thinking about my long trek up Route 116, it occurs to me that the continuing vitality of our poetry of place is an adaptation as remarkable in its way as that of the club moss. This highway, and the culture it stands for, are permanently disturbed ground, torn by every passing car; and in comparison with the standards of Wordsworth's Lake District, the social continuity is likewise ripped up, right along the yellow dotted line. Into such a world today's poets edge, in a project of reinhabitation and cohesion: adamant advance close to the ground.

The evolutionary advantage of club mosses is that they propagate themselves in two different ways: by spore dispersal from above and by runners under the ground. The second method is particularly advantageous when they find a niche suddenly ready for whatever inhabitant or community can possess it quickly. The localizing, particularizing impulse is very evident in Snyder, Berry, and Pack. But they have also drawn their powers of adaptation from buried runners; a prior generation of American poets put them in a position to possess the broken ground. Many poets could be identified as preparing for contemporary poets of place. Williams, Roethke, and Rexroth would certainly be important names on such a list. But in trying to relate the grounded writing of our contemporaries to Wordsworth's unified, but distant, world, I turn for mediation to two other poets, and to two of their poems in particular: Stevens's "Final Soliloquy of the Interior Paramour" and Frost's "Directive." To connect Wordsworth with such a poet as Berry, through their common affinity with Frost, is to enrich the soil of our experience of nature today. Resonances may thus be understood as rhizomes, and a pattern of disruption in human and natural order may be perceived as temporary, within the larger, unifying flow.

Poetry's power is always that of wholeness and expansion. This is Wallace Stevens's perpetual consolation. The beleaguered self, seemingly shut in from a fragmentary world, really only needs to be more clearly understood. In "The Final Soliloquy of the Interior

Paramour," Stevens explores the unity and consolation of perceiving the poet's mind, his lighted room at evening, and the world as one.

> Light the first light of evening, as in a room
> In which we rest and, for small reason, think
> The world imagined is the ultimate good.
>
> This is, therefore, the intensest rendezvous.
> It is in that thought that we collect ourselves,
> Out of all the indifferences, into one thing:
>
> Within a single thing, a single shawl
> Wrapped tightly round us, since we are poor, a warmth,
> A light, a power, and miraculous influence.
>
> Here, now, we forget each other and ourselves.
> We feel the obscurity of an order, a whole,
> A knowledge, that which arranged the rendezvous.
>
> Within its vital boundary, in the mind.
> We say God and the imagination are one . . .
> How high that highest candle lights the dark.
>
> Out of this same light, out of the central mind,
> We make a dwelling in the evening air,
> In which being there together is enough.[11]

Insight comes as a resolution of identity: the mind, reflective under lamplight, encompasses the world, becomes the world, and gains the finely textured externality with which to comprehend itself. This is the simple fact on which all poetry is based. The mind and the world are mutually informing, and thus take part in a larger reality beyond reason's dualism and all of its isolating discriminations. Wordsworth's "something far more deeply interfused" of Book I of *The Prelude* is an apprehension of this same inclusive truth. I think that Stevens's most important word in the poem is "dwelling," in the next-to-last line. The light, the shawl, and God Himself are all important only as "a room / In which we rest." The project of poetry is like the task Adam and Eve face at the end of Milton's Book XII: to trust in Providence that we can make this world our home. The unity of Stevens's "central mind" is valuable precisely for the multiplicity which it comprehends; familiarity with one's place brings with it liberty to look up and see the stars. Stevens speaks here to the necessity to build a home; and to do so, as his language throughout implies, necessitates a discipline of localizing and limitation: "first," "small," "this," "one," "single," "here," "now," "boundary." Like his disciple Pack, Stevens has always recognized an affinity between strict meter and the compassionate expansions of feeling and perception: there is a need, "since we are poor," for "a warmth, / A power, a light. . . . "

"The Final Soliloquy" sums up so much in Stevens's poetic achievement, but it is a hymn, not a creed or a meditation. A current of warm feeling always runs beneath the surface of Stevens's lapidary restraint, and in this poem it becomes an outpouring of emotion for the beauty of the world in which he lives, the world which he in living has made. It is also a poem which depends upon the fullness of his other poetry for its completion. It lacks the banks of flowers arrayed throughout "Notes toward a Supreme Fiction," the sharply felt human contacts and withdrawals of "Le Monocle de Mon Oncle." "The Final Soliloquy," in its more general and abstract character, thus invites the challenges confronting all late evening, firelight unities: Is the world included in the mind's expansiveness really more concrete and particular than the musing mind itself? Does the dwelling "in which being there together is enough" finally accommodate a world of *individuals*, of "counter-love, original response"? Turning toward Frost, as this fragmentary quotation from "The Most of It" suggests, I want to consider these questions in the context of "Directive." That poem seems to me a helpful bridge for the various vagrant ideas wandering across this essay. (It is at the same time the chasm below, waiting to swallow them up; but let the bridge stand for now.) It responds to Stevens's version of "the mind as its own place," while also pressing the claims of "otherness" put forward by the world, with its relics of lives outside our own.

My problem, as I tried in company with the Cumberland Beggar to hitch a ride up Route 116, was one of increasing disconnection. The beauty of sunset when I started out—connected with the power of Wordsworth's poetry and the memory of a recent moment of warm community centered on that poetry—had drawn together England and Vermont, our century and the last, my life and the lives of those driving the highway. It was after the sun had gone down and the air turned cold, and after rejection by those I looked to for rides had intervened between me and the seminar's friendship, that my "central mind" began to wobble on its axis. I wanted to put the world together again, but in terms that could acknowledge the afternoon's entropic turn. I needed, in order to place myself again in history and in Vermont, a directive.

Back out of all this now too much for us,
Back in a time made simple by the loss
Of detail, burned, dissolved, and broken off
Like graveyard marble sculpture in the weather,
There is a house that is no more a house
Upon a farm that is no more a farm
And in a town that is no more a town.
The road there, if you'll let a guide direct you
Who only has at heart your getting lost,
May seem as if it should have been a quarry—
Great monolithic knees the former town
Long since gave up pretense of keeping covered.
And there's a story in a book about it:
Besides the wear of iron wagon wheels
The ledges show lines ruled southeast-northwest,
The chisel work of an enormous Glacier
That braced his feet against the Arctic Pole.
You must not mind a certain coolness from him
Still said to haunt this side of Panther Mountain.
Nor need you mind the serial ordeal
Of being watched from forty cellar holes
As if by eye pairs out of forty firkins.
That sends light rustle rushes to their leaves,
Charge that to upstart inexperience.
They think too much of having shaded out
A few old pecker-fretted apple trees.
Make yourself up a cheering song of how
Someone's road home from work this once was,
Who may be just ahead of you on foot
Or creaking with a buggy load of grain.
The height of the adventure is the height
Of country where two village cultures faded
Into each other. Both of them are lost.
And if you're lost enough to find yourself
By now, pull in your ladder road behind you
And put a sign up CLOSED to all but me.
Then make yourself at home. The only field
Now left's no bigger than a harness gall.
First there's the children's house of make-believe,
The playthings in the playhouse of the children.
Weep for what little things could make them glad.
Then for the house that is no more a house,
But only a belilaced cellar hole,
Now slowly closing like a dent in dough.
This was no playhouse but a house in earnest.

Your destination and your destiny's
A brook that was the water of the house,
Cold as a spring as yet so near its source,
Too lofty and original to rage.
(We know the valley streams that when aroused
Will leave their tatters hung on barb and thorn.)
I have kept hidden in the instep arch
Of an old cedar at the waterside
A broken drinking goblet like the Grail
Under a spell so the wrong ones can't find it,
So can't get saved, as Saint Mark says they mustn't.
(I stole the goblet from the children's playhouse.)
Here are your waters and your watering place.
Drink and be whole again beyond confusion.[12]

Like all of Frost's best poems, "Directive" simultaneously discloses and obscures its meanings, as the poet practices that art
which he described as "proper enigmatical reserve." But the poem's
main continuity is its exploration of human estrangement from nature and from human history alike, and its demonstration that to
become reconciled with one of the two realms is finally only possible
through reconciliation with the other. In the opening lines, Frost
frames an invitation to retreat that responds to my experience of
disappointment on Route 116, and to all our modern longings for
vanished wholeness: "Back out of all this now too much for us /
Back in a time made simple by the loss / Of Detail. . . . " But Frost's
propositions carry the seeds of their own destruction; they turn out,
like Wordsworth's affirmations, to be cast in negative terms. The
benign wholeness we attribute to human community with nature in
an earlier time depends on loss and foreshortening. Detail gives way
to the underlying pattern that connects. Like the vanished river
bank in Wendell Berry's "The Slip," Frost's "house that is no more a
house" opens, through its absence, a space for understanding and
connection. In his version the paradox, at its heart so much like the
Christian sense of dying into new life, is that of getting lost in order
to find oneself.

The discoveries of getting lost are augmented in "Directive" by
the bewilderment of differing time frames. The ruts of wagon
wheels recall the tide of settlers into the New England hill farms,
two hundred years ago; they suggest as well the region's depopula-
tion just a couple of generations later, as droves abandoned their
flinty fields for the promise of Midwest and Far West. The glacial
grooves in exposed rock record a similar advance and retreat across

the terrain—both a geological parallel to the farmers' history and the event which scraped away New England's soil and itself assured the settlers' downfall. And these ironic relations between the movement of glaciers and men, analogy, causation, disproportion, are all cast into a distanced past by the intervening time frame of the hardwood trees—"Where were they all not twenty years ago?"—that have overwhelmed the remnants of orchards. Frost's history of the changing landscape is an accurate one. But in his dreamy and overlapping sequence of temporal perspectives—human, geological, arboreal—Frost also accomplishes his poetic strategy of disorientation and re-inclusion: "And if you're lost enough to find yourself / By now, pull in your ladder road behind you / And put a sign up CLOSED to all but me. / Then make yourself at home." Like the "hidden valley" into which Wordsworth leads his reader at the beginning of "Michael," this poem forms its own enclosure. The abandoned farming landscape frames the meditation, but the poem no less thoroughly surrounds the vanishing field around the cellar hole. Like the adjoining hilltop villages, human history faded into the agricultural landscape which was its expression. "Both of them are lost," but in the relics of decay and interchange there is a haunted circle in which the present, imagining all that *has* been lost, may lose itself, and make itself complete.

The vanished farms are only the expression of a more general fact: the perpetual *otherness* of human beings to each other, which community must continually find ways to overcome. The mediation of nature, the emotional significance of place, is no less necessary in mediating human relations than are human associations for enriching our response to place. And in both human and natural orders, mediation is the child of loss. This nub of the poem is touched when Frost writes that, "Your destination and your destiny's / A brook that was the water of the house." Humanity and the nonhuman landscape draw life from the same elemental source. The vanishing house and field serve to make the miracle of origination clear. In decay the soil finds its health, from which new growth may come. For Frost, all of the world, not just the soil, expresses what he calls in "West-Running Brook" "this backward motion toward the source." As he writes in that poem,

> Our life runs down in sending up the clock.
> The brook runs down in sending up our life.
> The sun runs down in sending up the brook.
> And there is something sending up the sun.[13]

Frost is most serious when, as at the end of "Directive," he is at his most arch. With the broken goblet from the playhouse of long-dead children, he concludes the poem with a sacrament of communion: "Here are your waters and your watering place. / Drink and be whole again beyond confusion." The wholeness is with the children, and it is achieved through the tribute of a poet's playfulness. But it also encompasses a union with the "house in earnest," through the intercession of the "house of make-believe." In a similarly compound way, Frost's communion is with nature, both the cold mountain brook and the underlying principle of wholeness from which is springs.

To achieve the unity of life and poetry rooted in the earth is to listen to the voices of the dead, and to affirm the necessity of one's own decay. In the decay of one's culture, as well, there is an enhanced community with people in other times, whose way of life also settled back into the hills. It is for this reason that the remnants of stone cellar walls serve, like the "straggling heap of stones" in "Michael," to ground Frost's imaginative response in a larger circuit of natural process. As I made my slow pilgrimage up Route 116, I passed between bleached stands of corn ready to be chopped up for forage. The stillness and gravity of death always inform the meaningfulness of a landscape one has chosen for his life. In his poem "The Clearing," Berry writes,

> The farm is the proper destiny
> here now and to come.
> Leave the body to die
> in its time, in the final dignity
> that knows no loss in the fallen
> high horse of the bones.[14]

The beauty of chosen collapse in place, song rising from downward decay, joins the September sunset, the memory of beggars and of farmers long gone, and the gifts of poets cultivating their art amid a landscape of concrete and speed. A culture of the land coalesces in an hour before the coming of dark.

SECTION II

A Something Given

The Footpath of Tradition

Just as the wasteland and the wilderness are reconciled through earth's circuit of soil-building decay, the landscape and the imagination may be united through the process of walking. The mind's flicker of attention from the earth to its own associations seems on one level to have an inescapably binary quality. But mental sunlight and clouds are also borne out under a larger sky in the meandering circuit of the poet's walk. Walking becomes an emblem of wholeness, comprehending both the person's conscious steps and pauses and the path beneath his rising and falling feet.

Walking, as readers of Wordsworth have always recognized, is one of *The Prelude*'s organizing principles. M. H. Abrams writes of the poem, in *Natural Supernaturalism*, that

> . . . after the period of childhood, its chief episodes are Wordsworth's own wanderings through the English countryside, the Alps, Italy, France, and Wales—literal journeys through actual places which modulate easily into symbolic landscapes traversed by a metaphorical wayfarer. This organizing figure works in two dimensions. In one of these, *The Prelude* represents the life which the poet narrates as a self-educative journey. . . . In the second application, the poet repeatedly figures his own imaginative enterprise, the act of composing *The Prelude* itself, as a perilous quest through the uncharted regions of his own mind.[1]

The two dimensions of Wordsworth's walk which Abrams identifies are finally inseparable. My focus, however, is on those passages referring directly to the poet's physical path over the earth. Wordsworth's understandings of history, of poetry, and finally of the integrity of his own life may all be related to these depictions of himself walking.

As the poet prepares to set out on his walk in Book I of *The Prelude*, he issues a declaration of independence:

> The earth is all before me. With a heart
> Joyous, nor scared at its own liberty,
> I look about; and should the chosen guide
> Be nothing better than a wandering cloud,
> I cannot miss my way. I breathe again!
> Trances of thought and mountings of the mind
> Come fast upon me: it is shaken off,
> That burthen of my own unnatural self.
> The heavy weight of many a weary day
> Not mine, and such as were not made for me.
> Long months of peace (if such bold word accord
> With any promises of human life),
> Long months of ease and undisturbed delight
> Are mine in prospect. . . . [2]

A primary ingredient of this passage is Wordsworth's relief at being outside the city again, away from the alienating life of "many a weary day / Not mine." To walk into the valley of poetry is for him at the same time to turn his back on the haunts of other men, in pursuit of his own separate soul and of his own art. In lines 87–93 of Book I he writes,

> . . . casting then
> A backward glance upon the curling cloud
> Of city smoke, by distance ruralised;
> Keen as a Truant or a Fugitive,
> But as a Pilgrim resolute, I took,
> Even with the chance equipment of that hour,
> The road that pointed toward the chosen Vale. [3]

Wordsworth's language in lines 14–16 and in line 93 echoes Milton's description, in Book XII of *Paradise Lost*, of Adam and Eve setting out from the Garden of Eden:

> The world was all before them, where to choose
> Their place of rest, and Providence their guide. [4]

In framing *The Prelude*'s opening with such resonant lines, Wordsworth suggests a *return* to the garden, an escape from the history and problems of fallen man. This invasion is reflected both by the use of these lines to begin, rather than conclude, Wordsworth's epic and by the substitution of "earth" for "world" in line 14. Although Wordsworth is not altogether consistent in his use of "world," his tendency in *The Prelude* is to employ it for the realm of *society*; sometimes, as in lines 354–57 of Book IV, he directly opposes the human *world* to the power of existence in nature and the *earth*:

> When from our better selves we have too long
> Been parted by the hurrying world, and droop,
> Sick of its business, of its pleasures tired,
> How gracious, how benign, is Solitude.[5]

In the second hundred lines of *The Prelude* there is a faltering in the blithe confidence of Wordsworth's beginning. His sense of creative power adequate to support the poet in place of Providence is "soon defrauded." The wobbling of confidence implicit earlier in his triple self-description as truant, fugitive, and pilgrim now collapses entirely and, in lines 267–78, he eventually sees himself as

> Unprofitably travelling toward the grave
> Like a false steward who hath much received
> and renders nothing back.[6]

Turning toward the garden, he seeks to turn away from prison-society, but finds instead that he cannot outpace the shadow of his own anxious dividedness. The Parable of the Talents, with its "false steward," thus comes to express Wordsworth's growing awareness that he must make a creative response to culture and to nature alike. Indecisiveness, disappointment, and the city itself all persist as important elements of the poem and of his own life; the garden's tempered response is unavailable to Wordsworth on any permanent basis. The curling cloud of city smoke is *always* over his shoulder.

Though Wordsworth is unable to extricate his life from the troubled mass of humanity, he nevertheless keeps a very jaundiced eye on human culture and "what man has made of man." The influence of Milton is everywhere in Wordsworth's poetry, and sometimes, gazing at the moon, he remembers Spenser; but it is only through a continual return to earth that his own bond with humanity and a vital culture can be renewed. A thoroughgoing critique of tradition and culture winds through *The Prelude*, from the discussion of student life at Cambridge to the devastating sequence of disappointments following his first great hopes for France's revolution. Western man, Wordsworth would agree with Jeffers and Bly, has fallen into a false sense of culture, which is maintained in its artificiality through isolation from the wisdom of earth. A central statement of this critique occurs in Book XIII.

> There are who think that strong affection, love
> Known by whatever name, is falsely deemed
> A gift, to use a word they would use,
> Of vulgar nature; that its growth requires
> Retirement, leisure, language purified
> By manners studied and elaborate;
> That whoso feels such passion in its strength
> Must live within the very light and air
> Of courteous usages refined by art.
>   . . . .
> Yet, in those wanderings deeply did I feel
> How we mislead each other; above all,
> How books mislead us, seeking their reward
> From judgments of the wealthy Few, who see
> By artificial lights; how they debase
> The Many for the pleasure of those Few;
> Effeminately level down the truth
> To certain general notions, for the sake
> Of being understood at once, or else
> Through want of better knowledge in the heads
> That framed them; flattering self-conceit with words,
> That, while they most ambitiously set forth
> Extrinsic differences, the outward mark
> Whereby society has parted man
> From man, neglect the universal heart.[7]

Wordsworth's concern here for "the universal heart" is typical of *The Prelude* in its entirety: he wishes to return to his origins in nature not, finally, in order to leave society behind, but as a corrective and restorative measure. Wherever a man turns, the contradictions of his situation emerge anew; all progress toward wholeness must therefore, like a river or like a walker across hilly country, take a meandering course. To walk away from the close world of cities and books is itself an important early bend in such a meander. Thoreau expresses a similar insight in the opening paragraph of his essay on "Walking": "I wish to speak a word for Nature, for an absolute freedom and wildness, as contrasted with a freedom and culture merely civil,—to regard man as an inhabitant, or a part and parcel of Nature, rather than a member of society. I wish to make an extreme statement, if so I may make an emphatic one, for there are enough champions of civilization: the minister and the school-committee and every one of you will take care of that."[8] Where "judgments . . .

by artificial lights" are disruptive, in their rigidly hierarchical distinctions, to the unity of man and nature, walking achieves a human circuit at the meeting of sky and earth.

Though *The Prelude* was first conceived as preparation for a greater, visionary work, it remains Wordsworth's most fully realized poetic statement—a prelude which introduces only itself. Similarly, the poet's walking has no final destination: though the trail ascends mountains in Books VI and XIV, and though Wordsworth experiences moments of vision and transfiguration along the way, there is no spot outside the process where life can rest for long. The exaltation and disappointment of Book I establish a dialectical framework which includes even the poem's lofty conclusion as just one phase in an ongoing cycle. The irony of insight for Wordsworth is that it always comes at a particular place and a particular time. To stand in one spot or hold to one creed is thus not to retain one's vital unity but to lose it; integrity is the circuit of vision completed in each step. Though, at the start of Book I, Wordsworth writes, "It is shaken off, / That burthen of my own unnatural self," his remains a story moving through time, space, and personality. In a walk, as in a life, there is no one point providing a summary or explanation: circling through the distraction and liberation of terrain, life comes to understand itself in passing.

For Wordsworth, in *The Prelude*, walking is a process of reconciliation: it provides the dynamic unity of his life. One of the most important dimensions of such reconciliation is indicated in the opening lines of Book II:

> Thus far, O Friend! have we, though leaving much
> Unvisited, endeavoured to retrace
> The simple ways in which my childhood walked;
> Those chiefly that first led me to the love
> Of rivers, woods, and fields.[9]

Wordsworth struggles throughout his poetry with the problem of how a personal identity may comprehend both one's experiences in the past and the personality's present moment. He is troubled by discrepancies in the sequence of his selves, and the most helpful response to such perplexity is to walk, remembering, through the immediacy of the world. To retrace the paths of childhood is to experience, for the walk's duration, the present and the past as one. The familiar landscape is the repository for early emotions which that terrain itself first called forth. To return to such hills is a renewal of childhood identity and a wedding with the earth. As Words-

worth writes in "Michael," describing the shepherd's deep identification with the valley where he labors,

> Those fields, those hills—what could they less?
>   had laid
> Strong hold on his affections, were to him
> A pleasurable feeling of blind love,
> The pleasure which there is in life itself.[10]

Wordsworth, throughout *The Prelude*, finds that to walk back
through childhood's landscape is to rediscover the paths "that first
led me to the love / Of rivers, woods, and fields." Wordsworth's
genius is one of understanding apparently hopeless oppositions as
stages in a subtle and life-giving *sequence*. The adult's complex emotions derive from "the simple ways" of the child in nature. For this
reason, to walk familiarly over the earth is to be reconciled with
oneself in a circuit of rediscovery, wholeness, and belonging.

The latter part of Book II speaks to the way seeming dichotomies
flow together into the unifying process of a life:

>   . . . 'Twere long to tell
> What spring and autumn, what the winter snows,
> And what the summer shade, what day and night,
> From sources inexhaustible, poured forth
> To feed the spirit of religious love
> In which I walked with Nature.[11]

Day and night, summer and winter are only unified within the
sequence of a year. Like walking, weather has no norm and no
conclusion: it must move to be itself. This is why reconciliation,
rather than resolution, is the word for Wordsworth's poetic achievement. Reconciliation is the acceptance of differences, not their elimi-
nation or merger. It is a circling dialectic that yields no synthesis
beyond a certain watchful affirmation. "Guide," by A. R. Ammons,
is a poem which addresses Wordsworth's imagery of life's walk,
while also expressing the impossibility of achieving any resolution
through such a circuit:

> You cannot come to unity and remain material:
> in that perception is no perceiver:
>   when you arrive
> you have gone too far:
>   at the Source you are in the mouth of Death:
>
> you cannot
>   turn around in

the Absolute: there are no entrances or exits
   no precipitations of forms
to use like tongs against the formless:
   no freedom to choose:

to be
   you have to stop not-being and break
off from *is* to *flowing* and
   this is the sin you weep and praise:
Origin is your original sin:
   the return you long for will ease your guilt
and you will have your longing:

   the wind that is my guide said this: it
should know having
   given up everything to eternal being but
direction:

how I said can I be glad and sad: but a man goes
   from one foot to the other:
wisdom wisdom:
   to be glad and sad at once is also unity
and death:

   wisdom wisdom: a peachblossom blooms on a particular
tree on a particular day:
   unity cannot do anything in particular:

are these the thoughts you want me to think I said but
   the wind was gone and there was no more knowledge then.[12]

There is no absolute unity available for existence in a physical, and
thus temporal, world. Rather, going from one foot to the other,
human life takes its passage through a universe of particulars. Ammons's poem does not deny the reality of "the Absolute." But, like
the similarly capitalized "Death," it is not a state you can "turn
around in." The vital circuit will invariably break "and you will have
your longing." Meanwhile, though, having recognized that "unity
cannot do anything in particular," the poet looks back down to his
feet. To gain the duration of a life requires that a person be reconciled with his own irresolution.

Wordsworth's walk, like Ammons's wind, shows him glimpses of
a world of resolution into which he, while living, can never enter. In
his solitary separation from the city's masses, and in his communion
with the inwardness and quietness of nature, the poet is drawn
toward a certain stillness from which he is at the same time repelled.

It is the resolution of inertness, as reflected in the Old Cumberland Beggar, or in the dead girl of "A Slumber Did My Spirit Seal":

> No motion has she now, no force;
>   She neither hears nor sees;
> Rolled round in earth's diurnal course
>   With rocks, and stones, and trees.[13]

Wordsworth's insight in this stanza is into a reality fulfilling his desire for oneness with nature. But it is a reality allowing for neither individuality nor focused perception, and one that immerses the poet in a mysterious sleep. The only response to such a consummation and annihilation is one of ambivalence: right foot, left foot.

The clearest example in *The Prelude* of Wordsworth walking around a resolution which he cannot choose is in a passage near the end of Book IV. It is the episode beginning at line 370, where Wordsworth narrates how, one autumn evening, he "left a flower decked room" in which

> . . . spirits overwrought
> were making night do penance for a day
> Spent in a round of strenuous idleness.[14]

The poet's disapproving tone echoes his depiction of the city in Book I and anticipates the treatment of London in Book VII. He distances himself from the noisy and distracting human round, setting out by himself on a more ambitious path: "My homeward course led up a long ascent." His passage is from people to nature, noise to silence. But the momentum of setting out is such that he almost carries too far into what Jeffers calls "the beauty of inanimate things." Except for the voice of an unseen brook, like the voice of Ammons's wind, "All else was still; / No living thing appeared in earth or air. . . . " It is in such an hour that Wordsworth comes upon the "uncouth shape" of the veteran, motionless by the roadside. In his bleak disregard, the man is like a voice for the quiescent night, and for the estrangement of the poet's own heart.

> . . . a more meagre man
> Was never seen before by night or day.
> Long were his arms, pallid his hands; his mouth
> Looked ghastly in the moonlight: from behind,
> A mile-stone propped him; I could also ken
> That he was clothed in military garb,
> Though faded, yet entire. Companionless,
> No dog attending, by no staff sustained,
> He stood, and in his very dress appeared

> A desolation, a simplicity,
> To which the trappings of a gaudy world
> Make a strange background.[15]

"Meagre," "ghastly," "companionless," the returning veteran embodies Wordsworth's own turning away from the "gaudy world." But in these same attributes he resembles a "pallid" corpse "propped" against a milestone—showing Wordsworth how far he has himself traveled toward death. Such an apparition throws the poet back upon himself and guides him toward a recognition of his precarious walk between the extremes of distraction and a cold resolution.

To escape too far from life is to become "a desolation." In his manner, impassive almost to the point of inertness, the veteran recalls both the Cumberland Beggar and the leech-gatherer of "Resolution and Independence." Wordsworth's response to the encounter here is also pointedly reminiscent of Jesus' parable of the Good Samaritan. The walking poet meets a stationary figure, who has apparently given up all power of movement; he pulls the soldier from the eddy of his "mild indifference," into the current of his own walk and of his life. What follows is a gradual process of revivification.

> I said, in pity, "Come with me."
> He stooped, and straightway from the ground took up
> An oaken staff by me yet unobserved—
> A staff which must have dropt from his slack hand
> And lay till now neglected in the grass.[16]

The veteran, thus encouraged, moves from the spot where he had become a monument to resignation; in picking up the staff, he also takes up a world of human companionship, with its inevitable "trappings."

As they walk along together, Wordsworth asks questions to stimulate in the veteran a warmer interest in his own life. But the account also reveals, as did the conclusion of "Resolution and Independence," a questioner with complex, and partially unrealized, motives.

> Nor could I, while we journeyed thus, forbear
> To turn from present hardships to the past,
> And speak of war, battle, and pestilence,
> Sprinkling this talk with questions, better spared,
> On what he might himself have seen or felt.
> He all the while was in demeanour calm,
> Concise in answer; solemn and sublime
> He might have seemed, but that in all he said

> There was a strange half-absence, as of one
> Knowing too well the importance of his theme,
> But feeling it no longer.[17]

One motivation of such insistent questioning is to continue to draw the frail soldier out of his quietude; like the walking, it is a way to warm a man whose limbs have grown cold. When the poet finally—like the Good Samaritan at the parable's end—entrusts his charge to the care of wayside cottagers, the movement back into the protective, responsive human sphere has also been fulfilled:

> . . . and in a faltering voice,
> Whose tone bespake reviving interests
> Till then unfelt, he thanked me. . . .[18]

It is also apparent, though, and acknowledged in retrospect, that the poetic walker's eagerness in talking with the veteran also derives from his own needs. He could not "forbear" raising questions which, considering the present weakness of his companion, would have been "better spared." It seems likely, in view of the passage's larger context in Book IV, that Wordsworth's headlong swoop upon the stark moonlit figure was impelled by two emotions even more pressing than his pity. On the one hand, the solitary man represents an ideal of detachment from the noisy world. Even in his feeble state he can offer an "apt admonishment" similar to the leech-gatherer's; he rebukes, by the very fact of his continuing existence, the buzzing, anxious distractions of the social whirl. Even as the poet leaves him, with a recommendation that he *seek* aid in future difficulties, the soldier's tone, like the leech-gatherer's, is one of sublime independence:

> At this reproof,
> With the same ghastly mildness in his look,
> He said, "My trust is in the God of Heaven
> And in the eye of him who passes me!"[19]

On the other hand, the fact that, in meeting such a human embodiment of solitude and silence, Wordsworth feels compelled to enliven him also reflects alarm at the embodiment of his own impulse. The veteran's "ghastliness" answers to Wordsworth's insight that beyond a certain line the stillness of solitary communion with nature is the same as death. In reviving the inert figure he meets and warms a side of himself, in this strange encounter on a silent road. The entire episode—like the beginning of Book I and so many other intense moments in Wordsworth's poetry—is a process by which the poet tries, through reaction and compensation, to attain that tempered awareness which he describes, in line 72 of Book II, as "a quiet independence of the heart." One cannot both subside into the peacefulness of "mute insensate things" and still retain a capacity for warm, unmediated response. Walking, though, is a way in which one's pulsing life may be cooled by a quietness different from repose.

Wordsworth's poetry may be read as a walk along a single road. At one end of it is childhood, with its spontaneous gladness and vitality, while at the other is the motionless conclusion to "life's long pilgrimage." In such a poem as the "Ode: Intimations of Immortality . . . ," he intuits a grand circle of which life's course forms only one arc. But the poet's conscious experience cannot take him beyond the two end-points of the mortal road, so that the only circuits he can achieve are backward and forward loops along that finite line. Only through the ambivalent repetition and reaction does his life take on an infinite aspect within this bounded course. Finding that his life's walk takes him further from the unconsidered joys of childhood, he first hastens toward a peaceful resolution of the misgivings of self-consciousness. But as the air cools and the solid earth itself subsides beneath his feet, he turns back in alarm to places where he has known a landscape of energy and response.

Wordsworth's troubling richness as a poet derives from this oscillation of warmth and cold, life and death. Similar to Freud's treatment—more an interweaving than an opposition—of Eros and Thanatos in *Beyond the Pleasure Principle*, Wordsworth acknowledges that only in *relation* to the eventual cessation of individual life can the warmth of personal experience be sustained. In moving through *The Prelude*, Wordsworth's two most charged thoughts are of his childhood and his death. The way in which this alternation becomes a *sequence* is especially clear in Book V, lines 364–459. In his first section of that passage, up to line 388, he tells of the Boy of Winander, whose oneness with nature through a "shock of mild surprise" is so much like Wordsworth's own negative leadings in Book I. Following a terse indication of the Boy's death, in line 389, Wordsworth moves to a meditation in the churchyard, where.

> . . . when my way has led
> On summer evenings, I believe that there
> A long half hour together I have stood
> Mute, looking at the grave in which he lies![20]

Then, in line 426 and following, the poet moves back to a memory of his own childhood, when, with "half-infant thoughts," he "was roving up and down alone, / Seeking I knew not what." He makes special mention of one day when he stood silent beside a lake, watching grappling irons raise a drowned man, whose "ghastly face" was like that of the roadside apparition of Book IV.

Wordsworth's trajectory in the entire passage is from childhood to death to childhood to death; and death is associated each time with those moments of standing quietly that occur in the course of a walk. In *The Prelude*, as in "Michael," when Wordsworth moves across the landscape it is often at graves and ruins that he pauses; they are the landmarks of resolution between human and natural terms. But the wholeness and beauty of such meditations on death are pervaded by a coldness from which the poet must soon depart. Wordsworth walks through places he could not survive, returning, like the benighted veteran, to the cottage of human comprehension. But though the stillness beside the Boy's grave may be only for the duration of "a long half hour," it suffuses the other hours of life. It bestows on humanity's brief span the transience and mitigation of preciousness. Leaving home, Wordsworth gains the possibility of a return.

One of the most moving passages in *The Prelude* speaks to the way walking binds up the human seasons of cold and warmth into the wholeness of a landscape and a year. Occurring near the beginning of Book VII, it presents a moment of revivification for the poet, after a slackening in the poem's composition which he has just described.

> But I heard,
> After the hour of sunset yester-even,
> Sitting within doors between light and dark,
> A choir of redbreasts gathered somewhere near
> My threshold,—minstrels from the distant woods
> Sent in on Winter's service, to announce,
> With preparations artful and benign,
> That the rough lord had left the surly North
> On his accustomed journey. The delight,
> Due to this timely notice, unawares
> Smote me, and, listening, I in whispers said,
> "Ye heartsome Choristers, ye and I will be
> Associates, and, unscared by blustering winds,
> Will chant together." Thereafter, as the shades
> Of twilight deepened, going forth, I spied
> A glow-worm underneath a dusky plume
> Or canopy of yet unwithered fern,
> Clear-shining like a hermit's taper seen
> Through a thick forest. Silence touched me here

No less than sound had done before; the child
Of Summer, lingering, shining, by herself,
The voiceless worm on the unfrequented hills,
Seemed sent on the same errand with the choir
Of Winter that had warbled at my door,
And the whole year breathed tenderness and love.[21]

The most important words in the passage are, for me, "going forth."
The wholeness of the poet's experience comes in a sympathetic departure from fixed, solitary order. But it is also a departure into, as
well as away from, order. The robins, fleeing from winter, bring it
with them. In the songs which mark their seasonal migrations,
Wordsworth finds an encouraging accompaniment to his own poetic
efforts, "unscared by blustering winds." He goes forth from his
house to be with the birds and to let the earth give him its unfore-
seen gift. The glowworm lingering in the cooling landscape carries
out in its own way the robins' "errand": just as they brought winter
and the North into the poet's room, the worm retains the light of
summer in an "unwithered" niche of "the unfrequented hills." Like
winter's voice in a house's warmth, or sunglow beneath a canopy of
fern, Wordsworth's is the poetry of mitigation. Redbreast, worm,
and poet escape from death into ambiguity and comradeship. A
solitary man walks into the darkness to rediscover sympathy.

In addition to its power to reconcile a man with the contradictions of his own life, walking represents one mode of relationship
with tradition. Lionel Trilling has spoken of the development of
"adversary culture" in the twentieth century. But a similar fear of
being trapped by diminishing civilization can be recognized
throughout cultural history, particularly in the incessant *traveling*
within the epic tradition. In *The Odyssey* and *The Aeneid*, both the
wholeness and the pathos of human life are expressed in terms of
movement across the surface of the earth. And in *The Divine Com-
edy* and *Paradise Lost,* the figure of the poet himself becomes the
traveler whose journey the poem charts. Those two poets' forms
of motion are more spectacular than Wordsworth's earthbound
walk; Dante ascends the terraces of Purgatory, and Milton, in the
invocations to Books I, III, VII, and IX, takes wing in finding his
own precarious way between hell and heaven. But like Wordsworth, Dante and Milton strive on their own journeys to synthe-
size a tradition against tradition—a true culture that redeems the
abuses of history. In the ambivalence of their regard for history
and culture, they move, like him, from foot to foot—solitaries
going self-consciously forth to meet the world.

Wordsworth's closest affinity as a poetic walker may be with the seventeenth-century Japanese poet Bashō. In drawing such a comparison, I am aware of moving far afield from the network of nineteenth- and twentieth-century writers in English with whom this book has been principally concerned. But it is a connection that reflects a vision of cultural synthesis to which I have been led by Gary Snyder and R. H. Blyth. Such wholeness as this book possesses is, after all, personal: an attempt to define the unity of tradition and nature insofar as I have been able to register it within my own experience and emotions. Some central figures, such as Blake, Emerson, and Whitman, have not exerted nearly as powerful an influence on my personal order as have others like Wordsworth and Eliot. As Whitehead teaches, reality is inevitably contingent and relative—a momentary "grasping" of pattern which he refers to as a "prehension." By the same token, Bashō has helped me to organize my understanding of Wordsworth and the poetry of nature. He is valuable to the book's larger argument just because he does corroborate and amplify Wordsworth's insights from within such a different cultural context.

There is a clarifying, purifying effect, particularly within the poetry of nature, as major lines of response reinforce each other, while others come to seem nonessential. Time is culture's winnowing fan, and a poet like Wordsworth becomes more precious to our sense of tradition at the same time that other aspects of the writing and thought of his day mean less and less to us. Space, too, as Thoreau notes in "Walking," offers a clarifying oblivion. His statement in this regard is particularly noteworthy in relation to the cultural developments of the post–World War II era, as American thought begins to integrate Asian models:

> We go eastward to realize history and study the works of art and literature, retracing the steps of the race; we go westward as into the future, with a spirit of enterprise and adventure. The Atlantic is a Lethean stream, in our passage over which we have had an opportunity to forget the Old World and its institutions. If we do not succeed this time, there is perhaps one more chance for the race left before it arrives on the banks of the Styx; and that is in the Lethe of the Pacific, which is three times as wide.[22]

To travel west for Thoreau meant moving into new encounters with both the wilderness and the reorientations of Asian culture; in either case, one experienced a healing forgetfulness of convention's trivial strictures. But certain kinds of forgetting are the prologue to right remembering, as we turn back eastward to study our newly recollected origins. Like Wordsworth's, Thoreau's is a single road along which we walk, forward and backward, amassing a meaningful life through the process of discrimination and forgetfulness.

The most important connection of Bashō's *Narrow Road to a Far Province* and *The Prelude* is that in both works the process of walking serves as a poetic vehicle for unification. Mind and earth flow together in the process of the body's motion, and observation and imagination come to pervade one another. In the opening of *Narrow Road*, Bashō addresses this mingling of earth's processes with the cycle of a human life: "The passing days and months are eternal travellers in time. The years that come and go are travellers too. Life itself is a journey. . . . And some poets of old there were who died while travelling."[23] Like *The Prelude*, Bashō's book is the poem of a life. The ambivalent quality of the poet's walk is brought out even more forcefully, in this pilgrimage to the north of Japan's principal island, Honshu, by the fact that it is primarily a prose account, with haiku interspersed. The haiku accord with Wordsworth's "spots of time" and with his mountaintop visions. With the exceptions of such transcendent visions, Wordsworth's narrative and descriptive verse in *The Prelude* often possesses a directness about which he admonishes his readers in the 1800 Preface; some individuals will find his poems so barren and prosaic, he says, that they "will look round for poetry, and will be induced to inquire by what species of courtesy these attempts can be permitted to assume that title."[24] For Wordsworth and Bashō, though, poetry illuminates the narrative by which it is conveyed, just as it comprehends the humblest particulars of existence. In taking a walk, these poets, like Gary Snyder, draw a wide circle; the measure of their success is the inclusion of elements which would not otherwise have been considered poetic.

Bashō finds, as does Wordsworth, that in walking through the world he encounters past and present together in a single sphere of experience. Out of such an interfusion comes poetry. His is literally a pilgrimage, following the particular footpath taken by the poets Saigyō and Sōgi in the twelfth and fifteenth centuries; and all along the way he takes his landmarks principally from poetry. Such a frame of mind makes for a complex interplay for the walker, among present experience, memories of past poets, and the poet's own artistic expressions of the moment. An example of such complexity appears in *Narrow Road* after Bashō has passed the poetically celebrated barrier at Shirakawa and is asked by another poet for his impressions.

> "After the rigours of the long journey," I replied, "I was weary in body and spirit, and with my soul enthralled by the beauty of the scene, and my heart pierced through thinking of those bards of yore, I had little inclination for composing poetry.

For verse, it did suffice
To hear the northern peasants sing
As they planted rice.

> That was all I wrote. After all I could hardly pass that barrier without writing a single line."

> Using my triplet as a beginning, we took turns and composed three sets of linked verse.[25]

The poet's creative expression comes only after the merger of the present, on the level of physical sensation, and the past, as represented by the work of earlier poets. His verse acts to encapsulate that moment of combination, so that it may in its turn serve as the basis for a future sequence of responses. Walking is the vehicle for such an ongoing sequence; but poetry also contributes, as the repository of an accessible personal past, to the synthesis of each new moment. To any reader of Wordsworth, the haiku included in the passage from Bashō recalls "The Solitary Reaper." In the concluding four lines from that poem Wordsworth achieves an encapsulation like Bashō's: imagination closes the circle of perception, so that human moments may be bound into the sheaf of a life.

> I listened, motionless and still;
> And, as I mounted up the hill,
> The music in my heart I bore,
> Long after it was heard no more.[26]

There is one last point I want to make about Bashō's comments after crossing the barrier at Shirakawa. His haiku's three lines, in addition to commemorating an intense moment within the pilgrimage, provide the foundation for a social occasion, as a group composes linked verses extending Bashō's, in the conventional manner of the day. Through poetry, the individual's moment enters into a widening circle of sympathy. And in this way it illustrates the general principle by which a meaningful past can connect the individual with a meaningful present. The memory of earlier poets, after all, gave the emotional charge to Bashō's weariness at the barrier. For most of Wordsworth's poetic career, his own distant childhood simi-

larly added a necessary dimension of nostalgia to his experiences in
the present. Even when he was a boy, as depicted in Book III,
Wordsworth haunted ruined abbeys on islands in the Lake District.
Since ruins existed in both past and present, they offered the boy an
experience of temporal and natural unification. Like the ruins of
memory later in his life, they disclosed the foundations of identity.

The problem for poets who are related to each new present
through the mediation of the past is how to maintain a quality of
freshness in their experience. In exploring this issue I want to consider a comparison first suggested by R. H. Blyth, that passionate
interpreter of Japanese culture to the West: "Haiku record what
Wordsworth calls those 'spots of time,' those moments which for
some quite mysterious reason have a peculiar significance . . . a
kind of *satori*, or enlightenment, in which we see into the life of
things."[27] Because the haiku and the spot of time are on one level
outside of time and personality, they are able to provide a basis for
vitalizing connection. In Book XII of *The Prelude* Wordsworth defines
his phrase in these terms:

> There are in our existence spots of time,
> That with distinct pre-eminence retain
> A renovating virtue, whence, depressed
> By false opinion and contentious thought,
> Or aught of heavier or more deadly weight,
> In trivial occupations, and the round
> Of ordinary intercourse, our minds
> Are nourished and invisibly repaired;
> A virtue, by which pleasure is enhanced,
> That penetrates, enables us to mount,
> When high, more high, and lifts us up when fallen.
> That efficacious spirit chiefly lurks
> Among those passages of life that give
> Profoundest knowledge to what point, and how,
> The mind is lord and master—outward sense
> The obedient servant of her will. Such moments
> Are scattered everywhere, taking their date
> From our first childhood.[28]

Wordsworth analyzes here the process by which a moment of experience is transformed into a usable past, from which further life can
be derived. In an illuminating passage following shortly after that
above, Wordsworth goes on to show how poetry in particular may
become a sort of therapeutic locus—like a miracle-working shrine—
where one may draw on the vitality of the past:

                                So feeling comes in aid
Of feeling, and diversity of strength
Attends us, if but once we have been strong.
Oh! mystery of man, from what a depth
Proceed thy honours. I am lost, but see
In simple childhood something of the base
On which thy greatness stands; but this I feel,
That from thyself it comes, that thou must give,
Else never can receive. The days gone by
Return upon me almost from the dawn
Of life: the hiding-places of man's power
Open; I would approach them, but they close.
I see by glimpses now; when age comes on,
May scarcely see at all; and I would give,
While yet we may, as far as words can give,
Substance and hope to what I feel, enshrining,
Such is my hope, the spirit of the Past
For future restoration.[29]

In talking about the vitalizing past, I have gradually turned back
to the central concern in Section I for a sense of tradition that is
harmonious with nature. The discussion of Eliot, Jeffers, and Snyder
centers around the need to avoid a fossilized, conventionalized
sense of culture, through maintaining a creative and open-ended
relation between past and future. Blyth expresses this sense of a *true*
tradition in saying that haiku should be as "near to life and nature
as possible, as far from literature and fine writing as may be, so that
the asceticism is art and the art is asceticism. This kind of thing we
see in Chuangtse and Hanshan, Thoreau, Wordsworth, and Clare;
and also in Bach, Giotto, Eckhart, Spinoza, Socrates, Cervantes,
Conrad, Stevenson; in Bashō and Issa. We cannot divide a certain
kind of life from a certain kind of art, the truth from the beauty."[30]
He extends this sense that tradition really has to do with "a certain
kind of life" in a sentence, from another volume, which Wendell
Berry has admired: "Poetry is not the words written in a book, but
the mode of activity in the mind of the poet."[31]

Bashō and Wordsworth, through attention to distinct moments of
vision, lead their readers into a stream of feeling connecting them
alike with other human beings and with the earth. Poetry, like culture or the health of the soil, comes to be understood as an ongoing
process of reformulation. It is a cycle of action and reaction, like
Thoreau's passage east and west, or like Wordsworth's turnings
between birth and death on the path of his life. In the 1800 Preface,

Wordsworth describes the way in which the particles of experience flow together in a stream of poetry and light:

> . . . our continued influxes of feelings are modified and directed by our thoughts, which are indeed the representatives of all our past feelings; and, as by contemplating the relation of these general representatives to each other, we discover what is really important to men, so, by the repetition and continuance of this act, our feelings will be connected with important subjects, till at length, if we be originally possessed of much sensibility, such habits of mind will be produced, that, by obeying blindly and mechanically the impulses of those habits, we shall describe objects, and utter sentiments, of such a nature, and in such connection with each other, that the understanding of the Reader must necessarily be in some degree enlightened, and his affections strengthened and purified.[32]

Through Wordsworth's power of repetition and connection, reader and poet alike enter into that dynamic relation with other people which deserves the name of culture. Walking through a world of impressions and of associations, the poet weaves a personally significant past, and one with a continuing power to produce, finish, and absorb the new moment. The fulfillment of each moment is also its conclusion, after which it can only be understood in a further temporal relation, rather than in any abstraction or codification. Geoffrey Hartman speaks of "the temporalization of insight" in Wordsworth's "broken windings": insight is inseparable from a given moment, and, like that moment, is thus a particle in a stream. For a similar reason, there seems to me a *localization* of Wordsworth's vision. Step by step, the poem of a life re-centers itself. There is an inevitable melancholy in such an itinerant vision of human existence, a quality of loneliness, *sabi*, which Blyth ascribes to haiku in particular, and which has to do with the poignant transfer of spirit from place to place. Only by a continual uprooting can a person remain at home in the world. Bashō seems to acknowledge this aching inevitability in the sad lines of his narrative's close:

> It is already autumn, so I shall set off once more, in a boat, for Futami-ga-Ura shore where the clams are so delicious, but now alas,
>
> > Sadly, I part from you;
> > Like a clam torn from its shell,
> > I go, and autumn too.[33]

Since there is no place in nature to invest our lives' particular marriages with the earth, poetry becomes an important means to perpetuate true natural response.

As in the reliance of cultural renewal upon the process of decay, there is an apparent paradox in the heightening of immediate natural experience by moments which art has encapsulated and separated from the larger flow. The separable quality of art is one about which Wordsworth expresses the deepest misgivings. In Book V of *The Prelude*, entitled "Books," he laments the foreignness of written records to the ongoing, eternal dimension of humanity.

> Oh! why hath not the Mind
> Some element to stamp her image on
> In nature somewhat nearer to her own?
> Why, gifted with such powers to send abroad
> Her spirit, must it lodge in shrines so frail?[34]

The dream of the Arab, the stone, and the shell, which immediately follows these lines in Book V, reflects the mind's unfulfilled desire for a harbor beyond temporality. Written formulation can so easily become inert, or even come to exert a deadening influence. Literature, as Blyth has emphasized, can contribute to a tradition that thwarts the circuit of vital response in which it no longer participates. In Book III, Wordsworth depicts "blind Authority beating with his staff / The child that might have led him."[35]

Wordsworth's problem with books is finally a problem with integrating the past, and relates once more to the ways in which Bashō and Wordsworth, embedding haiku and spots of time in their narratives, strive for vitalizing expression. A *glancing* contact with the past is called for, back and forth between the earlier experience of freshness and its present possibility. Renewed contact with the usable past must be as fleeting as is the passing experience of the present, lest one be captured by the closed reality of a formulation. Tradition, within such an understanding, becomes a peripheral swirl, focusing attention vividly on the center of immediacy. Bashō's glancing regard for the past reflects his own training in Zen Buddhism. Blyth has compared haikus' spots of time with *satori*, the moment of insight when dualistic categories fall away. An experience of such power, though, like any revelation, too easily begets a theology interfering with subsequent revelations under different circumstances. Shunryu Suzuki-roshi, who founded a Sōtō Zen monastery in the mountains near Robinson Jeffers's California home, has written that to escape bondage to past moments of release, "we should always live in the dark empty sky. . . . Even if the flashing of enlightenment comes, our practice forgets all about it. Then it is ready for another enlightenment."[36] The service of past enlightenment, then, is to bring a person out again under the dark and empty sky, to counsel stillness, and to go away.

The dynamic of such self-obscuring enlightenment, such self-erasing writing, may be related to Hartman's discussion of Wordsworth's paradoxical fidelity to nature:

> Traveling along a *via naturaliter negativa* [Wordsworth] finds that the senses have a life of their own, an anagogical dialectic which emancipates him from them, above all from the tyranny of visuality. The euphrasy and rue which purged his eyes were Nature's own, not Vision's. The stay with nature became, therefore, a moral act: a fidelity beyond what nature itself seemed to urge. The poet's "return" was a self-covenanting on the part of imagination or will, a heroic curriculum that enlisted memory or duty in order to temper skylarking desire. . . . It is a paradox, though not an unfruitful one, that he should scrupulously record nature's workmanship, which prepares the soul for its independence, out of respect of nature. His greatest verse *still takes it origin* in the memory of given experiences to which he is often pedantically faithful. He adheres, apparently against nature, to natural fact.[37]

There is a close parallel in Wordsworth's writing to this "self-covenanting" with a nature that would otherwise have led him beyond itself: just as he is faithful to nature out of gratitude for its transcendent intimations, he is loyal to poetry because of the ways it points him back toward a vital union with nature. Poetry obviously provides the access for Wordsworth's *readers* to his vitalizing spots of time. But for the poet, too, his poetry is the record, or the map, of moments otherwise lost:

> . . . and I would give,
> While yet we may, as far as words can give,
> Substance and life to what I feel. . . .[38]

Wordsworth is grateful to poetry for its readiness to lead him back to nature. As Blyth writes of the spirit of haiku, "The words are less important than the sensation . . . that gave birth to them, that hardly existed however as a cause until the effect arose. From the expression we go back to the impression. . . ."[39] Book I of *The Prelude* enacts Wordsworth's discovery of this necessary dialectic of impression and expression. His first attempt to find *independent* ex-

pression having failed, he moves into the regular walking alternation of sensation and reflection that is to be the dynamic of his
poetry. The beginning of Book I is not the last time Wordsworth is
to stumble in forgetting the need for such reciprocation. Even at the
conclusion of Book XIV, we find him overreaching in his claims for
poetry's dominance over the earth:

> . . . what we have loved
> Others will love, and we will teach them how;
> Instruct them how the mind of man becomes
> A thousand times more beautiful than the earth
> On which he dwells. . . . [40]

But such extreme assertiveness, as Hartman has shown, always
brings Wordsworth to a standstill; he is destined, by the nature of
his poetry and of the earth alike, to be "a borderer."

My concern throughout this book is for poetry's achievement of a
dynamic balance between seemingly opposed terms, but those
terms themselves shift, as the individual's relation with his world is
considered under different aspects. Among the polarities which
must be reconciled if a vital identity or culture is to be achieved are
those of the past and the present, poetry and nature, imagination
and observation, society and the individual. But the most basic expression of this dividedness in human experience, and the one to
which Wordsworth's walking dialectic may be related most directly,
is the apparent opposition between body and mind. *The Prelude's*
clearest statement about how one's division may be reintegrated
comes in Book II—the hymn to the baby in his mother's arms. Body
and mind are united because both are joined with the earth, through
the corresponding agencies of gravity and feeling. Wordsworth's
lines present the physics of identity: those principles of wholeness
which persist throughout the world's transformations.

> Blest the infant Babe,
> (For with my best conjecture I would trace
> Our Being's earthly progress,) blest the Babe,
> Nursed in his Mother's arms, who sinks to sleep
> Rocked on his Mother's breast; who with his soul
> Drinks in the feelings of his Mother's eye!
> For him, in one dear Presence, there exists
> A virtue which irradiates and exalts
> Objects through widest intercourse of sense.
> No outcast he, bewildered and depressed:
> Along his infant veins are interfused

The gravitation and the filial bond
Of nature that connect him with the world.
    . . . .

For feeling has to him imparted power
That through the growing faculties of sense
Doth like an agent of the one great Mind
Create, creator and destroyer both,
Working but in alliance with the works
Which it beholds.—Such, verily, is the first
Poetic spirit of our human life,
By uniform control of after years,
In most, abated or suppressed; in some,
Through every change of growth and of decay
Pre-eminent till death.[41]

Gravity's filial bond is a connection with the physical world. Gravity, as experienced by a person in its effects on his body, is after all the most basic of feelings. And feelings, as Whitehead has shown, are the gravity of personality's sphere: "Feelings are vectors; for they take what is *there* and make it *here*." Through its expression of both body and mind, poetry spirals around the fields of both these forms of gravity. The body or the mind in isolation would fall into entropic collapse, "abated or suppressed." But the counter-pulls of earth, drawing out the mental circle, and of self-consciousness, always seeking to organize and recombine the world of sensation, maintain the possibility for poetry's dynamic equilibrium.

In the following chapter I explore ways in which the poetry of Denise Levertov and William Everson is illuminated by the body's radiance. They reveal the poet's encounter, walking through the world, with the universe of his own body. Chapter 6 follows A. R. Ammons's unification of the spinning world with the circuit of his *mental* sphere. These three contemporary poets, with their impressive and sustained achievements, also work out implications of Wordsworth's circular narrative. Whitehead includes his own magnificent achievement in the judgment that Western philosophy consists of footnotes to Plato. With a similarly nonreductive intent, I would say that many of the most valuable responses to nature in contemporary poetry follow in the footsteps of Wordsworth.

Bodies of Vision

WORDSWORTH'S walk through the world embodies the human dialogue with nature. His poetry's unity is that of an oscillating process, within which human awareness moves between sensuous investment in the world and an absorption of the world in the reflective mental order. But even in such a comprehensive art there is clearly a powerful impulse to idealization, brought into balance only as it is thwarted, sometimes harshly, in its over-reaching imaginary projects. This dynamic of correction through conflict with nature is apparent throughout *The Prelude*. One response to a sense of the mind as an overreacher is to seek for a way of more fully vesting human consciousness in the *body* during the walk of life and art. Wordsworth himself, in Book XII, acknowledges a need for the body's redeeming connections with the earth. The manifold nature of bodily experience serves to distract a person from single-mindedness.

> I speak in recollection of a time
> When the bodily eye, in every stage of life
> The most despotic of our senses, gained
> Such strength in *me* as often held my mind
> In absolute dominion. Gladly here,
> Entering upon abstruser argument,
> Could I endeavour to unfold the means
> Which Nature studiously employs to thwart
> This tyranny, summons all the senses each
> To counteract the other, and themselves,
> And makes them all, and the objects with which all

Are conversant, subservient in their turn
To the great ends of Liberty and Power.[1]

Schopenhauer, a contemporary of Wordsworth, constructed his treatise on *The World as Will and Idea* around the belief that only the body can penetrate into the real world that is beneath the surface of mental vision.

> . . . we can never arrive at the real nature of things from without. However much we investigate, we can never reach anything but images and names. We are like a man who goes round a castle seeking in vain for an entrance, and sometimes sketching the facades. And yet this is the method that has been followed by all philosophers before me.
>
> In fact, the meaning for which we seek of that world which is present to us only as our idea, or the transition from the world as mere idea of the knowing subject to whatever it may be besides this, would never be found if the investigator himself were nothing more than the pure knowing subject (a winged cherub without a body). But he is himself rooted in that world; he finds himself in it as an *individual,* that is to say, his knowledge, which is the necessary supporter of the whole world as idea, is yet always given through the medium of a body. . . .[2]

From Schopenhauer there has developed an antirational, or bodily, tradition in the West. On the face of it, this line running from Schopenhauer to Nietzsche to Freud is an antitraditional tradition, calling into question the idealistic, dualistic, analytical foundations of Western culture. But it has also been a central influence on modern thought: similar to the Schopenhauerian irony by which the body's knowledge supports the mental order is that by which the antirationalists connect modern consciousness with the very tradition against which they violently react. These ironies speak to the Introduction's concerns. In explicitly rejecting the intellectual and cultural traditions of the West, poets unavoidably have interpreted and synthesized them, endowing otherwise inert forms with new life. By turning to the body as a vehicle for knowledge of the world, a poet enters a dialectic corresponding to Wordsworth's: plunging into the body, as toward the sky, calls forth a complex process of correction from the other dimensions of human experience.

To discuss poetry's sensuous revelations inevitably runs the risk of reducing the bodily to the mental, of violating the poets' impulse. So much of contemporary poetry conveys a warning against attempts at understanding it primarily within an intellectual or historical framework. There are finally two reasons, however, why a reader who is attempting to be respectful and tactful may still hope to articulate an understanding of such writing and to relate it meaningfully to the rest of his life and to his tradition. One is that the poet, too, in working with language, is engaged in a balancing act: words, which can be so abstract, are called on to convey sensation and emotion. Poetry in this way provides a model for wholeness of expression that is encouraging to any sincere consideration of the meanings and implications of poems. There is inevitably an affinity, both in frustrations and in possible achievements, among all attempts at attaining a voice of authenticity and concrete precision. The second reason that a value may be conceived in teaching or discussing the most antirational, antitraditional poetry is that in its polemic it exercises leverage on the cultural mass. Written discussion of such art is one way to clarify, for oneself and for others, its significance for our culture. It provides, at its best, a medium through which new bodies of vision may move and interact.

In her poem "Artist to Intellectual (Poet to Explainer)," from the volume *Life in the Forest*, Denise Levertov both shows the value of an awareness centered in the body and protests against the reductive analysis which is so inimical to such bodily vision. This is a poem which touches on several important issues to be developed in the course of the chapter.

> i
>
> 'The lovely *obvious!* The feet
> supporting the body's tree and its crown
> of leafy flames, of fiery
> knowledge roaming
> into the eyes,
> that are lakes, wells, open
> skies! The lovely
> *evident*, revealing
> everything, more mysterious
> than any
> clueless inscription scraped in stone.
> The ever-present, constantly vanishing,
> carnal enigma!'
>
> ii
>
> 'Do I prophesy? It is
> for now, for no future.
> Do I envision? I envision

what every seed
knows, what shadow
speaks unheard
and will not repeat.
My energy
has not direction,
tames no chaos,
creates, consumes, creates
unceasing its own
wildfires that none
shall measure.'

iii

'Don't want to measure, want to be
the worm slithering wholebodied
over the mud and grit of what
may be a mile,
may be forever—pausing
under the weeds to taste
eternity, burrowing
down not along,
rolling myself
up at a touch, outstretching
to undulate in abandon to exquisite rain,
returning, if so I desire, without
reaching that goal the measurers
think we must head for. Where is
my head? Am I not
worm all over? my own
orient!'[3]

Levertov's immediate antagonism is to "measurers" who would
hold a ruler's edge to the waverings and indirections of life. In the
course of her polemic, though, she also sets up positive criteria for
distinguishing the values of her art from such a linear approach. One
such value is that of *presentness*, as opposed in Section i to the "clue-
less inscription scraped in stone" and in Section ii to prophecy or
vision of *future* things. Her emphatic present corresponds to one side
of Wordsworth's ambivalent art: the side of immediate sensation un-
snared in memory or reflection. Her desire in this poem is for a walk
without meditation, a mind like an empty sky. The present is where
the body lives, and in Section iii the opposition of body and mind is
most fully developed: "Where is / my head? Am I not / worm all
over?" The side of Wordsworth's poetry which answers to Levertov's
emphasis here is seen in the conclusion of his climb up Mount Snow-

don, in Book XIV, where his sudden perception of light on the ground redemptively deflects a mind intent on a limited, foreseen goal. But her poetry is more exclusive than Wordsworth's in this regard. Whereas he could see himself in company with the glow-worm and the robins' choir, she wants to strike the human term from the equation, to be only a tree, a seed, a shadow, a worm. Headless spontaneity, intent upon its own sensation, is the poem's ideal.

"Artist to Intellectual" is an ironically linear poem. As the heavily stressed lines of Section i suggest, it voices an anger that finally exemplifies the reductiveness against which it protests. Ours is a culture that has placed too much value on the analytical, discriminating aspects of awareness, those associated by recent physiological research with the brain's left hemisphere. The price for such one-sidedness has been an often brutal carelessness about the delicate balance of organic wholeness. However, a reaction that values the sensual and emotional faculties to the *exclusion* of the analytical aggravates rather than corrects the problem of human estrangement from the world. To celebrate the headless body in a poem in a book is a self-deception, just another angle on what Buddhists would call dualism. The only way truly open if we are to move beyond the nightmare of history and wake up to "the lovely / *evident*" is an integration, through passionate attentiveness, of intellect with the irreducible wholeness of life. And Levertov, like Wordsworth, is finally a poet who grows through reacting to her own reactions, through both ratifying and enlarging her passions within a circuit of understanding.

Denise Levertov's emphasis on a bodily relation with the world reflects her intense political commitments. She was in the forefront of poets writing, reading, and demonstrating against the Vietnam War, and has continued to work against racism at home and the reign of nuclear terror in foreign relations. Technological civilization has been so alarming in its political outgrowths that she mistrusts it deeply. In a poem from *The Freeing of the Dust* entitled "May Our Right Hands Lose Their Cunning," she opposes "exquisite dumbness" and "warm wholeness" to the finely calibrated products of abstract intelligence.

> Smart bombs replace
> dumb bombs. 'Now we can aim
> straight into someone's kitchen.'
>
> Hard rice
> sprays out of the cooking pot
> straight into the delicate jelly of eyes.

Invisible pellets,
pointed blobs of mist,
        bite through smooth pale-brown skin
        into perfect bodies,
chewing them into bloody mincemeat.
This is smart.

        There is
a dumb fellow, a mongoloid,
40 years old, who, being cherished,
learned recently to read and write,
and now has written a poem.
        'Summer in the West when
          everything is quiet
        And clear, with everything
          beautiful and green.

        With wild flowers of all colors,
          and a small water creek,
        And a beautiful sky. And
          the trees,' he wrote,
forming the letters carefully, his tongue
protruding, 'are very still.
        And sometimes a small breeze.'
He has been cherished,
slowly learned
what many learn fast, and go on
to other knowledge. He
knows nothing of man's devices,
        may die without discovering that
he's dumb, and they
are smart, the killers.

And the uncherished idiots,
tied in cots, smelling
of shit—
        exquisite dumbness,
guaranteed not to know,
ever, how smart
a man can be,
        homo faber of laser beams, of
quaintly-named, flesh-directed, utterly ingenious
mutilating spit-balls,
        yes,
the smartest boys, obedient to all the rules, who never
aimed any flying objects across the classroom,
now are busy with finely calibrated equipment

fashioning spit-balls with needles in them,
that fly at the speed of light multiplied
around corners and into tunnels to arrive
directly at the dumb perfection of living targets,
icily into warm wholeness to fragment it.

We who
        know this
tremble
at our own comprehension.
Are we infected,
viciously, being smart enough
to write down these matters,
        scribes of the unspeakable?
We pray to retain
something round, blunt, soft, slow,
dull in us,
not to sharpen, not to be smart.[4]

This is a poem that urges us—to follow Levertov in adapting bibli-
cal language—"If thy right hand offend thee cut it off." Cut off that
whole side of human behavior governed by the brain's left hemisphere. The poem's terms reveal even more clearly, however, the
conflict that was also at the heart of her "Artist to Intellectual": in
defense of the organic principle, the poem sacrifices its own organic
wholeness. Though the poet prays ". . . to retain / something
round, blunt, soft, slow / dull in us," her poem, like much of Levertov's specifically political writing, is rhetorical, disembodied in the
service of anger. She employs rhetoric to oppose other, destructive
rhetoric. But in her outrage at the pain of bodies she runs the danger
of making poetry a means to an end, and thus reflecting the reductive projects of mental will. As an admirer of Levertov, I have always appreciated the courage of her commitment and the way in
which, with poems like these, she has entered the struggle against
warfare and antihuman technology. But it is nevertheless important
to acknowledge that in "May Our Right Hands Lose Their Cunning"
she speaks for, but not with, the body: it has been left behind.

The threads of implication easily become tangled at this point in
the discussion, so it may serve a useful purpose to return to the
concept of the body's *presentness* from "Artist to Intellectual." The
preciousness of a rounded physical order, of the "perfect bodies"
mutilated by our "smart" weapons, is such that Levertov strives
to be a champion, in the political arena, on behalf of the body's
tender beauty. But fierce partisanship, in its intense engagement

with history and no less burning hopes for the future, can neglect the senses' present. A poem may become a self-sacrificial departure from that which it would save; poetry's body starves itself into angularity so that the body of the world may not be destroyed. Levertov's choice in this regard might be considered a Bodhisattva poetry, divesting and deferring its own fulfillment for the sake of others.

Her sacrificial trajectory may be contrasted with the larger political development in Wordsworth's poetry; she chooses linearity over ambivalence. In Books IX, X, and XI of *The Prelude,* concerning his "Residence in France," Wordsworth registers his own vast hopes and subsequent disappointment in the French Revolution. For him no less than for Levertov, intense natural experiences led to a desire for human liberation, a social harmony and beauty analogous to nature's. As the Revolution promising such a breakthrough darkened, however, he extricated his passions from the political struggle and founded instead a more hermetic union between himself and nature; poetry, not politics, became the way for sharing with other men his own relation to nature. Book X, in fact, presents political passions in the terms of disease, or as a storm disordering man's unity with nature and with himself:

> Amid the depth
> Of those enormities, even thinking minds
> Forgot, at seasons, whence they had their being. . . .[5]

Having himself experienced such disorientation, and having seen the devastation to which it led, Wordsworth looks again for wholeness in poetry's aesthetic and psychological rendering of the human bond with nature. His decision to pull back into the relativizing personal voice is evident when, after a stirring passage on the battle against Robespierre, he writes,

> But these are things
> Of which I speak, only as they were storm
> Or sunshine to my individual mind,
> No further.[6]

In Book XI, as Wordsworth looks back at his hopes of the Revolution, his language recalls the opening of Book I, where there was a similar assertion of escape from ambiguity. In both areas of his life disillusionment leads back to self-absorption, and whatever hope remains is in a hazy future, not in any immediate prospect for independence.

> . . . thus hope,
> From her first ground expelled, grew proud once more.
> Oft, as my thoughts were turned to human kind,
> I scorned indifference; but, inflamed with thirst
> Of a secure intelligence, and sick
> Of other longing, I pursued what seemed
> A more exalted nature; wished that Man
> Should start out of his earthy, worm-like state,
> And spread abroad the wings of Liberty,—
> Lord of himself, in undisturbed delight—
> A noble aspiration! *yet* I feel
> (Sustained by worthier as by wiser thoughts)
> The aspiration, nor shall ever cease
> To feel it. . . . [7]

Wordsworth's communion, in Book VII, with the glowworm on the wintry heath offered a possibility for comradeship between humanity and the rest of creation, in contrast with Denise Levertov's headless, uncomraded worm in "Artist to Intellectual." But in this more politically oriented passage from Book XI, the caterpillar's "earthy, worm-like state," once the poet has despaired of a ready appearance by liberty's wings, retires instead into a cocoon's long isolation. Levertov rejects such poetic self-containment. Like Wordsworth, she traveled in the wake of revolution, but the bodily suffering she saw in Vietnam broke open her poetry's impulse to rounded, sensual enclosure.

In the 1800 Preface Wordsworth writes that his ambition in the *Lyrical Ballads* was "at all times to look steadily at my subject." Levertov, seeing the bodies maimed by American bombs, finds that in her poetry she cannot look *away*. The second stanza of her poem "In Thai Binh (Peace) Province" reads,

> And for the moment all my tears too
> are used up, having seen today
> yet another child with its feet blown off
>   a girl, this one, eleven years old,
> patient and bewildered in her home, a fragile
> small house of mud bricks among rice fields[8]

Levertov insists that the wounded girl is more than just a "storm . . . to my individual mind"; the body's image prevents the poem's appeasement. Throughout the Western tradition, poets have tried to find in their artistic order a healing perspective on suffering that would otherwise find no remedy in this world. For Levertov, it is equally important that pain be shown *unredeemed* in poetry, as a goad to changing its causes in the human order. In her use of line-breaks, too, Levertov's poetry conveys a personal response very different from the mediating tradition and cadence of Wordsworth's blank verse: "all my tears too / are used up." It is a quiet voice, but one that refuses to be shaped into acquiescence. In "Goodbye to Tolerance," from the same volume of poems as "In Thai Binh (Peace) Province," she disassociates herself from "genial poets":

> . . . neutral fellows, seers of every side.
> Tolerance, what crimes
> are committed in your name.[9]

It is also true, however, that Levertov's political commitment is part of an alternating dynamic in her poetry that is much like that in Wordsworth's. He enacted a pattern in which the striving for visionary independence led inevitably to its own collapse; in returning to nature he drew fresh strength from the source of his creativity, then gradually built toward further ambitions of transcendence. Levertov's course seems to me parallel. To be so bitterly wide awake to the suffering body of humanity and the physical world is to waste away, consumed, as Simone Weil was, by the fever of your own compassion. For Levertov, though, the political fervor that makes her vision of the world gaunt also makes her want to continue to be strong. And so she must also return in her poetry to the simple, rounded presentness of the natural world for sustenance. As "Matins" and so many of her other poems indicate, direct experience of the sensuous world is a replenishing communion, a way to nourish sacrificial love. Her poem entitled "Not Yet" centers on the poet's *need* for such sacramental return.

> A stealth in air that means:
>
> the swallows have flown
> south while I flew
> north again.
>
> Still, in the quiet there are
> chickadees,
> to make me grudgingly smile,
> and crickets curious about
> my laundry put out to bleach
> on brown grass.
>
> So I do smile.
> What else to do?
> Melancholy is boring.

And if the well goes dry—
and it has;
and if the body-count goes up—
and it does;
and if the summer spent
itself before I took it
into my life—?

Nothing to do but take
crumbs that fall from the chickadee's table
—or starve.
But the time for starving is not yet.[10]

When the eyes have been fixed on the wounded surface of the world, one can only recover, to move and speak again, by remembering a different way to see—as Levertov says in an earlier poem, "With Eyes at the Back of Our Heads":

. . . the way to the mountain will clear,
the mountain we see with
eyes at the back of our heads, mountain
green, mountain
cut of limestone, echoing
with hidden rivers, mountain
of short grass and subtle shadows.[11]

The healing communion which nature holds out to human beings come, from its presentness and its otherness. It is the host through which the spirit's transubstantiation may be celebrated. William Everson, who wrote during the middle of his poetic career as Brother Antoninus, celebrates the saving otherness of nonhuman nature in his beautiful poem "A Canticle to the Waterbirds."

Clack your beaks you cormorants and kittiwakes,
North on those rock-croppings finger-jutted into the rough
  Pacific surge;
You migratory terns and pipers who leave but the temporal
  clawtrack written on sandbars there of your presence;
Grebes and pelicans; you comber-picking scoters and you
  shore-long gulls;
All you keepers of the coastline north of here to the Mendo-
  cino beaches;
All you beyond upon the cliff-face thwarting the surf at Hecate
  Head;
Hovering the under-surge where the cold Columbia grapples at
  the bar;

North yet to the Sound, whose islands float like a sown flurry
   of chips upon the sea;
Break wide your harsh and salt-encrusted beaks unmade for
   song
And say a praise up to the Lord.

And you freshwater egrets east in the flooded marshlands
   skirting the sea-level rivers, white one-legged watchers of
   shallows;
Broad-headed kingfishers minnow-hunting from willow stems
   on meandering valley sloughs;
You too, you herons, blue and supple-throated, stately, taking
   the air majestical in the sunflooded San Joaquin,
Grading down on your belted wings from the upper lights of
   sunset,
Mating over the willow clumps or where the flatwater rice
   fields shimmer;
You killdeer, high night-criers, far in the moon-suffusion sky;
Bitterns, sand-waders, all shore-walkers, all roost-keepers,
Populates of the 'dobe cliffs of the Sacramento:
Open your water-dartling beaks,
And make a praise up to the Lord.

For you hold the heart of His mighty fastnesses,
And shape the life of His indeterminate realms.
You are everywhere on the lonesome shores of His wide
   creation.
You keep seclusion where no man may go, giving Him praise;
Nor may a woman come to lift like your cleaving flight her
   clear contralto song
To honor the spindrift gifts of His soft abundance.
You sanctify His hermitage rocks where no holy priest may
   kneel to adore, nor holy nun assist;
And where His true communion-keepers are not enabled to
   enter.

And well may you say His praises, birds, for your ways
Are verved with the secret skills of His inclinations,
And your habits plaited and rare with the subdued elaboration
   of His intricate craft;
Your days intent with the direct astuteness needful for His
   out-working,
And your nights alive with the dense repose of His infinite
   sleep.
You are His secretive charges and you serve His secretive
   ends,
In His clouded, mist-conditioned stations, in His murk,

Obscure in your matted nestings, immured in His limitless
 ranges.
He makes you penetrate through dark interstitial joinings of
 His thicketed kingdoms,
And keep your concourse in the deeps of His shadowed world.

Your ways are wild but earnest, your manners grave,
Your customs carefully schooled to the note of His serious
 mien.
You hold the prime condition of His clean creating,
And the swift compliance with which you serve His minor
 means
Speaks of the constancy with which you hold Him.
For what is your high flight forever going home to your first
 beginnings,
But such a testament to your devotion?
You hold His outstretched world beneath your wings, and
 mount upon His storms,
And keep your sheer wind-lidded sight upon the vast perspec-
 tives of His mazy latitudes.

But mostly it is your way you bear existence wholly within the
 context of His utter will and are untroubled
Day upon day you do not reckon, nor scrutinize tomorrow,
 nor multiply the nightfalls with a rash concern,
But rather assume each instant as warrant sufficient of His final
 seal.
Wholly in Providence you spring, and when you die you look
 on death in clarity unflinched,
Go down, a clutch of feather ragged upon the brush;
Or drop on water where you briefly lived, found food,
And now yourselves made food for His deep current-keeping
 fish, and then are gone;
Is left but the pinion-feather spinning a bit on the uproil
Where lately the dorsal cut clear air.

You leave a silence.. And this for you suffices, who are not of
 the ceremonials of man,
And hence are not made sad to now forgo them.
Yours is of another order of being, and wholly it compels.
But may you, birds, utterly seized in God's supremacy,
Austerely living under His austere eye—
Yet may you teach a man a necessary thing to know,
Which has to do of the strict conformity that creaturehood
 entails,
And constitutes the prime commitment all things share.

For God has given you the imponderable grace to *be* His
    verification,
Outside the mulled incertitude of our forensic choices;
That you, our lessers in the rich hegemony of Being,
May serve as testament to what a creature is,
And what creation owes.

Curlews, stilts and scissortails, beachcomber gulls,
Wave-haunters, shore-keepers, rockhead-holders, all cape-top
    vigilantes,
Now give God praise.
Send up the strict articulation of your throats,
And say His name.[12]

Everson's canticle to the birds is an exhortation for them, in their
turn, to lift their songs to God. Theirs becomes, in this way, a
service of mediation: they are capable of a directness of response to
the world beyond the human. The waterbirds' life is in the holy
present, across which there falls no shadow of anxiety or regret;
they "assume each instant as warrant sufficient of His final seal."
Because they are determined in their songs—"the strict articulations
of your throats"—as in the rest of their behavior, they achieve a
fullness of harmony with that divinity immanent in the natural
order: "But mostly it is your way you bear existence wholly within
the context of His utter will and are untroubled." In some ways
Everson's cosmic design here is parallel to Dante's, since the souls in
the *Paradiso* are also blessed precisely because of the perfect accord
of their wills with God's: "E'n la sua volontade e nostra pace," "In
His will is our peace."[13]
    Dante is unable to remain in the luminous order of heaven for
long, but must descend to earth to articulate his experience as best
he can within the limits of mortal language. Everson, in a similar
way, must pitch his song to harmony across the chasm of his own
humanity: "You keep seclusion where no man may go, giving Him
praise; / . . . . / And where His true communion-keepers are not
enabled to enter." As the second of these quoted lines makes clear,
Everson's parallel with Dante is finally accomplished through an
inversion. The birds are closer to God and the earth because *lower* in
a scale of free-will, self-consciousness, and, in accord with orthodox
theology, spiritual authority—"our lessers in the rich hegemony of
Being." Though he sings to the waterbirds, Everson is not able to
talk to them in the Franciscan spirit of fraternal love: they are both

purer in their presentness and, by another measure, less conscious than man, "Outside the mulled incertitude of our forensic choices."

Its Catholic vocabulary notwithstanding, Everson's poetry resembles that of Robinson Jeffers, who struggles to free himself from humanity, or even from organic life, in his desire for a granite oneness with reality. Like Jeffers, Everson is thus involved in a paradoxical affirmation, couched in terms that question the validity of the affirming self. Such a stance results from passionate rejection of traditional anthropocentrism, with its disregard for the worth of the nonhuman world, and for the nonintellectual dimensions of human reality as well. In an essay entitled "The Giant Hand," from Everson's book *Fragments of an Older Fury*, about Robinson Jeffers, he defends the poetic principle that

> . . . the initiating locus of energy (the archetype) must determine the configuration of its effect. To maintain otherwise is to betray the fact that the actual motive in play is not to register the naked truth of the subject, its essence, its truth of being, but is rather to situate it in our mental world, a secondary thing, locate it in some power-complex in the ego (Tradition, Politics, Religion, etc.), imposing definition from without. While all art is admittedly born of the tension between these two psychological polarities, the *creative* writer inevitably takes the plunge into the depths of the former. . . .[14]

Everson's values lead him to reject both conventionally based judgments of proper poetic form and the brutal subordinations of warfare and technology. Such impositions are alike in taking the immediate experience of the physical world to be "a secondary thing." The waterbirds of his canticle, by virtue of being "lesser," become *primary* in their value and contribution. Clearly, the realms of mind and personality, and of the cultural history informing them, may no more be eliminated from human consciousness than may the body and the physical world. What is possible, however, is a shift of emphasis. This is the tangled reality which Everson acknowledges, I believe, in his statement that there are two *psychological* realities between which the creative writer discriminates. Emotions are invariably registered in the mind and in language as well as in the body. Yet it is also true that mental responses may involve an identification with values and realities beyond the mental sphere. The writing of A. R. Ammons, which the next chapter treats, is centrally concerned with poetry's possibility for embodying the mind's identification with the earth.

In its own terms, "The Canticle to the Waterbirds" also achieves a primary and present quality beyond the endless relativism of self-consciousness. Because he values the birds' nonhuman presentness, the poet is closely attentive to their particular lives and cries. This is a *catalog* of birds, like the catalogs filling the pages of *Leaves of Grass*. Especially in Everson's first two stanzas and in the last one, there is an ecstatic listing that identifies the eye and ear with all of the specifics of a world of creatures. Delight in the dimensions of creation thus makes the poem's body conform to the body of the world, in the same way that the long breaths of the verse echo the cries of wheeling, mixed flocks of birds at surf's edge: "Curlews, stilts and scissortails, beachcomber gulls." Although all human knowledge occurs in the waves and undertow of consciousness, the poet *can* go beyond the *idea* of waterbirds, as he uses human language to sing their songs with them.

There is a great tradition of birdsong in American poetry. Whitman's "Out of the Cradle Endlessly Rocking" bursts at its crises into the whistling, slightly varied reiteration of the mockingbird calling for his mate:

> Hither my love!
> Here I am! here!
> With this just-sustain'd note I announce myself to you,
> This gentle call is for you my love, for you.[15]

And Denise Levertov's piercing hymn to the white-throated sparrow, "Claritas," as it strives to attain the ringing purity of the bird's voice, concludes with imitation:

> Sun
> light.
>   Light
> light light light[16]

This is the grace conveyed in the cries of Everson's waterbirds: their "direct astuteness" to the natural order gives the poet a worthy model for imitation. The poet's eye and ear, fixed on the birds, practice obedience to the world.

> Yet may you teach a man a necessary thing to know,
> Which has to do of the strict conformity that creaturehood
>   entails
> And constitutes the prime commitment all things share.
> For God has given you the imponderable grace to *be* His
>   verification.

Through poetry, human awareness gains a medium in which to practice fidelity to the ongoing creation of the world. Its admonition, like that of the Psalm verse (34:8) from which Levertov took the title for one of her volumes, is "O taste and see that the Lord is good." Poetry serves as the liturgy for a communion of the senses.

The sensuous dimension of language, its incarnation of a wisdom shattering preconceived forms, is one way the body becomes a vehicle beyond abstraction. And, through attentiveness to the human body's messages from the natural creation, the world itself comes to be perceived as a body. In "Ebb at Evening," from William Everson's most recent book of poetry, *The Masks of Drought,* the ocean and the human cycle of fertility express one another. In the alternation of human and nonhuman images there is not a clear pattern of metaphor, with one order having primacy. Rather, there is the reflection of a quiet moment, at the hesitant turning of inner and outer tides, when the oneness of the world is fully evident. Between the inevitable rising and falling of dualisms, natural and human, comes a respite of attentiveness. In such a gathered moment, to identify the human body with the ocean is to gain a power of participation in nature beyond all *ideas* of its goodness or beauty. Such identification was the vital achievement of myths in those cultures which understood more clearly than ours how to live by them. But in the rhythms and shape of a poem's embodying attentiveness there may be a similar reconciliation of human consciousness and its world.

> Tide-turn: and the surf
> Swept back from the shore,
> Crouched shuddering on its flat mat,
> Unable to rise.
>
> When the tide
> Hunkers low like this on squat hams
> Everything bates breath.
>
> It is the solstice, the hip of the year
> Bent double, the body of earth
> Clenched for passage, time's Ancient art, the deep
> Rite of renewal.
>
> In the evening ebb, as the sun
> wallows under a skirt of cloud and flares low,
> Many people came forth to traverse the beach,
> Seeking shells, stones, strange fragments of drift,
> Seeds of the lost fecundity
> Borne back to their lives.

Now the sun is gone.

            But the cloud
Defers, sidling offshore. For a moment
The beach, in the oblique
Bifurcation of dusk, confronts the west,
Immense and abstract, a massive slab.

The neap tide turns.

And the dark
Drops.

          And the sea,
An awakening woman,
Simultaneously rising and turning, impulse
Groined in the ripple of immense repose,
The sea
Stands up in her bed and stares.[17]

So many of our most valuable poems of integration are set at evening and the ebb. With the grey light, things that seemed distinct in the strong outlines of noon begin to merge. The eye at such an hour can see only with imagination's aid, and, correspondingly, the human projects of the day drop away in the quietness of body and mind. Day's end and the ocean's ebb are our models for the beauty of giving up, a relinquishment to which, I argue, Jeffers's and Eliot's struggling poetry finally leads. For Snyder, Berry, and Pack, as well, poetry is a process of investing the isolated, isolating, consciousness in an order larger than itself. Labor makes rest sweet; noonday prepares a blessing for evening's first cool hours; the mind's fire, having resisted the tyranny of rigid forms, while all the time raging for its own new orders, finally quenches itself where the tide lies down at the end of the day. It is not so easy to *learn* obedience to the beauty of what is. Just as it is the tired body that can rest, the will gives acquiescence only after something is finished and done. The tide's ebb and sunset are two times attentiveness to the earth can guide us to the peace of presentness.

The seasonal turnings and suspensions offer their own admonitions, too, when the air is like a finger to the lips. In Levertov's poem "The Coming Fall," such a gathered moment is recorded. It is a poetry of serene descriptiveness, fragments of experience and reflection unlinked by propositions. Like the forty-year-old man's poem she includes in "May Our Right Hands Forget Their Cunning," this is a poem very close to immediate impressions—colors and coolness quietly noted in an autumn hour before the coming of dark.

The eastern sky at sunset taking
The glow of the west:
                    the west a clear stillness.

The east flinging
nets of cloud
to hold the rose light a moment longer:
                    the western hill dark to blackness.

The ants
on their acropolis
prepare for the night.

The vine among the rocks
heavy with grapes

the shadows of September
among the gold glint of the grass

among shining
willow leaves the small birds moving

silent in the presence of a new season.
                    . . . .

In the last sunlight
human figures dark on the hill
outlined—
a fur of gold
about their shoulders and heads,
a blur defining them.
                    . . . .

Down by the fallen fruit in the old orchard
the air grows cold. The hill
hides the sun.

A sense of the present
rises out of earth and grass,
enters the feet, ascends

into the genitals, constricting
the breast, lightening
the head—a wisdom,

a shiver, a delight
that what is passing

is here, as if
a snake went by, green in the
gray leaves.[18]

This is the body's moment, mind and eye subsiding under the slow pressures of breath and gravity. Separations grow less clear as the sun goes down. The "fur of gold" re-animalizes human figures on a darkening hill, so that they may step again into the physical world.

Poetry and
the Mind's Terrain

In his book-length poem *Sphere: The Form of a Motion*, A. R. Ammons writes, "we are not half-in and / half-out of the universe but unmendably integral."[1] The one long sentence that is *Sphere* curves out to encompass the birch and shale of landscape closely observed, curves back to join the circle of imagination's "new coherences"; Ammons's interwoven lines express his "integral" vision of mind and earth. But his voice is also that of a man talking to himself, worrying out the wholeness of his poetry: the surface of his world divides and locks along its own fault-lines. Wendell Berry identifies Ammons as a "nature poet," one whose art "has an implicit and essential humility, a reluctance to impose on things as they are, a willingness to relate to the world as student and servant, a wish to be included in the natural order."[2] Harold Bloom values a different aspect of Ammons's poetry, regarding the "ecological and almost geological" strain as his "largest flaw as a poet," a "literalness" which, "allied to a similar destructive impulse in Wordsworth and Thoreau, attempts to summon outward continuities to shield the poet from the mind's own force." Bloom finds that Ammons's more significant concern is for an identity transcending natural specifics, in the tradition of Emerson, Whitman, and "American Orphism."[3]

These two essays dealing with Ammons—Berry's "A Secular Pilgrimage" and Bloom's chapter on Ammons from *Ringers in the Tower*—treat elements which must be reconciled if one is to comprehend his larger natural vision. Ammons is indeed a poet of mind, and of human loneliness within the natural world. But a reading of

Ammons also makes apparent that the mind's swerve is persistently determined by the "literalness" of natural fact: nature's order, which is above all an intricate process, brings the redemption of continual disorder and deflection to the mind's otherwise self-centered round. For Ammons, integral can mean both isolated and reunited.

As he tries to relate mind and nature convincingly to one another, without sacrificing the substantial existence of either, Ammons enters into a conversation initiated by the English Romantics. The poetry of Wordsworth and the process-thought of Whitehead are especially valuable in suggesting a context for Ammons's contribution to this ongoing exchange. There are two important ways in which Wordsworth anticipates Ammons's resolution of the conflicting claims by nature and mind to ultimate reality. The more obvious of these is the fact that, like Wordsworth, Ammons is a walker. As Chapter 4 discusses, Wordsworth walks through *The Prelude* in a way that gives continuity to his diverse responses to nature. Both imaginatively and physically, he is always moving around; but motion is the integrating dimension of a quest. Climbing a mountain and strolling through London take on for Wordsworth a relation more complex than contradiction, as they are linked in the larger progress of a life. In much of his poetry Ammons, too, is on his feet and moving. A poem such as "Guide," already discussed in connection with Wordsworth, invokes a man's walk through the world, each step recentering the horizons in a balanced field of vision and reflection: "how I said can I be glad and sad: but a man goes / from one foot to the other." Ammons's special contribution comes in the ironic richness of his self-awareness. He is always conscious of walking through his own mind, and of the way the mental and terrestrial spheres express each other's particulars, as they spiral together through the unifying processes of poetry.

Wordsworth's "Michael," with its identification of a landscape and a life, anticipates Ammons's exploration of the process through which mind and nature invest each other with a larger reality. For the purposes of this discussion, I want to look briefly at the beginning and the end of "Michael," as Wordsworth frames his rural tale with an elaborate interfolding of the landscape and the imaginative world. The poet begins by alerting the reader to a region removed "from the public way," where "the mountains have all opened out themselves, / And made a hidden valley of their own." Only through the guidance of poetry, that is, does one find and enter this valley. Wordsworth continues,

> Nor should I have made mention of this Dell
> But for one object which you might pass by,
> Might see and notice not. Beside the brook
> Appears a straggling heap of unhewn stones!
> And to that simple object appertains
> A story.[4]

The entire poem can be read as showing how a story, on its deepest level of meaning, can appertain to an object which is itself conveyed and contained *by* the story.

At the conclusion of "Michael" our view moves slowly away from the aged shepherd, laboring at the project that was to have been a covenant between his son and him: the final image is "the unfinished Sheep-fold," "beside the boisterous brook of Green-head Ghyll." The heap of stones reflects the reality of Michael's existence in nature, the way in which "Those fields, those hills—what could they less? had laid / Strong hold on his affections, were to him . . . . The pleasure that there is in life itself."[5] Our thoughts and feelings tie us into the natural scene which is their context: the "world" is always personal. The landscape is the mind's coherence, its features the landmarks of thought. Poetry is the medium, for Ammons as for Wordsworth, within which mind and nature interfuse.

"Michael," more than any other of Wordsworth's poems, reverberates with Ammons in its sense of the landscape's own cycles. In "Tintern Abbey," despite the ruin's tumultuous past, the landscape presents the poet with an apparent stability by which to gauge *his* alteration; but "Michael" is the poem of alteration in nature. By the poem's end the shepherd's cottage is gone—"the ploughshare has been through the ground / On which it stood"— and agriculture has erased the pastoral life. Process is at the center, too, of Ammons's natural experience, and it is through such process that he finds himself, again and again, at one with nature: natural stability would only mean human separation. He apprehends the world moment by moment, as his poetry follows the revolutions of outward reality.

Whitehead, who acknowledges his own debt to Wordsworth, is the philosopher whom Ammons's concern for process continually recalls. In *Process and Reality* Whitehead makes a statement that would serve as a motto for much of what Ammons has written: "Each creative act is the universe incarnating itself as one, and there is nothing above it by way of final condition." In this volume Whitehead produces his most thorough critique of Western philosophy, with special attention to Locke, who played such a large part in stimulating Romantic anxiety concerning nature and mind. White-head's argument concludes:

All modern philosophy hinges around the difficulty of describing the world in terms of subject and predicate, substance and quality, particular and universal. The result always does violence to that immediate experience which we express in our actions, our hopes, our sympathies, our purposes, and which we enjoy, in spite of our lack of phrases for its verbal analysis. We find ourselves in a buzzing world, amid a democracy of fellow creatures; whereas, under some disguise or other, orthodox philosophy can only introduce us to solitary substances, each enjoying an illusory experience.[6]

Individuals may be cut off, in their self-consciousness, from the "objective" reality of metaphysics. For Whitehead, however, this fact does not plunge us into dualism, but rather confirms his statement that "the universe is always one, since there is no surveying it except from an actual entity which unifies it."[7]

In his chapter on Ammons to which I have referred, Harold Bloom cites a passage from Emerson's essay '"Circles"; for Bloom, these lines reflect the poet's false identification with *Ananke*. I find, however, that Emerson's lines, like Ammons's poetry, speak to the freedom within nature's order as well as to the necessity. Natural process continually liberates Ammons from what would otherwise be the hardening circles of the *mental* order. In Emerson's formulation, "the natural world may be conceived as a system of concentric circles, and we now and then detect in nature slight dislocations which apprise us that this surface on which we stand is not fixed, but sliding."[8] The significant shift from Emerson to Ammons is in the perception that dislocations are perpetual, not "now and then," and that they make available a human fertility of imagination corresponding directly to nature's superficial instability. The Jersey shore, where Ammons lived at one time, figures in many of his poems: its constant motion of wind and sand meets the movement of his accommodating mind. "Dunes" is a brief poem staking a poetic claim in the marginal world at the continent's shifting edge, where nature's universal dislocation is easiest to detect:

> Taking root in windy sand
>   is not an easy
> way
> to go about
>   finding a place to stay.

A ditchbank or wood's edge
  has firmer ground.

In a loose world though
  something can be started—
a root touch water,
  a tip break sand—

Mounds from that can rise
  on held mounds,
a gesture of building, keeping,
a trapping
into shape.

Firm ground is not available ground.[9]

In its brevity and the directness of its closing statement, "Dunes"
could be read as an epigraph for Ammons's best-known poem,
"Corsons Inlet." That poem too is set at the seashore, but in its
greater complexity *embodies* what "Dunes" says. It is like Everson's
"Canticle to the Waterbirds" or Levertov's "The Coming Fall," in an
inclusiveness of observation that keeps any one image or statement
from becoming dominant. "Corsons Inlet" is not a self-contained
poetic artifact but a terrain into which the reader may step. Verse
records the scattered impressions and reflections of the poet walking
by the shore. The body's motion carries the mind, alert and moving,
through a world of shifting sand and waterline, minnows and wind.
Instead of the conflict of stationary, opposed orders, the walk brings
ordered flux. Accordingly, the poem has a journalistic quality in
parts, presenting scraps of information about how the sky turns
overcast, an egret stalks an unseen prey. Only in the circumambula-
tory integrity of the poem are these events connected.

I went for a walk over the dunes again this morning
to the sea,
then turned right along
    the surf

            rounded a naked headland
            and returned
along the inlet shore:

it was muggy sunny, the wind from the sea steady and high,
crisp in the running sand,
    some breakthroughs of sun
  but after a bit

continuous overcast:

the walk liberating, I was released from forms,
from the perpendiculars,
     straight lines, blocks, boxes, binds
of thought
into the hues, shadings, rises, flowing bends and blends
          of sight:

               I allow myself eddies of meaning:
yield to a direction of significance
running
like a stream through the geography of my work:
   you can find
in my sayings
               swerves of action
               like the inlet's cutting edge:
          there are dunes of motion,
organizations of grass, white sandy paths of remembrance
in the overall wandering of mirroring mind:
but Overall is beyond me: is the sum of these events
I cannot draw, the ledger I cannot keep, the accounting
beyond the account:

in nature there are few sharp lines: there are areas of
primrose
   more or less dispersed:
disorderly orders of bayberry; between the rows
of dunes,
irregular swamps of reeds,
though not reeds alone, but grass, bayberry, yarrow, all . . .
predominately reeds:

I have reached no conclusions, have erected no boundaries,
shutting out and shutting in, separating inside
          from outside: I have
          drawn no lines:
          as

manifold events of sand
change the dune's shape that will not be the same shape
tomorrow,

so I am willing to go along, to accept
the becoming
thought, to stake off no beginnings or ends, establish
          no walls:

by transitions the land falls from grassy dunes to creek
to undercreek: but there are no lines, though

change in that transition is clear
as any sharpness: but "sharpness" spread out,
allowed to occur over a wider range
than mental lines can keep:

the moon was full last night: today, low tide was low:
black shoals of mussels exposed to the risk
of air
and, earlier, of sun,
waved in and out with the waterline, waterline inexact,
caught always in the event of change:
    a young mottled gull stood free on the shoals
    and ate
to vomiting: another gull, squawking possession, cracked a
    crab,
picked out the entrails, swallowed the shot-shelled legs, a
    ruddy
turnstone running in to snatch leftover bits:

risk is full: every living thing in
siege: the demand is life, to keep life: the small
white blacklegged egret, how beautiful, quietly stalks and
    spears
            the shallows, darts to shore
                    to stab—what? I couldn't
        see against the black mudflats—a frightened
        fiddler crab?

            the news to my left over the dunes and
reeds and bayberry clumps was
            fall: thousands of tree swallows
            gathering for flight:
            an order held
            in constant change: a congregation
rich with entropy: nevertheless, separable, noticeable
        as one event,
                    not chaos: preparations for
flight from winter
cheet, cheet, cheet, cheet, wings rifling the green clumps,
beaks
at the bayberries
    a perception full of wind, flight, curve,
    sound:
    the possibility of rule as the sum of rulelessness:
the "field" of action
with moving, incalculable center:

in the smaller view, order tight with shape:
blue tiny flowers on a leafless weed: carapace of crab:
snail shell:
       pulsations of order
broken down, transferred through membranes
to strengthen larger orders: but in the large view, no
lines or changeless shapes: the working in and out, together
      and against, of millions of events: this,
          so that I make
          no form of
          formlessness:

orders as summaries, as outcomes of actions override
or in some way result, not predictably (seeing me gain
the top of a dune,
the swallows
could take flight—some other fields of bayberry
      could enter fall
      berryless): and there is serenity:

      no arranged terror: no forcing of image, plan,
or thought:
no propaganda, no humbling of reality to precept:

terror pervades but is not arranged, all possibilities
of escape open: no route shut, except in
   the sudden loss of all routes:

      I see narrow orders, limited tightness, but will
not run to that easy victory:
      still around the looser, wider forces work:
      I will try
   to fasten into order enlarging grasps of disorder, widening
scope, but enjoying the freedom that
Scope eludes my grasp, that there is no finality of vision,
that I have perceived nothing completely,
      that tomorrow a new walk is a new walk.[10]

Ammons is determined to impose "no form of / formlessness" on
the "millions of events"; he wants, like the bayberry along the
dunes, only "disorderly orders." In the midst of this flow, in the
course of his walk, the poet can say, "I allow myself eddies of
meaning: / yield to a direction of significance / running / like a
stream through the geography of my work." In "Corsons Inlet," as
in his other lengthy poems, Ammons's drift is celebration. And the
key word for his experiences of such significance is "eddies": affir-

mation coalesces in a moment, and then the flow of events continues past. It is a word that recalls Whitman:

> I effuse my flesh in eddies and drift it in lacy jags.

> I bequeath myself to the dirt to grow from the grass I love,
> If you want me again look under your bootsoles.[11]

Effusions and eddies cannot be compressed into discrete orders,
because they are continually merging with the larger disorderly
orders of the world. Ammons's rhythms and syntax convey the
world's constant reformulation. David Kalstone's analysis of this
effect in "Saliences" is equally descriptive of "Corsons Inlet":
"Nouns are suspended in a chain of participial explosions . . . you
almost feel that the verbal motion is more important than the mix-
ture of abstractions and particulars swept along."[12] Such a dynamic
vision of reality leads, in Ammons, to a certain modesty of statement, though accompanied by the broadest ambitions for connectedness and for participation in the natural order: "I see narrow
orders, limited tightness, but will / not run to that easy victory: / still
around the looser, wider forces work: / I will try / to fasten into
order enlarging grasps of disorder. . . ." Like Berry and Pack, Ammons practices a poetry of "proud humility." But where they root
their poetry in the chosen landscapes of personal experience, he
finds his art among the shifting winds and dunes of process, the
country where every walk must follow a wavering shore.

"Corsons Inlet" has a great deal in common with that other extended meditative poem, "Sunday Morning." But Ammons's final
stanza underlines the poems' crucial difference. Stevens's natural
order, after the collapse for him of the Christian system, is "an old
chaos of the sun," and his tone is a mingling of nostalgia and exhilaration in the freedom that comes with submission to universal entropy: these are the complex feelings compressed into the poem's
last line, "Downward to darkness, on extended wings." For Ammons, though, the emphasis is on the way in which nature and the
poet alike break open old orders continually, to liberate the materials
from which new orders may be "grasped." Decay is, as we have
seen, a central process of human experience as of the earth, and is in
both realms a renewing dynamic. Accordingly, the world of Ammons's poetry is always presented as a freshly emerging event. In
Science and the Modern World, Whitehead generalizes the creative dimension of each moment in this way: "An event is the grasping into
unity of a pattern of aspects."[13] And in Ammons's poems the se-

quence of natural shifts and the path of human consciousness are tied into just such a pattern of coherence, in an ecologically balanced art.

Like walking, ecology is one of Ammons's chief formal metaphors. It relates to his knowledgeable fascination with nature's intertwined specifics (*Sphere:* "touch the universe any where you touch it / everywhere"), and it also speaks to the loose balance of poetic form and experience affirmed by the last stanza of "Corsons Inlet." In *Tape for the Turn of the Year,* Ammons develops this concept most explicitly:

> *ecology* is my word: tag
> me with that: come
> in there:
> you will find yourself
> in a firmless country:
> centers and peripheries
> in motion,
> organic,
> interrelations![14]

Later on in *Tape*'s entry of "27 Dec:" he continues his development of this aesthetic:

> don't establish the
> boundaries
> first,
> the squares, triangles,
> boxes
> of preconceived
> possibility,
> and then
> pour
> life into them, trimming
> off left-over edges,
> ending potential:
> let centers
> proliferate
> from
> self-justifying motions![15]

Ammons's dislike of fixed boundaries relates both to what he sees and how he says it. Unlike the majestic blank-verse stanzas of "Sunday Morning," "Corsons Inlet" presents a thoroughly irregular verse form, with the wavering left margin responding to the eddies of perception. Ammons's poetry does not line up and march but holds together in a dense, unhierarchical order of suspension, like a flock of seabirds wheeling above the surf.

It is Ammons's vision of "a firmless country" that accounts, at least in part, for his poetry's richness of formal innovation. Through his variable margin, inherited from Williams, he brings a range of phrases and rhythms into his poetry which a more regular cadence would scarcely allow. And Ammons carries this technique beyond the three and four tabs of Williams's verse, achieving a distinctively intricate shuttle of lines. The more even verse forms of *Tape for the Turn of the Year* and *Sphere: The Form of a Motion* equally reflect his need for a medium which will accept the world's "disorderly order." To the eye they at first seem more narrowly bounded than the shorter pieces—a "long thin poem" whose lines are limited by the adding-machine tape on which it is written, and *Sphere*'s unvarying stanzas of four triplets, each line composed of five to seven beats. But visual regularity serves chiefly as a sort of funnel, allowing Ammons to pour his eddies and fragments into poetry. Both of the works are single unbroken sentences, with colons serving to mark the breaths and to link the poetic elements of variable length. In both cases, order is not inherent in the tightness of stanza and line but in the meandering current of each poem as a whole.

In Ammons's two book-length poems, the center is everywhere. The poetry of inclusiveness, rather than of hierarchical ordering, is founded on the understanding that only in specific events, not in abstractions, do we discover the world. As Ammons writes in "Guide,"

> wisdom wisdom: a peachblossom blooms on a particular
> tree on a particular day:
>   unity cannot do anything in particular:[16]

Interest in nature's dynamic particularity, and a conviction of the inherent importance of each particular, weave together the diverse levels of Ammons's writing—his explicit statements about ecology, his inclusiveness of subject matter and interest in science, his open-ended, constantly re-centering verse forms. The intensity with which the poet notices and appreciates the details of the natural world fuses mind and nature; it bears out Whitehead's claim, already cited in connection with Wordsworth: "Feelings are 'vectors'; for they feel what is *there* and transform it into what is *here*."[17]

Ammons's writing is poetry of the mind in that it describes (transcribes) these vectors. It is poetry of nature because its "feeling" is for the passing beauty of this physical world. If the world's beauty were not always passing out of the world, poetry would not be necessary. But as it is,

> poetry has
> one subject, impermanence
> which it presents
> with as much permanence as
> possible.[18]

This passage, from a late section (entry of 31 Dec:) of *Tape for the Turn of the Year*, balances another moment near the poem's beginning (entry of 8 Dec:):

> how like a gift
> the memory
> of bird and empty tree!
> how
> precious
> since we may not have
> that configuration
> again:[19]

Nature's wind of process revives the subsiding mind, and a blink of waking surprise records and remembers the preciousness of a moment already vanishing. This is the human pact with the world. And it is one which recalls Whitehead's God in *Process and Reality*, the "Poet of the World" who gains concrete existence from the physical world and lends it, in turn, an eternal aspect: "Thus God is to be conceived as one and as many in the converse sense in which the World is to be conceived as many and as one. The theme of Cosmology, which is the basis of all religions, is the story of the dynamic effort of the World passing into everlasting unity, and of the static majesty of God's vision, accomplishing its purpose of completion by absorption of the World's multiplicity of effort."[20] I quote this theological passage from Whitehead not out of any desire for Ammons's apotheosis, but as a model for how nature's multiplicity and the poet's unifying vision inform and authenticate one another. Poetry, too, poises its majesty in the midst of process. At the end of *Sphere* the mind and nature meet in vivid repose, in the knowledge that "if light warms a piney hill, it does nothing better at the / farthest sweep of known space:"[21]

"Identity" reveals, more precisely than any of Ammons's other poems, the way in which nature supplies the mind's terrain:

> 1) An individual spider web
>   identifies a species:

an order of instinct prevails
          through all accidents of circumstance
          though possibility is
high along the peripheries of
spider
          webs:
          you can go all
          around the fringing attachments

          and find
disorder ripe,
entropy rich, high levels of random,
          numerous occasions of accident:

          2) the possible settings
          of a web are infinite:

          how does
the spider keep
          identity
          while creating the web
          in a particular place?
          how and to what extent
          and by what modes of chemistry
          and control?

it is
wonderful
          how things work: I will tell you
                    about it
                    because

it is interesting
and because whatever is
moves in weeds
   and stars and spider webs
and known
                    is loved:
          in that love,
          each of us knowing it,
          I love you,

for it moves within and beyond us,
          sizzles in
winter grasses, darts and hangs with bumblebees
by summer windowsills:

          I will show you
the underlying that takes no image to itself,

cannot be shown or said,
but weaves in and out of moons and bladderweeds,
        is all and
    beyond destruction
    because created fully in no
particular form:

           if the web were perfectly pre-set,
           the spider could
    never find
    a perfect place to set it in; and

           if the web were
perfectly adaptable,
if freedom and possibility were without limit,
           the web would
lose its special identity:

    the row-strung garden web
keeps order at the center
where space is freest (interesting that the freest
           "medium" should
           accept the firmest order)

and that
order
           diminishes toward the
periphery
      allowing at the points of contact
           entropy equal to entropy.[22]

Hyatt Waggoner and others have pointed out what a characteristic subject of American poetry the spider and its web provide, from Edwards to Frost. Ammons, though, gives the image a triple importance: as a model of natural order amid flux, of human meaning in a physical world, and of the reflective voice in "nature poetry." The poem's first section is bracketed by two propositions from Ammons the naturalist which prepare, in turn, for the question to which the rest of the poem is a response: "how does / the spider keep / identity / while creating the web / in a particular place?" In the remainder of "Identity" Ammons responds both to these lines and to the more general question of how the mind is housed in nature. For him, as for Wordsworth, nature is "the anchor" of the mind. In the image from "Tintern Abbey," however, "purest thoughts" float fathoms high above the anchor's grounding in the ocean bed, whereas in Ammons the mind is anchored *within* nature, among the twigs and outcrops that surround the poet and make his world.

The spider web, like all of nature's precious particulars, is worthy of the poet's consideration, "because whatever is / moves in weeds / and stars and spider webs / and known / is loved." In the particular of the spider's web, interwoven into the poem's sequence, we see "the underlying that takes no image to itself." Through attentiveness to natural form, the poet voyages beyond all forms. Yet poetry itself, though it may invoke transcendent visions, retains its irreducible formal dimension. Like a walk by the ocean or in the woods, a poem may direct one's gaze toward "the underlying," but it always accomplishes this in terms of a passage *through* form. Thus it is Ammons's concern for what is "beyond destruction" that turns his gaze back to nature's awaking and disappearing instances. Ammons might be called, in the term Geoffrey Hartman applies to Wordsworth, "a borderer." But within his poetry's order of departures and returns, Ammons's main interest is not in the placement of a disputed boundary; rather, it is in walking around, and around, the falsely divided region of personal experience, until mind and nature are encompassed in a "valley of their own."

Ammons's sphere of concerns may be centered on almost any natural event to which the poet turns. But in "Identity" the spider web, with its own formal circularity and balance, shows especially clearly the place of human meaning in the world and of the natural world in poetry. The science of ecology confirms the indivisibility of natural process: each feature of a landscape must be understood with reference to the whole, just as the habits of each creature reflect, and depend upon, the larger community of life around it. Yet within nature's system of constraints, specific beauty and identity remain real. In the web, Ammons gives us a metaphor for his own indivisible poetry, in which the necessities of nature frame the beauty and originality of his vision. His special attentiveness as a poet is to "the points of contact" between the mind and nature, and within the entropic, looping margins of his poetry he supports the concentric identities of them both.

Excursion:
Winter Without Snow

Despite temperatures at or below normal for the season, much of New England received no major snowfalls in January and February of 1980. This essay records the disorientations and disclosures of such a winter.

Clearing

The cold months settle into Vermont as a gradual clarification. First comes the simplicity of subtraction. The golden warblers, which rush through our wood at the rate of one new species a day in May, all have retired for the duration. On a winter's walk I can count on seeing the same handful of hardy birds—red-breasted nuthatches, black-capped chickadees, tree sparrows, jays, evening grosbeaks, and the two smaller sorts of woodpecker, downy and hairy. A friend has taught me how to make the chickadee's sibilant distress call, which fills the trees around me with mixed flocks of curious chickadees and nuthatches. They hop up to my face, cocking their heads first on one side then on the other, to fix me with a bright stare. So few birds, but so fully disclosed, are in perfect equation with summer's hints and fragments, the numerous songs half heard among the leaves and the flashes of color at the edge of vision. A green cloud lifts and these little lives perch, day after day, on the sharp twigs, to be seen.

Last week we crossed Lake Champlain at the Crown Point Bridge and drove on into the Adirondacks for a day-hike up Noonmark. It is the perfect mountain for such an outing in midwinter: the ascent and return are short enough to allow for slow walking and frequent stops, yet the view from the top, of Giant and the Upper and Lower Wolfjaws, is unsurpassed. Hiking along the trails we spotted all our familiar birds from Vermont, as well as an enormous pileated wood-pecker. As in the Green Mountains, we could see deep into these bare woods to where the sharply etched branches began to fuse into a patina on the pewter horizon. But looking down the slope from the crest, we saw a new way in which wintry woods disclose them-selves. The rosy cast of paper birches' buds and twigs and the pale green of aspens swirled and gathered in highly defined patterns several miles away and two thousand feet below. A plant-ecologist could probably look at such an interchange of color and say what various conditions of soil and moisture underlie it. But failing such lore, we could still appreciate this game of *Go* in forest tones; the masters' strategy evades the novice, but the beauty of patient, oblique response is inescapable.

The most notable thing about our hike up Noonmark was some-thing we did *not* see. This winter in west-central Vermont, even with the average temperature for January and early February poised around fifteen degrees, there has been little snow. And here too, climbing up above four thousand feet in a region where snow is usually yards deep by the middle of winter, there were just a few inches on the ground—loosely packed, as if the dry, cold air had sucked out and crystallized whatever sparse water lay in the rocks. There were no white drifts on the boughs of these hemlocks and fir, nothing to pull them earthward or to make them look, by contrast, black. This year the second half of winter's clarification, namely its campaign of concealment, has never come. There is no white blan-ket setting off the trunks' stark posts or highlighting the filigree of branch, twig, and bud. A thin crust remains, unmelted, from De-cember's inconclusive flurry, but it is pierced everywhere by winter weeds and beds of frozen leaves. The smooth curves that always make me think of deep sleep, of shoulders and back relaxed, are nowhere in sight today. Intricacy meets an eye looking for repose.

The clarity of winter's usual snowy dream is a quality our writers of nature have known how to appreciate. Aldo Leopold tells us, at the beginning of *Sand County Almanac*, that "the months of the year, from January up to June, are a geometric progression in the abun-dance of distraction . . . . January observations can be almost as simple and peaceful as snow, and almost as continuous as cold."[1] Much is stripped down; much that is left is removed from sight by the covering snow. A person standing in this field of sleep can feel a new attentiveness awaking in himself. It is not that those natural phenomena left out to view are inherently more interesting from a human perspective than those we lose sight of, but that, as Leopold

suggests, the movement and variety of summer distract our attention from any one thing. Winter holds up objects in high relief—
tree, boulder, bird—for our most careful regard. It invites us to be
still and cool, to let one curve, one color truly enter the mind. In the
chapter of *Walden* entitled "The Pond in Winter," Thoreau asserts,
"If we knew all the laws of Nature, we should need only one fact, or
the description of one actual phenomenon, to infer all the particular
results at that point."[2] Every chapter of *Walden* testifies as well to the
complementary truth, that to know one "fact" fully is to understand
through it all of nature's laws and relations. Such a conviction informs Thoreau's desire "to transact some private business with the
fewest possible obstacles." Winter's austerity accords well with a
mission of strategic isolation. "Nature is a discipline,"[3] Emerson
says, and winter can teach us how to eliminate distractions, how to
begin again with the essentials.

A winter landscape is like a Zen garden. One reacts first to a
refreshing simplicity of setting, but soon the sparseness of the
garden's obvious "features" and the superficial randomness of their
arrangement engage the eye and the mind: the few things that *are*
there gather significance until they become a configuration at the
center of meaning. The similar properties of a snowy world may
account for the way, throughout *Pilgrim at Tinker Creek*, Annie Dillard returns to waking dreams about the Eskimos. Seal hunters,
mesmerized in their kayaks amid undifferentiated whiteness, lose all
power of action or speech. Wolves lick themselves to death on the
grease-smeared blades of sharpened knives set out for such a purpose. A starkness of white and red reduces consciousness to certain
basic truths, the material fact of this spinning globe, the pervasive
struggle of living forms upon its surface. Summer's foliage, as well
as the variety and fertility of its animal life, perpetually suggest just
what they never allow the time or space for us to realize clearly: the
vast simplicity of life sacrificed to life, fragile threads of warmth
drawn through a world largely inert. Dillard finds a sacramental
quality in the arctic terrain, a revelation of the altar and the cup
immanent in this "nibbled and nibbling" life. In the chapter called
"Northing," she brings this strain to its clearest articulation: "A kind
of northing is what I wish to accomplish, a single-minded trek toward that place where any shutter left open to the zenith at night
will record the wheeling of all the sky's stars as a pattern of perfect,
concentric circles. I seek a reduction, a shedding, a sloughing off."[4]
Her imagery recalls Dante's lines, from the *Purgatorio*, on the wheeling stars God spins like a lure, to draw us up into the perfect order

of His will. White on black, the stars and the snow are aspects of nature that turn us away from earth's complexities.

At the heart of our most characteristic and enduring American responses to nature is an ambivalence, a turning from the fecundity of Tinker Creek to dreams of the Beaufort Sea and back again. Emerson testifies to his "child's love" for "my beautiful mother," but also declares, "The best moments of life are these delicious awakenings of the higher powers, and the reverential withdrawing of nature before its God."[5] The integrity of Emerson or Dillard is in not denying either the immediate sensuous beauty or the transcendental impulse. And, at least in New England or Virginia, nature confirms the artist's divided mind. In spring we start up from our dream of blank reality; summer is the abandonment of Vision for vision, as we, with Emerson, "expand and live in the warm day like corn or melons"; autumn comes and we fall into a reverie on the end of things; and then the world turns white once more. The forest floor is hidden from view, but—to borrow Emerson's phrase—the seasons have "already transferred nature into the mind, and left matter like an outcast corpse."[6] This is one winter, however, when the snow has stayed away, and the transfer between nature and mind is of a different order.

Relics

Outdoors, in February of other years, our gaze always travels up. In the muffled silence, the tones washing the snow at our feet insist upon angles of light in the northern sky, pale blue at noon, lemon with the setting sun, darker blue as night comes on. Sight is colored by the hour, sucked up through the trees' capillary fans, streaming out into thin air. This year, with no snow, the eye hugs the cluttered ground; this is obviously no polished mirror, meant to reflect the magnitudes of sky, but a lens, objective, refracting closer facts. There is no snowshoe experience of treading silently through clouds, but instead a crunch of leaves and twigs with every step. It's like walking over a floor littered with egg shells, a sensation guaranteed to defeat the visionary dream winter otherwise abets.

On the trail in Ripton, crunching up with friends to see the beaver lodge, I was amazed at the numbers of bright green club mosses flourishing in crumbly banks along the way. Within six inches of the ground was a second forest, but most winters we would never have guessed it was there. On broad patches of ice, where springs made a last run for it, then froze when winter came around the corner, we found another surprise. At first it seemed that certain areas of ice had been mysteriously dyed red. Looked at a little closer, the pigment appeared to be some dry, pulverized material—lichen? Then, when my face was finally near enough, I could see that the individual flecks were in constant motions, insects, millions of them, splashed along the trail in sizzling masses. I had read about springtails, or snow fleas, as one of the dominant insect forms in winter. The field guides described them, however, as black, not this collective shout of color.

The cities of hopping springtails suit the general busy feeling of the woods this winter. No curtain has been drawn decorously before the ramshackle disintegration of used forms. The skeleton has come out of the closet. Filling in for snow, brown leaves pile up in their own drifts among the trees. It is too cold for shed branches to rot, so they lie around, grow brittle, and fall apart. Even when I stand still, sounds of falling, cracking, groaning, hissing seem, with comic excess, to issue from all sides. Sound carries forever through these unobstructed woods. The log-truck at Middlebury Gap, shifting down to make the grade with a full load, lifts the noise of its engine to us, across the miles. Our friends, talking and laughing as they start up the beginning of the trail, are also audible way up here. The hilarity of today's hike reflects the fact that this winter has turned out to be an especially happy one for outings with others. Transcendental vision seems often to exclude the pleasures of society. Annie Dillard ventures forth alone, and Thoreau, writing in his cabin by the frozen pond, chooses not to make much of his dinner parties in Concord. But the fractured consciousness of our group's January hikes has found a terrain perfectly accommodating to its fits and starts.

The abundance of sensory messages, of all manner of fine detailing, does not eliminate the mysterious quality of winter in Vermont. But visionary abstraction is crowded out by a welter of numinous "facts," each of which seems able to tell us all, if only we could divine the code. One sits cross-legged in the Zen garden, then notices that instead of a single, beautiful boulder, there are dozens of them. Bamboo creaks, leaves rattle down, yet each sensation remains intensely meaningful. This bewilderment of significance has to do with the *uncanny* quality of frozen woods without snow. Ice bends branches into dramatic arcs, it seals moss-covered rocks into smooth bowls. Look again, we are told; looking, we find runes, unfamiliar as they are profuse.

The beaver pond had been frozen for weeks when we reached it and slid across to investigate the lodge. No snow obscured the ice, and it was an enticing page we found written and rewritten under-foot. Much of the ice was milky and smooth, but cut with jagged blue seams deep within. Running, then sliding, in my treadless work-boots, I felt the change to a pebbled surface of clear ice overly-ing the smooth opaque. The old white continent had dipped under, a new one bubbled over the top. On the east side of the pond, large tufts of grass poked through, elegant arrangements bleached almost white except for a rare strawberry-colored blade twisted in. Around each gathering of grass the ice opened into an elaborate circle of lacework. Such intricate, balanced beauty without any human maker finds one side of the brain wanting to laugh it off as accident, or to dismiss it with the apt analogy. But the exquisitely patterned pond cannot be swept away; it is just one more thing winter does, whether we notice it or not.

The most startling difference between this winter and others is finally in the hayfields, not in the woods. It is usually the smooth whiteness of fields that sets the key for everything else in the land-scape. Last week, though, as I was walking in Cornwall through a chain of broad fields leading down to Otter Creek, my eye was mastered by the sharp silhouettes of the weeds. The frost and the little bits of snow we had received matted the old grass down and left the plentiful weeds to stand out as if on display. The stiff, thick stalks and petrified clusters of tiny blossoms and leaves made me feel as if I were walking on an alien planet. Spore cases of the sensitive fern were much in evidence, so dramatic it was hard to believe their purposes did not include making me blink and stop for a better look. Out of each pale, stick-straight stalk, a foot or so in length, rise pairs of short twigs, branching at an angle nearly paral-lel with the main stem. And on each little branch is a double row of berries, so dark as to appear almost black. I halted by one of these small semaphores and took a single bee-bee–sized berry between my thumb and finger. It yielded a fingertip full of spores, hundreds of thousands of them, finer than dust.

The stiffness of winter weeds makes them seem like self-contained artifacts, giving the lie to the smooth continua of evolution, ecology, plant succession. If these little sculptures have been arrayed for each to have its full effect, however, the question is why, and by whom. Darwin, before the voyage of the Beagle, was already asking why the Lord had bothered to make 250,000 different types of beetle. In one regard, Darwin and the theory of evolution have helped us to account for the amazing proliferation of life forms. But certain questions return today, as I walk in this field of rattling perfection. Why should the sensitive fern bother to stage this startling spectacle along the trail? It seems, at this season, to be a drama without particular reproductive advantage, unless part of a grand design to carry out spore dispersion by the fingers of fledgling naturalists. We have learned more easily how to deal with springtime, to tell ourselves the force that through the green fuse drives the flower is nothing but genes seeking to replicate themselves. Our age, sentimental about its own skepticism, rather likes to have soft beauty blown away. Birds in the blossoming trees, and even the human lovers underneath, are only vehicles, we tell ourselves, for the thing that's real. Spring is a painted show; winter has taught us, as we believe, its deeper truth.

The million-weed field suggests a different point of view. Nature does not compliantly withdraw, leaving us face-to-face with a transcendent God. It intensifies fine definition, focuses high summer's sweep into particulars of spore case, seed, and stalk. Thickly clustered spears of mullein, rounded with brown flowerlets of varying size, recall the marble garlands on monuments to the fallen of World War I: cold carvings that loop among names of out-of-the-way places in Belgium and France. The upright mullein affects us as the floral ornaments are meant to—so many brittle buds that will never open beneath this sky—but our emotion here in the field finds a circuit to complete. Down at the base of the mullein's shafts are grayish leaves that will last through the winter, fuzzy and perfectly soft. New life bides its time among last season's husks. "Lamb's ears," said a friend, and rubbed one on our Rachel's cheek.

Chicory, with faint reminders of blue in the drab purses pacing the crooked stalk, cattails splitting to show they're nothing but seeds and sails, packed tight and given a skin, Joe-Pye weed, with touches of down scattered among its tiny, many-pointed stars—all poise in this world of sharp contrasts, showing how the passage of time is captured in one moment and one form. In such ways the weeds announce that they are merely dormant, not dead, that they do not go away; we usually just don't notice them. Beauty is the vehicle for life, but the opposite is also true. In this field we see what summer made for us as a farewell gift. Plants, no less than Wordsworth, may have their days bound each to each by natural piety. And when all is said, our visions of withdrawal and transcendence may reflect the simpler fact that we, being large carnivores in a northerly zone, are

driven to seek an annual cave in the mind and to spend the winter
dreaming of snow. Like burdocks and bears, we are quiet for a
season, as the earth whispers its course.

Return

Sometimes, when there are perplexities for which daytime allows no
resolution, the best idea is to stay up all night. Sleep and dreams are
usually the wiser road to morning, but waking night does offer its
own quiet suspension, in which the *conscious* mind has time to
think, time. At night, pressing issues may be unpressed, leisurely
looked at from all sides. Objects in the house emerge into greater
clarity, the abstraction of furniture yielding up a particular, comfort-
able chair, an afghan. A boiled egg, toast, a cup of tea, become a
communion with the hour. This winter without snow is such a
night, a chance, now that we're not sleepy anymore, to see life
clearly and to see it whole.

Near the end of *Process and Reality*, Whitehead distills that massive
and overwhelmingly precise book into two lines of the old hymn:
"Abide with me, / Fast falls the eventide."[7] His philosophy of organism is an attempt, he says, to acknowledge those two perceptions of
the world which the hymn also addresses. We look at the world and
see transience, and we look at the world and see something eternal.
Often such perceptions are in an alternation, like summer and
winter; but then there are seasons like this, asking us to draw the
circle. The definiteness of winter weeds, coupled with their mystery,
answers to Whitehead's call for a mutually informing relation between the calibrations of science and the dreams of religion and art.
We want a vision that is focused in this field.

As winter was beginning, a friend pointed out that the bleached
flowerheads of Queen Anne's Lace continued opening and closing
each day. These little cups of twigs and seeds remember, while we
are turning our thoughts to the cold, that the earth still takes its spin
around the sun. I awoke this morning, February 15, 1980, to find
that it had snowed a couple of inches—powdery snow, but plenty to
keep the earth tucked in smooth for the rest of the day. When
flowerheads unfurl today, small globes of snow that have formed on
the clustered crown will sift down into each widening cup. At dusk,
the closing twigs will gather snow inside and hold it there during
the night. Milkweed, snow-weed.

SECTION III

The Science of the Heart

CHAPTER

7

Structures of
Evolving Consciousness

THE ENCOUNTER of poetry and science provides a context within which to draw together this book's main strands. In attempting a fresh, authentic response to the earth, today's poets have often begun with a sense of opposition between the body's presentness in nature and the paired terms *past* and *mind*; to reconcile such a dichotomy, the poets considered here have worked at achieving an art of expansive particularity. Twentieth-century science assists the poets' project of reconciliation because of its increasingly comprehensive view of physical reality. This new scientific vision of the world has both attracted poets estranged from the Western humanistic tradition and helped to break down their sense of polarization between culture and nature.

Robinson Jeffers was in the vanguard of modern poets interested in science and frequently introduced scientific insights and terminology into his writing. But Jeffers, as Hyatt Waggoner has pointed out, generally maintains a sense of physical reality's "objective" separation from the human experience: within such a perspective he could speak of beauty as superfluous, love as a dream.[1] Such a conviction of the earth's reality as apart from any human point of view led him into what Whitehead calls "the fallacy of misplaced concreteness." Jeffers contributes to our vision of nature by locating nature beyond the exclusively human circle of values. Contemporary poetry and science rebalance Jeffers's expanded equation and rediscover a place in nature for human consciousness and culture.

Whitehead has been, along with Wordsworth, a major influence in my reading of contemporary poetry. *Science and the Modern World*

(1925) and its elaboration, *Process and Reality* (1929), comprise his widest-ranging critiques of Western civilization. Since Whitehead's day, a number of outstanding writers have tried to bridge the gap between scientific and artistic apprehensions of the world. But because of his scientific authority, his love of poetry, and his organic rendering of tradition, his cultural synthesis remains for me the fullest and most compelling. Whitehead finds in the *defiant* love of nature, as expressed by poets from Wordsworth to Jeffers, a reaction to the seventeenth-century turning in human thought. The rise of philosophical dualism and that of scientific materialism were simultaneous, Whitehead argues, and led to a neglect of nature and the human heart which only the poets effectively protested. But the early twentieth century's revolutions in physics—the general theory of relativity, quantum mechanics, the uncertainty principle—have undermined mechanistic science and allowed for a new conception of science which can more fully assimilate the testimony of poetry. Whitehead is a prophet of passionate process whose insights resonate with many of the achievements of our poets of nature. His insistence that emotion is essential to the universe's reality makes possible an ecstatic form of science.

In the final part of this chapter, after having considered Whitehead's historical analysis and the larger outlines of his philosophy of organism, I want to exemplify his "feeling" approach to the physical world with passages from two books of meditative natural history— Annie Dillard's *Pilgrim at Tinker Creek* and Peter Matthiessen's *The Snow Leopard*. These two writers seem to me to embody the human relation with the earth which Whitehead delineates. They also form a rich pairing with Snyder and Ammons, the poets on whom Chapter 8 focuses. Scientific awareness, in the rich contemporary genre which these two volumes represent, is augmented and fulfilled by human emotion and personal history. Similarly, verse is informed, its systems of metaphor generated, by the insights of science. In each case there is an expansiveness circling beyond superficial dualities. The earth is round, the complexity of natural relation luminous.

Whitehead views the seventeenth century as the beginning of a separation between human consciousness and the earth, and of a corresponding split between human thinking about values and quality and the quantitative, manipulative intelligence. He further perceives that the aesthetic and ethical faculties and the scientific pursuits have depended upon each other to confirm their isolating self-definitions. This mutual dependency within estrangement is explained in a passage from *Science and the Modern World:*

> The enormous success of scientific abstraction, yielding on the one hand *matter* with its *simple location* in space and time, on the other hand *mind,* perceiving, suffering, reasoning, but not interfering, has foisted onto philosophy the task of accepting them as the most concrete rendering of fact.
>
> Thereby, modern philosophy has been ruined. It has oscillated in a complex manner between three extremes. There are the dualists, who accept matter and mind as on an equal basis, and the two varieties of monists, those who put mind inside matter, and those who put matter inside mind. But this juggling with abstractions can never overcome the inherent confusion introduced by the ascription of *misplaced concreteness* to the scientific scheme of the seventeenth century.[2]

In the dichotomy of seventeenth-century thought, Whitehead sees the setting of a cultural trap, which has been sprung in the uncontrolled technological explosion of our own century. He finds this a challenge both for modern philosophy in particular and for *all* attempts at integral human existence. There has been, in short, a "divorce of science from the affirmations of our aesthetic and ethical experiences."[3] One reason for the divorce is the indisputable success of science in analyzing and manipulating the physical world, and the resultant readiness to call into question the *reality* of anything not quantifiable in its own systems and terminology. In his book on *The Domination of Nature,* William Leiss speaks of this "mastery of science [as] manifested in its ability to cast a 'veil of ideas' (*Ideenkleid*) over the nature experienced in everyday existence, that is, to treat the phenomena of nature as if they were purely mathematical-geometrical objects."[4] It is an exorcising mastery, a willingness to deny meaning to "nonverifiable" results of experience, whether conveyed by the rush of emotion or the productions of art. A statement ascribed to the great evolutionist George Gaylord Simpson is a breathtaking instance of such presumption. In emphasizing the importance of *Origin of Species,* he poses the question "What is man?" and then responds to it in this way: "The point I want to make is that all attempts to answer that question before 1859 are worthless and that we will be better off if we ignore them completely."[5] So much for the Book of Job, for *Hamlet,* and for *Faust!*

Scientific materialism can fall into a horrifying arrogance in its treatment of the world's body. Unwillingness to recognize spirit in the earth and its creatures finally wounds the same human beings who pursue such insensitive dealings with their world. In California several years ago, a scientist took a core sample of one of the few remaining bristle-cone pines, in an attempt to determine the age of this oldest of all living things on earth. His valuable coring-drill broke off in the wood and, with the permission of the Forest Service, he cut down the tree to get his tool back. Through treating the world as inert, we have diminished our capacity for work suffused with emotion and sympathy. This is the "smart" civilization Levertov rejects in her poem "May Our Right Hands Lose Their Cunning"; we cannot even be safe from ourselves unless we can register our power's implications in our guts.

The seventeenth-century split, in Whitehead's analysis, divorced science from its necessary emotional and aesthetic complements; it cut the nonscientific elements of our culture off from the amazing beauty and connectedness which science reveals in the physical creation. As he says in *Process and Reality*, "Greeks were ignorant in modern physics; but modern philosophers discuss perception in terms of categories derived from the Greeks."[6] It seems to be the case that by dividing culture into its scientific and humanistic components, we left each category in a dead end and forfeited the capacity to have a society enhanced by, and respectful of, the surrounding processes of nature. Since Whitehead wrote, there have been numerous attempts to bridge the gap between "the two cultures"; and, as this book argues, poetry has become one of the most important media of synthesis. But it remains equally clear that such impulses at reintegration constitute a *reaction* to the powerful reductive forces of our culture's dualism.

Whitehead would not be surprised by the role of current American poetry in reconnecting science with the immediate wholeness of human experience. According to his reading of history, it was the poets of the Romantic era in England who kept alive an alternative to the alienations of science and philosophy:

> The literature of the nineteenth century, especially in its English poetic literature, is a witness to the discord between the aesthetic intuitions of mankind and the mechanisms of science. . . . Wordsworth is the poet of nature as being the field of enduring permanences carrying within themselves a message of tremendous significance. . . . Both Shelley and Wordsworth bear witness that nature cannot be divorced from its aesthetic values; and that these values arise from cumulation, in some sense, of the brooding presence of the whole on its various parts.[7]

In the Preface to the 1800 edition of *Lyrical Ballads,* Wordsworth shows how strong an awareness he bore of the relation between his poetry and the science of his day. Both the need for feeling in our transactions with the physical world and an underlying *affinity* between science and poetry come out in this important passage from his Preface:

> The Poet . . . considers man and nature as essentially adapted to each other, and the mind of man as naturally the mirror of the fairest and most interesting qualities of nature. And thus the Poet, prompted by the feelings of pleasure which accompanies him through the whole course of his studies, converses with general nature, with affections akin to those which, through labour and length of time, the man of science has raised up in himself, by conversing with those particular parts of nature which are the objects of his studies. The knowledge both of the Poet and the man of science is pleasure; but the knowledge of one cleaves to us as a necessary part of our existence, our natural and inalienable inheritance; the other is a personal and individual acquisition, slow to come to us, and by no habitual and direct sympathy connecting us with our fellow-beings. The man of science seeks truth as a remote and unknown benefactor; he cherishes it in his solitude; the poet, singing a song in which all human beings join with him, rejoices in the presence of truth as our visible friend and hourly companion. Poetry is the breath and finer spirit of all knowledge; it is the impassioned expression which is in the countenance of all Science. [8]

Though Wordsworth's poetic vision opposes the inertness and detachment of scientific materialism, he implies in the passage quoted that there is the possibility for another mode of science, grounded, as is poetry, in the experience of pleasure. For a science of this sort, poetry represents a consummation, an integration of insight into a world of human response and relation. Wordsworth's poetry anticipates in important ways both Whitehead's vision of cosmic process and the scientific integrations of our new poetry of nature. He seems in the following sentences, also from the 1800 Preface, steadfastly to look beyond the science of his day to a more precise and less rigid acquaintance with the world: "If the labours of men of science should ever create any material revolution, direct or indirect, in our condition, and in the impressions which we habitually receive, the Poet will sleep then no more than at present, but he will be ready to follow the steps of the man of science, not only in those general indirect effects, but he will be at his side, carrying sensation into the midst of the object of science itself."[9]

What was an "object" is informed and vivified by the poet's sensation of it. Sensation, in this understanding, becomes a creative act, the evocation of a world within which objects may be bound in vital relationship. Whitehead addresses this same dimension of Wordsworth's poetry when he writes that the poet "always grasps the whole of nature as involved in the tonality of the particular instance. That is why he laughs with the daffodils, and finds in the primrose thoughts 'too deep for tears.' "[10] To insist on both the particularity and the wholeness of every moment is to purify the human experience of the world. It has a refreshing effect on the sense of identity in poet and reader alike, and offers a similarly purifying power to a science bewildered about its own character and value. Whitehead's advocacy of subjectivity and emotions in the pursuit of knowledge—what I have called "the science of the heart"—contradicts the more abstract sense of science which still generally prevails. But it is a perspective endorsed by many of the most distinguished scientists since Whitehead's day. The chemist Michael Polanyi is one who has confirmed the scientist's "passionate participation in the act of knowing": "As human beings, we must inevitably see the universe from a center lying within ourselves and speak of it in terms of a human language. . . . Any attempt rigorously to eliminate our human perspective from our experience of the world must lead to absurdity."[11]

As Whitehead asserts several times in the course of his writings, his purpose in elaborating a critique of scientific materialism is not to discount science, but rather to reform it. Science, in his view, has gone astray within the larger drift of culture. At its heart, though, is a valuable impulse of attentiveness and appreciation, as was acknowledged by Wordsworth in his Preface. The most positive and basic thing to say about science is that it "requires an active interest in the simple occurrences of life for their own sake."[12] Prior, in all senses, to systems and abstractions is the scientific impulse of observation; it is there that the poet may find a context harmonious with his celebrations. It seems to be an unstated rule that critics of a lifeless tradition illustrate their objections with a counter-heritage, a lineage of wholeness and immediacy. Like Blyth, Bly, or Berry, Whitehead defines his own history of life-giving attentiveness as one within which the fragmentary apprehensions of the world by art and science may be reconnected: "The craftsmen who executed the late medieval decorative sculpture, Giotto, Chaucer, Wordsworth, Walt Whitman, . . . Robert Frost, are all akin to each other in this respect. The simple immediate facts are the topics of interest, and these reappear in the thought of science as the 'irreducible stubborn facts.' "[13] Beneath the desiccations of its conventional style, science derives value from its "active interest in . . . simple occurrences"; even the linear measurements against which Levertov protests necessitate a continual return to physical immediacy.

The flat, impersonal style usual to scientific reports provides one reason why this affinity between science and art is so often obscured. I remember when, as a college junior, I handed in my first field report for a class on marine biology. The professor, a concerned teacher and an amiable man, turned it back to me with all personal pronouns excised and all verbs shifted into passive voice. He also crossed out the initial sentences, which tried to register the beautiful sunrise hours I had spent along the beach, while studying tidal variations in the populations of littoral snails. Both my physical presence on the granite shelf and my retrospective emotion had no place in science, it seemed; they were not allowable even if all of the other pertinent "facts" could also be included. The abstracted world remaining was still fascinating: brown and olive swirls of periwinkle shells, a silver meterstick against the granular, pale tan rock. But science had pared it down relentlessly, a purgation like the fire of Robinson Jeffers's anger, smouldering farther up the coast. Facts advanced shining out of the ocean's process, but soon subsided into the coordinate system of a rock whitening under the sun.

Scientific style is, in one way, a kind of shorthand, an economical way to transmit information. Beyond this fact, though, it seems to express a basic skepticism about the reliability of emotional or aesthetic information. A proud moment in the history of science was Galileo's confrontation with the Church; his muttered response to orthodoxy's insistence that the earth was motionless—"Still, it *does* move"—opposed the open eyes of scientific observation to the closed eyes of faith. What scientists, in the giddy revolutions of technology, seem often not to remember, however, is that science no less than religion rests on faith. And the faith of science is closely equivalent to that fidelity from which Wordsworth's poetry emerges: a conviction of the importance and connectedness of every detail of nature. In a beautiful passage from *Science and the Modern World*, Whitehead expresses the nature of science's fundamental, though often unrecognized, faith:

Faith in reason is the trust that the ultimate natures of things lie together in a harmony which excludes mere arbitrariness. It is the faith that at the base of things we shall not find mere arbitrary mystery. The faith in the order of nature which has made possible the growth of science is a particular example of a deeper faith. This faith cannot be justified by any inductive generalisation. It springs from direct inspection of the nature of things as disclosed in our own immediate present experience. There is no parting from your own shadow. To experience this faith is to know that in being ourselves we are more than ourselves: to know that our experience, dim and fragmentary as it is, yet sounds the utmost depths of reality: to know that detached details merely in order to be themselves demand that they should find themselves in a system of things: to know that this system includes the harmony of logical rationality, and the harmony of aesthetic achievement: to know that, while the harmony of logic lies upon the universe as an iron necessity, the aesthetic harmony stands before it as a living ideal moulding the general flux in its broken progress towards finer, subtler issues.[14]

Whitehead's philosophy of organism is itself a grand effort of connection. Because of the underlying affinity between art that is attentive to nature and the physical sciences, he wants to develop a process of thought that will comprehend them both; his philosophy's function, as he says in the introduction to *Science and the Modern World*, is "to harmonise, refashion, and justify divergent intuitions as to the nature of things."[15] Only through such a synthesis of the disparate elements of human experience may one achieve Whitehead's personal goal: "a fertilisation of the soul."[16] This concern with human fertility speaks to the main concerns of the Introduction and Section I. For Eliot, Whitehead's contemporary, a sterile culture and the sterility of individual experience were locked in an embrace that signified only death, with no prospect for regeneration. Eliot's fearful obsession, in *The Waste Land*, with the water of natural process and Jeffers's burning anger at human folly both express despair of any fruitful connection between man and earth. It is in reaction to such an impasse that the vitalizing understanding of decay emerges as so valuable. The attempts at rooted cultivation by Snyder, Berry, and Pack at once assume the collapse of a more general cultural order and reinitiate the cycle of fertility within a local context. In his effort of connection between science and a more personal and aesthetic appreciation of nature, Whitehead aids the process of refertilization.

Whitehead shows the fundamental similarity among aspects of experience which were held to be widely divergent. He consistently pursues an organic analogy in carrying out his own effort of reconciliation. Seeds' germination, the mating of animals, the intermingling of decay—all presuppose a common realm of chemistry; in the first of these two cases, only the elaborate and dependable symmetries of DNA allow reproduction to transform the elements in a filial image. For Whitehead, the cross-fertilization of human and natural realities, and of the scientific and aesthetic apprehensions of the world, are likewise only possible because these things were never essentially foreign to each other. The cycles of the earth and of human response to nature are fundamentally the same: in each case creativity and evolutionary expansiveness are ever-present. It is because of these deep genetic bonds that nature's gift to humanity—self-forgetfulness—and the human gift to nature—self-consciousness—are so valuable.

The basic fact about the universe, from the perspective of Whitehead's philosophy of organism, is that it is both creative and *self*-creative. As he writes midway through *Process and Reality*, "The universe is thus a creative advance into novelty. The alternative to this is a static morphological universe."[17] This statement, so rich in psychological and artistic implication, is also as accurate a description as modern science allows of the physical status of reality. Though *Process and Reality* was written over fifty years ago, Whitehead stood at the forefront of revolutions in physics whose significance is still being registered. One way, for our purposes, to generalize the emerging scientific worldview from which his writings began would be to say that it showed decay as essential to all of reality, inorganic as well as organic. There can be no "static morphological universe," because of the incessant atomic and subatomic transfer of energy. Another word for decay here would be relationship; in a universe of mingling self-surrender, and assimilation, even light responds to the world around it, bending in deference to a gravitational field. Just as in the case of culture, there is a breaking down of hierarchical distinctions in twentieth-century science. As Whitehead puts it in *Science and the Modern World*, "Science is taking on a new aspect which is neither purely physical, nor purely biological. It is becoming the study of organisms. Biology is the study of larger organisms; whereas physics is the study of the smaller organisms."[18] Like the science of ecology, culture too may be understood organically: it is the field of relationship between organisms and, as such, a complex organism in its own right. Everything that *is*, within Whitehead's context, may be understood as an organism, and that is the basis for his vision of a creative, fertile world.

Whitehead's understanding of the entire universe as an organism

of organisms means that the universe is always unified. But the
nature of such unity varies with every slight shift in space or time.
Einstein and Heisenberg, from their different angles, both emphasized the need to describe reality in relation to a point with a certain
location at a certain time and with a certain momentum; there are no
static absolutes in the physical world. Such a state of affairs is not,
for Whitehead, a defeat of the human urge for knowledge, but instead a triumph. For, since "an event is the grasping into unity of a
pattern of aspects," the creativity and relativity of human consciousness find themselves in a world answering to their own flow and
coalescence. In his attempt to "harmonise . . . divergent intuitions,"
Whitehead points to a view of science responsive to Wordsworth's
poetry, one which "always grasps the whole of nature as involved
in the tonality of the particular instance."[19] Just as Wordsworth, in
one of the profoundest insights of The Prelude, connects the force of
gravity with "the filial bond," Whitehead "attributes 'feeling'
throughout the actual world."[20] All of reality, on every level of our
perception, is dynamic and responsive. Human self-consciousness
thus presents no obstacle for unification with nature, when "each
actual entity is a throb of experience including the actual world
within its scope."[21]

For the poets considered in previous chapters, the relation of the
past to the present was a central problem. The philosophy of organism, too, takes this to be a crucial area for integration, since otherwise there would be only a broken chain of unified but isolated
"worlds," with no larger principle of wholeness. Like Eliot, for
whom tradition must be continually redefined, Whitehead shows
the present as always absorbing and surrounding the past. As he
says at one point in Process and Reality, "Causation is nothing other
than the outcome of the principle that every actual entity has to
house its actual world."[22] Later in that volume he expresses a similar
insight in these terms: "This passage of the cause into the effect is
the cumulative character of time."[23] Like a tree, with broadening
concentric rings, the world grows. But its growth, rather than being
located simply in space, takes place in the increasingly complex
relationship between everything that is and everything that has
been. Just as only decay can provide the new materials for life, only
the ceaseless transience of the world allows for nature's evolutionary
expansiveness. Moments, like points on the surface of the earth, are
thus related as "events disposed in an interlocked community."[24]

"Community" is a word highly characteristic of Whitehead's outlook. Even when he uses that other key word "evolutionary" in his

writing, it is in a more progressive sense than would be allowed in strict Darwinian theory. Nature, for Whitehead, is moving toward harmony, but not toward a definitive, focused embodiment like Teilhard de Chardin's "omega point"; it is instead a balanced accommodation, like those communities of biological interdependence which the post-Whiteheadian science of ecology has helped us to understand. Like the climax forest which represents for Snyder a richness of organic stability, the world of Whitehead's vision is a gathering of intricacy, energy, and balance. As a beautiful passage in *Science and the Modern World* says, "Such order as we find in nature is never force—it presents itself as the one harmonious adjustment of complex detail."[25] Such an emphasis on community as an ever-emerging harmony has an important bearing on the relation between the *tradition* of natural response and the immediacy of present experience. It is not, in Whitehead's vision, a matter of approaching a *conclusive* harmony. Climax forests, too, give way before the conditions of their own success; even before the coming of European settlers, the grand white pine forests of northern New England periodically shaded out their own seedlings and allowed the deciduous woods to come again. But at every stage the natural world incorporates the previous incorporations of available energy. Like the grooves on a boulder-erratic in the Green Mountains, the trees too convey the history of a slope; they transmit into the breaking present a community that extends through time as well as space. The world is a gate through which each present must pass, to embrace the past and assure its own perpetuation. Whitehead's terms for describing this speak to the dialectic of past and present in human consciousness as well as to the encompassing cycle of nature: ". . . life turns back into society: it binds originality within bounds, and gains the massiveness due to reiterated character."[26]

"Community" is synonymous for Whitehead with that dimension of the physical world he calls "the everlasting"—"the property of combining creative advance with the retention of mutual immediacy."[27] Such a vision of something binding past and present together makes possible a richness of relation between people and between individuals and nature. It is a continuity like that Wordsworth recalled in Book I of *The Prelude*—allowing past and present to flow into one another, but with their distinctiveness enhanced, not dissolved. So often the great seers of unity between man and nature express themselves in religious terms; though, like Whitehead's, their writings come out of a reverent impulse of attentiveness rather than out of any orthodox expectations. Writers from Thoreau to

Dillard have seen, in the woods, the countenance of the "everlast-ing." It is a vision of paradoxical transcendence, of a principle of unification found not in airy abstractions but in the amazing inter-twinings of this earth. Whitehead says this of the religious impulse arising from a world of connection in flux: "The vision claims noth-ing but worship; and worship is a surrender to the claim for assimi-lation, urged with the motive force of mutual love."[28]

Through understanding worship as chosen assimilation, it is possible to grasp the specifically human part in the evolving har-mony of nature. The philosophy of organism, building on the relativistic insights of modern physics, breaks down the hierarchi-cal separations between human beings and other elements of the world. "In a certain sense, everything is everywhere at all times. For every location involves an aspect of itself in every other loca-tion. Thus every spatio-temporal standpoint mirrors the world."[29] The most important benefit of such a perspective is that it effec-tively does away with the dualism between "subjective" human consciousness and an "objective" world, by attributing subjectivity to all of nature. Whitehead speaks of each phenomenon as a "prehension" of the entire world. The aspect of a prehension that is most fully *responsive* to the world—"conscious"—is what he calls the "superject":

> Thus an actual entity on its subjective side, is nothing else than what the universe is for it, including its own reactions. The reactions are the subjective forms of the feelings, elaborated into definiteness through stages of process. . . . The philosophies of substance presuppose a subject which then encounters a datum, and then reacts to the datum. The philosophy of organism pre-supposes a datum which is met with feelings, and progressively attains the unity of a subject. But with this doctrine, "superject" would be a better term than subject.[30]

As Wordsworth expresses in the "Infant Babe" of *The Prelude*'s Book II, feelings and identity, like one's body, are a reflection of the larger environment. This grounding of consciousness in the earth destroys any possibility for a mechanical relation with it. The more vivid the human response, the more clearly the person can understand her-self or himself as participating in and assimilated by a larger circle of feeling. Rachel Carson, who was trained as a biologist, nevertheless tried to break away from the "objective" voice in her writings, in the interest of a higher realism. In her book *The Sea Around Us* (1951), she writes, "If there is poetry in my book about the sea, it is not because I deliberately put it there, but because no one could write truthfully about the sea and leave out the poetry."[31]

For Whitehead, the distinctive quality of human consciousness is thus not estrangement but a possibility for acute awareness of other "subjectivity" throughout the universe. The senses' perception of the world—which he calls "presentational immediacy"—is at once an affirmation of kinship and a consolidation of individual identity. For, after all, human identity is a matter of perceived relation among the passing moments of a life, and "we—as enduring objects with personal order—objectify the occasion of our past with peculiar completeness in our immediate present."[32] Whitehead's achievement here is similar to what Hartman calls Wordsworth's *via negativa;* he achieves a human reconciliation with the world by demolishing any sense of thought as abstract. Not only is consciousness, in its primary "gravitational" forms, common to the entire creation, but it is always, even in its human expression, a manifestation of far larger realities: "Consciousness flickers; and even at its brightest, there is a small focal region of clear illumination, and a large penumbral region which tells of intense experience in dim apprehension. The simplicity of clear consciousness is no measure of the complexity of complete experience. Also this character of our experience suggests that consciousness is the crown of experience, only occasionally attained, not its necessary base."[33] A passage in A. R. Ammons's *Sphere: The Form of a Motion* speaks to this perception and illustrates why *Sphere* is for me the poem most fully embodying and illuminating Whitehead's system:

> . . . we are as in a
> cone of ages: each of us stands in the peak and center
> of perception: around us, in the immediate area of recent
>
> events, the planets make quickly-delivered news and the sun
> acquaints us of its plumes eight minutes old: but then
> the base widens dropping back in time through
>
> the spinal stars of spirals and deepens broadening into
> the core of our configuration with its ghostly other side:
> and then the gulfs and deepenings begin and fall away
>
> through glassy darkness and shadowy mind: antiquity on
> antiquity the removes unveil, galaxies neighbors and foreign
> cousins and groups of galaxies into the hazy breadths and
>
> depths the telescope spells its eye to trace: but here
> what took its beginning in the farthest periphery of event,
> perception catches the impact of and halts to immediacy,

the billion-year-old flint light striking chemical changes
into the eye: behold: the times break across one
another like waves in surfy shoals and explode into the

white water of instantaneous being: each of us stands in
the cone of ages to collect the moment that breaks the
deeper future's past through: each of us peak and center[34]

I have tried, in the first part of this chapter, to bring out the many
ways in which Whitehead's philosophy of organism prepares for our
contemporary nature poetry, with its own attempts at a synthesis of
poetry and science. A question remains, though, as to the immediate use of philosophical illumination, when the cone of experience
is, in its essence, dim. Why is it, for that matter, useful to study
literature, or to write about nature? These are questions around
which much of the book revolves in its concern for a dynamic reconciliation of the human and the natural. One of our greatest advocates of making dark regions light was Freud, but even he expressed
misgivings about the usefulness of rational analysis by itself. Simply
understanding the principles of psychoanalysis, Freud emphasized,
was as much use to a neurotic patient as "a menu-card to a starving
man."[35] For Freud, his theories only attained full value within a
cathartic therapeutic exchange. Whitehead, too, acknowledges the
need to go beyond an analysis of organism's wholeness to an experience of it: ". . . the true rationalism must always transcend itself by
recurrence to the concrete in search of inspiration. A self-satisfied
rationalism is in effect a form of anti-rationalism. It means an arbitrary halt at a particular set of abstractions. This was the case with
science."[36]

In turning at this point to a brief consideration of *The Snow Leopard*
and *Pilgrim at Tinker Creek*, my intent is to consider in more concrete
and sensuous form the implications of Whitehead's thought. It is
noteworthy that our day has seen a flourishing of the genre of
natural history, a form in which the scientific awareness of the
earth's processes is expressed in a highly imaginative, emotionally
charged voice. On the one hand, scientists such as Loren Eiseley,
Lewis Thomas, and Stephen Jay Gould have expressed the results of
their research in ways that also include their political, aesthetic
selves; the warmth and complexity of their emotion has flowed into
their science. On the other, adventurers and mystics, like Matthiessen and Dillard, have immersed themselves, and expanded their
fields of personal response, in the proliferating "data" of scientific

awareness. Traditional categories of literature and life are overturned by such books. It is interesting, in fact, how often, from Thoreau on, American literature's most intense engagements with nature have issued into uncategorizable books. Dillard and Matthiessen are, for me, fulfillments of Whitehead's vision, and in the power of their writing they forge an even closer connection between Whitehead and poets like Snyder and Ammons. Their books express a therapeutic exchange with the earth; for both author and reader, ecstatic science revivifies a human consciousness prone to abstraction and self-isolation. Dillard and Matthiessen answer Whitehead's call in *Science and the Modern World:* "What is wanted is an appreciation of the infinite variety of vivid values achieved by an organism in its proper environment. When you understand all about the sun and all about the atmosphere and all about the rotation of the earth, you may still miss the radiance of the sunset. There is no substitute for the direct perception of the concrete achievement of a thing in its actuality. We want concrete fact with a high light thrown upon what is relevant to its preciousness."[37]

"God and the World," the concluding chapter of *Process and Reality,* is the place Whitehead comes closest to the art of Peter Matthiessen and Annie Dillard. Arriving at the radiant poetry of this chapter after the difficult, highly technical precision of the book's middle chapters is like stepping into a sun-filled glade after hours of bushwacking through a New England forest. It is Whitehead's own best model for authentic, grounded vision in a self-creating world. The most basic connection among Whitehead, Matthiesen, and Dillard on this ground is that they all apprehend the synthesis of science and art in religious terms. Just as Whitehead develops a critique of the scientific and philosophical traditions, so in this chapter he interprets the religious tradition of the West in a way harmonious with *Pilgrim at Tinker Creek* and *The Snow Leopard.* To the various absolute, abstract gods who accompanied earlier visions of a "static morphological universe," Whitehead opposes the vision of "Galilean tenderness." Thus the Hebrew Moral Principle, the Greek Logos, and the Roman Emperor all give way, in the world of organism, to "a tender concern for all growing things," a worship of "the immediate present."[38] Annie Dillard and Peter Matthiessen both undertake their own voyages to the immediate. Dillard, in her seasons along the banks of a Virginia creek, holds the idea of a benevolent God, and the testimony of her eclectic reading, up to the disorienting rush of experience; she sings both the disillusionments and the transfigurations of open eyes. Matthiessen's trip to the Himalayas is at once a scientific expedition, a religious quest, and an encounter with the painful revelations of his own recent past. Out of the ironies of connection and separation in his journey, he too glimpses a wholeness beyond linear expression.

In *Process and Reality*, Whitehead treats as an emblem of ambivalent human consciousness the hymn lines "Abide with me, / Fast falls the eventide." This insight into the "everlasting" values in nature's transience is also a very central one for both *Pilgrim at Tinker Creek* and *The Snow Leopard*. Dillard acknowledges the paradoxical identity between the abiding and the passing in her choice of an epigraph for her volume, taken from Heraclitus: "It ever was, and is, and shall be, / Everliving Fire, in measures being / Kindled and in measures going out."[39] Since we have already paid attention to Levertov's and Whitehead's uses of the term, "measure" becomes a particularly helpful word for connecting Dillard's vision with those previously discussed. Levertov, in her poem "Artist to Intellectual," means by "measure" the analytical reduction of life's sensuous undirected body: she reacts against "reason" that meets the world only in terms of its own previously established categories. Whitehead, who in his critique of abstract thought fully agrees with Levertov, nonetheless finds a value in the human impulse to measure; it stems, for him, from attentiveness to the *things* of the world, as opposed to reliance on logical projections as to how things *should* be. The associated word for Whitehead is "concrete": we need to return to an immediate appreciation of the earth. And in the language of Whitehead's informed response to physical events there is also an affinity with Jeffers's need to dip his arms again in the beautiful river of Big Sur. For both men, "things" cool down the projects of the self-absorbed human heart. Dillard too finds that "measure" is the medium through which we may know the everlasting. Jakob Boehme saw the face of God in the gleaming reflection from a pewter plate, and Dillard finds it in every object to which she can open her spirit. Science, from such a perspective, becomes a form of worship; like Wordsworth's nature and Whitehead's true reason, scientific measurement transcends itself, leading through particulars to a luminous unity.

The transcendent significance of what in conventional human terms would be considered relatively "lowly" natural forms accounts for two characteristic features of Dillard's ironic vision. One of these is that, as in her fascinated attention to the horrors of "bugs," she dwells on test cases, on what she calls the ragged edge of nature; she is always trying to widen the scope of her comprehension, to approach in her own perceptions the multiplicity of the world. The other dimension of her attempt at inclusiveness is her humor. Hers is a world erupting in surprising "measures," amid which stands a bemused and moved human onlooker. The following passage from *Pilgrim at Tinker Creek* brings out the inclusive nature of what Whitehead would call her act of "worship":

> I am sitting under a sycamore by Tinker Creek. I am really here, alive on the intricate earth under trees. But under me, directly under the weight of my body on the grass, are other creatures, just as real, for whom also this moment, this tree, is "it." Take just the top inch of soil, the world squirming right under my palms. In the top inch of forest soil, biologists found "an average of 1,356 living creatures present in each square foot, including 865 mites, 265 springtails, 22 millipedes, 19 adult beetles and various numbers of 12 other forms. . . . Had an estimate also been made of the microscopic population, it might have ranged up to two billion bacteria and many millions of fungi, protozoa and algae—in a mere *teaspoonful* of soil." The chrysalids of butterflies linger here too, folded, rigid, and dreamless. I might as well include these creatures in this moment, as best I can. My ignoring them won't strip them of their reality, and admitting them, one by one, into my consciousness might heighten mine, might add their dim awareness to my human consciousness, such as it is, and set up a buzz, a vibration like the beating ripples a submerged muskrat makes on the water, from this particular moment, this tree. Hasidism has a tradition that one of man's purposes is to assist God in the work of redemption by "hallowing" the things of creation. By a tremendous heave of his spirit, the devout man frees the divine sparks trapped in the mute things of time; he uplifts the forms and moments of creation, bearing them aloft into that rare air and hallowing fire in which all clays must shatter and burst. Keeping the subsoil world under trees in mind, in *intelligence*, is the least I can do.[40]

The testimony of science directs human consciousness to what Gary Snyder has called the intelligence of the soil. And insofar as human consciousness can truly comprehend the soil's richness of life, it also becomes *identified* with that soil. In this connection it is interesting to see what an important part in the writings of both Dillard and Matthiessen is played by quotation from a wide variety of sources, for this seems to make their awareness even more like soil rich with diverse forms of life. Treasured texts decay and recombine in the mind, attaining at last a fertile unity. Science and literature, like the specifics of insect life and the quirks of personality, compose the ground beneath Dillard's transfiguring vision of "the tree of lights": the "dim awareness" of chrysalid butterflies augments the cone of Dillard's full awareness, driving out sparks from the "crown" of consciousness. Consciousness, as Whitehead's conclusion to *Process and Reality* also affirms, may thus become the clearest fulfillment of assimilation and identity: "The universe is to be conceived as attaining the active self-expression of its own variety of opposites—of its own freedom and its own necessity, of its own multiplicity and its own unity, of its own imperfection and its own perfection. All the 'opposites' are elements in the nature of things, are incorrigibly there. The concept of 'God' is the way in which we understand this incredible fact—that what cannot be, yet is."[41]

One of the values of juxtaposing Dillard and Matthiessen with Whitehead is that they bring out much more fully than he does the ironic *shifts* of human consciousness. The philosophy of organism addresses those moments, similar to spots of time, in which a person may participate consciously in the harmonious unity of the world. But such moments are hard to sustain; they occur in a vortex of counter-perceptions and desires. *Pilgrim at Tinker Creek* and *The Snow Leopard* can represent such swirl and coalescence precisely because Dillard and Matthiessen are, like Wordsworth, walkers. Revelation is housed in a moving human sphere of impression, expression, distraction, and recollection. Dillard, quoting Thoreau, describes her book as "a meteorological journal of the mind." Walking and looking, she heightens and clarifies the more muted ambivalence of *Process and Reality*, where Whitehead himself slowly moves from the overlapping, incremental precision of his epistemology to the grand generalizations of his unifying vision. One of Dillard's most strongly expressed conflicts is between her desire for a nonintellectual oneness with nature and the dogged sense of the value, and inescapability, of her own human intelligence. This wry passage from her chapter on "Fecundity" recalls Levertov's wish, in "Artist to Intellectual," for a headless enjoyment of life: "All right then, It is our emotions that are amiss. We are freaks, the world is fine, and let us all go have lobotomies to restore us to a natural state. We can leave the library then, go back to the creek lobotomized, and live on its banks as untroubled as any muskrat or reed. You first."[42] As the meditation continues, she acknowledges the unavoidable walking alternations of her experience—left foot and right, creek and library, a process comprehended, if at all, only in lyrical science's participation in the world.

Perhaps I don't need a lobotomy, but I could use some calming down, and the creek is just the place for it. I must go down to the creek again. It is where I belong, although as I become closer to it, my fellows appear more and more freakish, and my home in the library more and more limited. Imperceptibly at first, and now consciously, I shy away from the arts, from the human emotional stew. I read what the men with telescopes and microscopes have to say about the landscape. I read about the polar ice, and I drive myself deeper and deeper into exile from my own kind. But, since I cannot avoid the library altogether—the human culture that taught me to speak in its tongue—I bring human values to the creek, and so save myself from being brutalized.[43]

Finally, it is science that provides Dillard with the best metaphor for reconciling the diverse elements of her experience. One way to generalize the various dichotomies of culture and nature is as a question of how the recollected illuminations of earlier days may be related to the immediate experience of light in the present. And from the capacity of physics to describe light either in terms of particles or as the motion of waves, Dillard derives an impressive model of life's dynamic wholeness:

Here is the word from a subatomic physicist: "Everything that has already happened is particles, everything in the future is waves." Let me twist his meaning. Here it comes, the particles are broken; the waves are translucent, laving, roiling with beauty like sharks. The present is the wave that explodes over my head, flinging the air with particles at the height of its breathless unroll; it is the live water and light that bears from undisclosed sources the freshest news, renewed and renewing, world without end.[44]

Dillard's image makes it possible to appreciate more deeply Whitehead's saying in Process and Reality, "Completion is the perishing of reality: 'it never really is.' "[45] It is impossible to achieve a simultaneous experience of completion and immediacy: unity may only be understood as an ongoing process. The organic wholeness of the world is, in the words of D. H. Lawrence, "the wave that cannot halt."

In The Snow Leopard, Peter Matthiessen often echoes Dillard and Whitehead in his perceptions of "the eternal continuity of becoming."[46] His book is very helpful in rounding off this discussion, because, as a student of Zen, Matthiessen also ties this theme back directly to that affinity of Wordsworth with haiku and Buddhism which was touched on in Chapter 4. He writes at one point, "The Universe itself is the scripture of Zen, for which religion is no more and no less than the apprehension of the infinite in every moment."[47] As Matthiessen treks into the Himalayas, he comes upon such moments, stripped down to infinity by what Words- worth would call their "visionary dreariness"; they lie embedded in his narrative, possessing the evocative simplicity of haiku. A typi- cally unelaborated but resonant observation is this one: "At dusk, the northern sky is lavender. The cold lake nags at the gray pebbles, and there is no sign of a bird."[48] Infinity, as Wordsworth taught us, is an unexpected, deeply remembered bend in the path, left behind as quickly as it was encountered. In response to this comprehension of infinity within the bounds of human mortality, Matthiessen af- firms his own version of "Abide with me / Fast falls the eventide." For him, the model of paradoxical wholeness is the ancient Buddhist chant, *Om Mani Padme Hum*—the Jewel in the Heart of the Lotus. The perfection of the world can only be discovered in the midst of process.[49] To find the meaning of your life, you have to go on a pilgrimage in the world.

One of the richest features of Matthiessen's book is its ironic inter- folding of aesthetic and religious vision with science. Matthiessen's wildlife-biologist comrade is an admirable, intriguing character, but in his pursuit of science he sometimes manifests a single-minded- ness at odds with the larger narrative inclusiveness. Over a quarter of the way into the book we read, "GS, too, has seen blue sheep, and later, after tents are pitched, he goes out and finds more. He returns at dusk, delighted—'The first data in a month and a half!' he cries."[50] The joke here is in such a narrowly defined sense of data, excluding the revelations and adventures with which the previous pages have been filled. These are the data of a science with no place for personal pronouns, appearing oddly thin in a book so suffused with a connective and highly emotional apprehension of the world.

But the valuable twist of Matthiessen's writing, as of Dillard's, is that he goes beyond this surface incompatibility of the scientific and the subjective; like Whitehead with his notion of the "superject," Matthiessen perceives data as the vehicles of intense, appreciative encounter with creation. Just as a scientific expedition gives impetus and form to a religious pilgrimage among Buddhist holy places, Matthiessen's own careful scientific observations heighten his sense of the deep significance of other sentient beings he meets along his trek. In his synthesis of scientific, aesthetic, and religious experi- ences, he embodies that complementary wholeness to which Whitehead continually points. The cultural critique in *Process and Reality* includes a judgment that "the philosophy of organism seems to approximate more to some strains of Indian, or Chinese, thought than to western Asiatic, or European, thought. One side makes process ultimate; the other side makes fact ultimate."[51] Whitehead's persistent complaints about scientific materialism might seem at first to contradict this other passage from *Science and the Modern World:*

> In the last two centuries there has been a long and confused impact of Western modes upon the civilization of Asia. The wise men of the East have been puzzling, and are puzzling, as to what may be the regulative secret of life which can be passed from West to East without the wanton destruction of their own inheritance which they so rightly prize. More and more it is becoming evident that what the West can most readily give the East is its scientific outlook. This is transferable from country to country and from race to race, wherever there is a rational society.[52]

Whitehead's point is not, however, to advocate analytical, scientific reasoning as a replacement for Eastern traditions, any more than he was, in the previous quotation, suggesting Asian culture as an alternative to that of Europe. Rather, his sense is that science focuses and corrects the larger dynamics of a given tradition, just as it profits, in its turn, from an enlarged definition of "data." The mutual illuminations of science and Asian thought have been brought out recently in such works as *The Tao of Physics* and *The Dancing Wu Li Masters.* But Matthiessen's book remains especially helpful as a concrete instance of such connection. Walking into the highest mountain range on earth, on what is simultaneously an expedition and a pilgrimage, he rediscovers, within the polarized field of his own personality, the circular wholeness of the earth.

To a charged mind, swirling with the particles of perception and the waves of emotion, all "facts" are numinous. The sudden sailing passage of a great lammergeier, the hoot of an owl at nightfall, at once fill and articulate Matthiessen's consciousness. Rather than being a narrow light, cutting through the dross of feeling and experience to isolate significant data, the mind becomes a nurturing medium of connection. As Whitehead's use of the word "vectors" implies, this is a psychology understandable in terms of the physics of motion. The details of the physical universe deflect, accelerate, or, momentarily, arrest such vectors, leading the mind to apprehend the global gravity centering its own swirl. In a beautifully informed meditation toward the end of *The Snow Leopard*, Matthiessen exemplifies this organic identity of landscape and mind:

> Against the faces of the canyon, shadows of griffons turn. Perhaps the Somdo raptors think that this queer lump on the landscape—the motionless form of man in meditation—is the defunct celebrant in an air burial, for a young eagle, plumage burnished a heraldic bronzy-black, draws near with its high peeping, and a lammergeier, approaching from behind, descends with a sudden rush of feathers, sweeping so close past my head that I feel the break of air. This whisper of the shroud gives me a start, and my sudden jump flares the dark bird, causing it to take four deep slow strokes—the only movement of the wings that I was ever to observe in this great sailer that sweeps up and down the Himalayan canyons, the cold air ringing in its golden head.
>
> Dark, light, dark: a raptor, scimitar-winged, under the sun peak—I know, I know. In such a light one might hope to see the shadow of that bird upon the sky.
>
> The ground whirls with its own energy, not in an alarming way, but in slow spiral, and at these altitudes, in this vast space and silence, that energy pours through me, joining my body with sun until small silver breaths of cold, clear air, no longer mine, are lost in the mineral breathing of the mountain. A white down feather, sun-filled, dances before me on the wind: alighting nowhere, it balances on a shining thorn, goes spinning on. Between this white feather, sheep dung, light, and the fleeting aggregate of atoms that is "I," there is no particle of difference. There is a mountain opposite, but this "I" is opposite nothing, opposed to nothing.
>
> I grow into these mountains like a moss. I am bewitched. The blinding snow peaks and the clarion air, the sound of earth and heaven in the silence, the requiem birds, the mythic beasts, the flags, great horns, and old carved stones, the rough-hewn Tartars in their braids and homespun boots, the silver ice in the black river, the Kang, the Crystal Mountain. Also, I love the common miracles—the murmur of my friends at evening, the clay fires of smudgy juniper, the coarse dull food, the hardship and simplicity, the contentment of doing one thing at a time: when I take my blue tin cup into my hand that is all I do. We have had no news of modern times since late September, and will have none until December, and gradually my mind has cleared itself, and wind and sun pour through me, as through a bell. Though we talk little here, I am never lonely; I am returned into myself.
>
> Having got here at last, I do not wish to leave the Crystal

Mountain. I am in pain about it, truly, so much so that I have to smile, or I might weep. I think of D and how she would smile, too. In another life—this isn't what I know, but how I feel—these mountains were my home; there is a rising of forgotten knowledge, like a spring from hidden aquifers under the earth. To glimpse one's own true nature is a kind of homegoing, to a place East of the Sun, West of the Moon—the homegoing that needs no home, like that waterfall on the upper Suli Gad that turns to mist before touching the earth and rises once again into the sky.[53]

Everything that Matthiessen knows and sees becomes, in this moment of revelation, one thing. And just as there is no opposition between his "I" and the mountain at which he steadily looks, so there is no separation between the nondualistic vision of Zen and his scientific apprehension of the Himalayan canyon-world. The eagle and lammergeier, coming to see if he is ready for a more direct bodily assimilation into the scene, speak beautifully to the truth of the world as an unbroken circuit of energy and life. Matthiessen is not ready yet to give up his individual physical identity, but in a glimpse beyond the surface of such separations he comes to understand how, in the words of the great Zen master Dogen, "body and mind fall away." As Matthiessen himself writes, "Between this white feather, sheep dung, light, and the fleeting aggregate of molecules that is 'I,' there is no particle of difference." Whitehead discusses the "satisfaction" that comes from such self-transcendence, when reason has gone beyond reason, and individuality has seen through its own isolation. For him, it is associated with the dimension of "width"—a renewed apprehension of the larger world from which narrow human consciousness first arose. Einstein once said, "The sensation of the mystical [is] the power of all true science."[54] Biochemistry and ecology serve to confirm and amplify the immediate intuition of identity among feather, dung, and man. Physics connects the "fleeting aggregate of atoms" with its swirling world. The function of scientific awareness' human gift of "width" is "to deepen the ocean of feeling," to make possible "the savouring of the complexity of the universe."[55] Matthiessen's vision of a "homegoing that needs no home" illustrates a wonderfully evocative phrase at the end of *Process and Reality*: "the particular providence for particular occasions."[56] Both writers perceive a world that is always whole, in which human feelings of estrangement can be healed at any moment by an act of openness and acceptance. In the words "homegoing" and "providence" they address as well Wordsworth's great revision of *Paradise Lost*. The past is only apparently separate from the present, as the man is only superficially different from the "mountain opposite." A consciousness ready to participate in this world of process finds that every moment can be a step into the wholeness of remembered gardens.

A Record of the Waves

T HE "FEELING" science which Whitehead invokes, and which Dillard
and Matthiessen in their different ways achieve, offers a healing and
augmenting vision. It addresses directly the cultural despair of the
twentieth century, the bitter sense of conflict between the natural
order and our more specifically human heritage. In the conclusion of
Chapter 1 I speak of the therapeutic impulse expressed, from time to
time, within the current of Jeffers's rage. And I think, finally, that the
healing aspect of his vision accords fully with Whitehead's understanding of wholeness: we need, in Jeffers's view, to look at the world
much more closely, to attain a clarity that sees through apparent
human/natural dichotomies and relocates humanity in a comprehensive design. His poem "Signpost" is one that follows such an angle.

> Civilized, crying how to be human again: this will tell you
>   how.
> Turn outward, love things, not man, turn right away from
>   humanity,
> Let that doll lie. Consider if you like how the lilies grow,
> Lean on the silent rock until you feel its divinity
> Make your veins cold, look at the silent stars, let your eyes
> Climb the great ladder out of the pit of yourself and man.
> Things are so beautiful, your love will follow your eyes;
> Things are the God, you will love God, and not in vain,
> For what we love, we grow to it, we share its nature.
>   At length
> You will look back along the stars' rays and see that even
> The poor doll humanity has a place under heaven.

Its qualities repair their mosaic around you, the chips of
   strength
And sickness; but now you are free, even to become human,
But born of the rock and air, not of a woman.[1]

The poem begins in bitterness, with "civilized" spat out to make a
start and "that doll" humanity flung roughly to one side. But as
Jeffers considers the lilies and communes with the silent rock, his
attentiveness gradually leaves anger behind: the "great ladder" of
creation rises above personal discords, and earth is fixed in the
parallax of the stars. Jeffers attains a distance sufficient to reconcile
"the chips" of this world. Modern science has led us, in fact, to
understand how directly human beings express the chemical composition of our earth, how the same twisting threads inform the cells of
a sequoia and a man, how our tissues' salts glisten also in the granite. In a way analogous to Wordsworth's "ministry of fear," Jeffers's
self-loathing propels him to a perspective of wholeness within
which his humanity once more has a place. Significantly, this poem
is a sonnet in the number of lines and the rhyme scheme. Rhythmi-
cally and in the length of its lines, however, it breaks with tradition.
This formal synthesis amplifies Jeffers's meaning on the thematic
level. Long breaths register the explosive impulse of his poetry,
while the sonnet form points to the possibility of a coherent natural
order within which humanity may also be included.

At the end of "Signpost" a residual bitterness does appear, as
Jeffers refers once more to "the poor doll humanity" and opposes
birth of the rock and air to birth of a woman. It seems that Jeffers
indicates an avenue of wholeness that he cannot himself pursue.
Perhaps his is, like Wordsworth's, a choice of faithfulness to a beloved and endangered landscape. In Gary Snyder and A. R. Ammons there is a fuller integration of the particular terrain with underlying processes of creation that also include mankind. Because
these two poets are so open to science, they are able to move beyond the opposition of culture and nature which Jeffers so often and
so fiercely maintains. Just as Jeffers begins from Eliot's vision of
culture as a wasteland, Snyder and Ammons proceed from Jeffers's
therapeutic implications. Theirs is the next step in the dialectic of
nature and culture, at once an extension of Jeffers's critique and a
return to a poetic vision of wholeness. Ammons writes in Section 28
of *Sphere*, "having finished the pyramid, one recalls / the circle."

For Snyder and Ammons, science both confirms and elaborates
the senses' testimony. It introduces the mind's dynamic complexity

into a world that answer to it and that surpasses it in a liberating way. And, beyond the high definition which knowledge of science gives the poets' natural observations, the scientific vision of process also informs their poems in a more general way. Ezra Pound declared the impossibility of a unified long poem, since it would inevitably break down into a series of short poems connected by prose. In Snyder's and Ammons's lengthier pieces, however, even though there are moments standing out in their lyric intensity, science provides comprehensive models of coherence: images and feelings decay and fructify, a diverse terrain is populated according to its possibilities, approaching an ecosystem's cycling balance. Moments achieve coherence within the connectedness of a larger world.

At one point in *The Real Work* Gary Snyder says, "it's a problem of love; not the humanistic love of the West—but a love that extends to animals, rocks, dirt, all of it."[2] Poetry suffused with science is an expression of such love; culture is encompassed and completed as "humanistic" love gives way to love for "all of it." In "Toward Climax," from *Turtle Island,* Snyder offers to our perplexed present the augmenting perspective of science, in an effort to set human history in a larger, and more hopeful, perspective than modern culture has usually achieved.

> I.
>
> salt seas, mountains, deserts—
> cell mandala holding water
> nerve network linking toes and eyes
> fins   legs   wings—
> teeth, all-purpose little early mammal molars.
> primate flat-foot
> front fore-mounted eyes—
>
> watching at the forest-grassland (interface
> richness) edge.
> scavenge, gather, rise up on rear legs.
> running—grasping—hand and eye;
> hunting.
> calling others to the stalk, and the drive.
>
> note sharp points of split bone; broken rock.
>
> brain-size blossoming
> on the balance of the neck,
> tough skin—good eyes—sharp ears—
> move in bands.

milkweed fiber rolled out on the thigh;
      nets to carry fruits or meat.

catch fire, move on.
eurasia tundra reindeer herds
sewn hide clothing, mammoth-rib-framework tent.

Bison, bear   skinned and split;
      opening animal chests and bellies, skulls,
        bodies just like ours—
pictures in caves.

send sound off the mouth and lips
formal complex grammars transect
      inner structures & the daily world—

big herds dwindle
      (—did we kill them?
      thousand-mile front of prairie fire—)
ice age warms up
learn more plants, netting, trapping, boats.
bow and arrow. dogs,
mingle bands and families in and out like language
      kin to grubs and trees and wolves

      dance and sing.
begin to go "beyond"— reed flute—
      buried baby wrapped in many furs—
great dream-time tales to tell.

squash blossom in the garbage heap.
      start farming.
cows won't stay away, start herding.
weaving, throwing clay.
get better off, get class,
makes lists, start writing down.

      forget wild plants, their virtues
      lose dream-time
      lose largest size of brain—

get safer tighter, wrapped in,
winding smaller, spreading wider,
lay towns out in streets in rows.
and build a wall.

drain swamp for wet-rice grasses, burn back woods,
herd men like cows.
have slaves build a fleet

raid for wealth-bronze weapons
horse and wagon—iron—war.

study stars and figure central
never-moving Pole Star King.

II.

From "King" project a Law. (Foxy self-
survival sense is Reason, since it "works")
and Reason gets ferocious as it goes for
order throughout nature—turns Law back on
nature. (A rooster was burned at the stake
for laying an egg. Unnatural. 1474.)

III.

science walks in beauty:

nets are many knots
skin is border-guard, a pelt is borrowed warmth;
a bow is the flex of a limb in the wind
a giant downtown building
        is a creekbed stood on end.

detritus pathways. "delayed and complex ways
to pass the food through webs."

maturity. stop and think. draw on the mind's
stored richness. memory, dream, half-digested
image of your life. "detritus pathways"—feed
the many tiny things that feed an owl.
send heart boldly travelling,
on the heat of the dead & down.

IV.

two logging songs

Clear-cut

Forestry. "How
Many people
Were harvested
In Viet-Nam?"

Clear-cut. "Some
Were children,
Some were over-ripe."

Virgin

A virgin
Forest
Is ancient; many-
Breasted.
Stable; at
Climax.[3]

Snyder's vision is on several levels an evolutionary one. Beginning with "salt seas," and their radical product the "cell mandala holding water," he shows how human life emerged from nature and took on its specific characteristics in thousands of years of shaping interchange with the rest of the natural world. Estrangement makes little sense from such an evolutionary perspective; rather, a "primitive" worldview, with its sacramental sense of hunting, is much closer to the poem's outlook. As Snyder remarks in one of the interviews of *The Real Work*, ". . . if we talk about the evolution of consciousness, we will also have to talk about evolution of bodies, which takes place by that sharing of energies, passing it back and forth, which is done by literally eating each other. And that's what communion is."[4] There is no antagonism, in such a view, between spirit and matter. Spirit develops *in* and *from* the earth; to be born of woman is, in that fact itself, to be a child of rock and air.

Such a firm sense of human evolution within the context of nature, both at the beginning of life and in every phase of our history, makes possible the affirmative response to which Jeffers's "Signpost" pointed. Mankind, within such a scientific understanding, may be seen as the product of certain natural processes, rather than being a foreign element of any kind. This is, once again, a saving paradox: in the degree to which human nature has been determined by the inclusive nature of the earth, people are liberated to claim kinship and participation in the physical creation. In *The Origin of Species* Darwin says, "When I view all beings not as special creations but as the lineal descendants of some few beings which lived long before the first bed of the Cambrian system was deposited, they seem to me to become ennobled."[5] Similarly, human culture seems to be ennobled when placed, as in "Toward Climax," in an evolutionary context. Unlike the entropic, monstrous sense of humanity which prevails in so much of Jeffers's poetry, the biological and anthropological view is hopeful in its open-endedness. Cultural decay may be understood as adaptation, as well as demise.

Darwin's early shift from Edinburgh to Cambridge reflected his inability as a medical student to stand surgery on unanesthetized patients. Perhaps this reaction foretold that gift of imaginative sympathy and tender-heartedness which is so evident in his various encounters with people and animals in *Voyage of the Beagle*. It is an intuitive sense of connectedness, rather than of isolated striving, that is at the base of his insight into evolution: an embracing vision often submerged in the mechanistic approaches of Darwin's successors, but fulfilled and amplified in evolution's outgrowth, the science of ecology. Snyder says in *The Real Work*, "As the evolutionary model dominated nineteenth- and twentieth-century thinking, henceforth the ecological model will dominate our model of how the world is—reciprocal and interactive rather than competitive."[6] And in "Toward Climax," just as human culture may be understood in evolutionary terms, it also needs to be seen within the ecological circle. In a pregnant sentence from his *Fundamentals of Ecology*, Eugene Odum writes, "We, as human beings, should not forget that civilization is just one of the remarkable natural proliferations that are dependent on the continuous inflow of the concentrated energy of light radiation."[7] In beginning to recognize the reality of interdependence and cooperation within the ecosphere, humanity has gained an enhanced capacity to reaffirm its community with the earth.

Early on in his poem, and in its chronology of human evolution, Gary Snyder introduces one of the key concepts of ecology: "watching at the forest-grassland (interface / richness) edge." The edge, or ecotone, is always a critical natural environment, and in the following passage Eugene Odum amplifies the significance of such a setting:

> An ecotone is a transition between two or more diverse communities as, for example, between forest and grassland or between a soft bottom and hard bottom marine community. . . . The ecotonal community commonly contains many of the organisms of each of the overlapping communities and, in addition, organisms which are characteristic of and often restricted to the ecotone. Often, both the number of species and the population density of some of the species are greater in the ecotone than in the communities flanking it. The tendency for increased variety and density at community junctions is known as the *edge effect*.[8]

The edge effect has been very obvious in the fluctuating populations of Vermont's wildlife. Farmers in the early nineteenth century cleared away most of the state's forests, but from the middle of the nineteenth century to that of the twentieth the abandonment of hill farms allowed the proportion of wooded lands to rise again from 20 percent to 80 percent of the total acreage in Vermont. The reversion of abandoned fields, as sumac and hawthorn pioneers advanced into ground once held by bleaching corn stalks, has created an environment abundant with edge. It is in such a terrain that white-tailed deer and game birds have risen in the past decades to their greatest numbers since European settlement. Edge is implicitly an environment that moves and—as the forest-pasture edge in Vermont has moved ahead of expanding woodlands—populations such as bear and moose, decimated by the early wave of agriculture, are also reestablishing themselves. Even the panther, long considered extinct in Vermont, is rumored to be reappearing; but no one who has seen these cats is willing as yet to say just where.

This back-and-forth movement of an edge, when its oscillations may be comprehended as a predictable pattern, is referred to by ecologists as a "pulse." It is a tidal ebb and flow of energies that, in its middle passage as well as its extremes, nurtures characteristic ecosystems. The anthropological perspective of Snyder's Section I shows human history in terms of the long progression of an edge—a clearing away of the nonhuman growth that involves a "thousand-mile front of prairie fire," the draining of swamps, burning of woods, the human race's reiterated "raid for wealth." It is against the background of such a history that the science of ecology offers its doubly redemptive vision. The clearing away of woods is, on one level, an attack on complexity, reflecting a ferociously abstract Reason and a rigidly hierarchical understanding of the world. When history's "raid" is viewed in terms of such an opposition between man and nature, it is easy enough to fall into the despair that led Robinson Jeffers to call for the destruction of his own species. But when human attention finally focuses on the moving edge itself, a fresh understanding of wholeness results: man may be seen once more within ecological terms. In the dynamic and diverse interface between humanity and nature there is a vision of wholeness which can transform the linear, technological advance Snyder describes; it provides an opportunity for a cultural maturity analogous to that of a climax ecosystem, one in which maximum energy is concentrated through balanced diversity. "Science walks in beauty" is a line that sums up much in Gary Snyder's poetry. Snyder characteristically works at the entangling edge of science and poetry, one at which the seemingly opposed dimensions of human experience may be perceived as throbs, systole and diastole, of a larger pulse. As in the long quotation from *The Real Work* around which Chapter 2 revolves, Snyder's achievement is that of a comprehensive vocabulary, an edge of language in which terrains are able to overlap. When he writes, "send heart boldly travelling, / or the heat of the dead & down," he simultaneously describes the soil's regenerative cycle of decay, the growth of poetry from fermenting tradition, and the way a science of the heart may arise from the retold story of humanity's exploitations and dualities.

In the *two logging songs*, with which "Toward Climax" ends, Snyder brings his narrative of human evolution into the present and shows how urgent is the need for science's new vision of beauty at the edge. The science of ecology brings culture's evolution back into a natural perspective, but only as human violations of the circuit of wholeness have brought it near a breaking point. In "Clear-cut," Snyder perceives the connection which Levertov also sees so clearly, between society's carelessness toward the natural world and an inability to maintain the sanctity of human bodies and human life. Clear-cutting a forest and blanket-bombing a city are both the results of blinding abstraction: service to a "reason" as dead to mercy as it is to the sensuous revelations of this earthly life. Our forestry methods and our wars reflect each other; to move into a more delicate relation with the woods is to establish a more tender basis of interaction among people as well. "Virgin" is a distillation of poetry's role in such a further evolution. Poetry, regardless of its subject matter, is the edge where new combinations of the mind's life and the world's emerge, where a new language of balance and discovery finds itself. When Snyder's poetry aligns its edge with the margin between culture and science, its achievement is a vocabulary of amplified inclusiveness. Like so much of his writing, this final song is both an accurate description of a forest and a resonant emblem. It takes many decades for a forest to achieve the balance and diversity which prevailed in North America's woodlands when Europeans first encountered them. "Virgin" thus equals "ancient"; both qualities are meaningful only in terms of process, rather than as static absolutes. "Climax," too, expands its significance to include "stable." Like Wordsworth's "woods decaying, never to be decayed," in Book VI of *The Prelude,* the climax forest falls into life, into the perpetual culmination of its present. Science supplies the terms for Snyder's nonhumanistic love; it transcends our human separateness and shows how the accumulation of finite elements attains a state of open-ended process.

In order to go further with the rich implications of "Toward Climax," I want to draw on two of A. R. Ammons's longer poems—*Sphere* and the "Essay on Poetics." Ammons everywhere reflects on the edge between poetry and the natural world, but in these poems he also speaks directly to the particular issues with which this chapter and the book as a whole deal. A passage from Section 72 of *Sphere* typifies Ammons's awareness of his work's edge:

> the
> poetic consciousness beginning at a center works itself out by
> incorporation until through craft, experience, insight, etc., it
>
> brushes in a fulsome way against the fulsomeness of nature
>   so that
> on the periphery it is so deeply spelt out that it can tangle with
> the coincidental[9]

Ammons's poetic ecotone is fulsome because it is rich in the elaborated energy of awareness. Intense self-consciousness and the observations of an informed eye are like the tidal wash of nutrients in the coastal ecosystems to which Ammons's poems so often recur: the tide's pulse is like the mind's flicker between observation and imaginative response. The abundance of life along the shore also reflects the mind's surging fecundity, and the precariousness of any given creature amid such change mirrors the transience of momentary human resolutions. Three long quotations from scientific monographs frame the conclusion of "Essay on Poetics." The one nearest the end is from "The Life of an Estuary," a *Scientific American* article by Robert M. Ingle, and contains these sentences: "Life in an estuary may be rich, but it is almost inconceivably dangerous. . . . Twice each day the ebb and flow of the tide drastically alter the conditions of life, sometimes stranding whole populations to die a high-and-dry or freezing death."[10] To survive at a rapidly moving edge, whether that of the salt tide or that of human culture in the twentieth century, demands great powers of adaptability. In this regard, Gary Snyder's world, no less than A. R. Ammons's, is one between the tides. But poetry which adapts itself to a closely experienced terrain also gains an added capacity for the transfer and concentration of energy. Attentiveness is enriched by the dynamic nature of reality.

As a poem meets and transcribes the features of landscape, a transfer inevitably takes place. Wordsworth recognizes in "Michael" that a poem may become a "hidden valley of its own," and that a human life may be defined through associations both with a landscape and with a poem's terrain. In "Essay on Poetics," after considering the relation between mind and landscape, Ammons writes,

A poem is the same way: once it is thoroughly known, it
  contains

its motion and can be reproduced whole, all its shapeliness
  intact,
to the mind at the same time the mind can travel around
  in it and
know its sound and motion: nothing defined can

be still: the verbal moves, depends there, or sinks into
  unfocused
irreality: ah, but when the mind is brought to silence, the
non-verbal, and the still, it's whole again to see how
  motion goes:[11]

To think about edge is to think about principles of relationship and
thus to move toward a perspective of greater complexity. A given edge
divides into its component environments: it proliferates new edges,
both between itself and each of the two environments by which it was
originally defined and within itself. Thus, as in "Michael" or in "Essay
on Poetics," the poem is at first perceived as the edge between the poet
and the outer landscape. But as the poem achieves its own "fulsome-
ness," it grows into a counterpart landscape, with the *poet* at the edge
between the page and its facing terrain. The marginal field grows into a
heavily wooded tract, its edges so interwoven in a web of life that each
relationship entangles all the rest. As Snyder says in Section III of "Toward Climax," "nets are many knots."

In the lines quoted above from "Essay on Poetics," Ammons implies a progression from the temporal order of experience, within
which objects or words are perceived in a sequence and with high
individual definition, toward a spatial wholeness, with all features
of a poem or landscape perceived simultaneously, and with relationship replacing sequence as the organizing principle. This expresses a
psychological reality—the mind's flicker between observation's specifics and imagination's completions. But it also reflects the scientific
understanding of process leading toward and reenacting a larger
stability. In this regard, as in others, his own knowledge of science
helps Ammons to affirm the ambivalent energies of his own mental
process. In Section 10 of *Sphere* he writes,

I mean, if one speaks of mysticism, it makes good science,
which is the best part of science, that it makes mysticism

discussable without a flurry: and yet, too, the discrete
annihilated, suddenly here it is, blandished and available:
things go away to return, brightened for the passage:[12]

Science possesses the liberating function Ammons ascribes to
"nothingness" in a late section of his poem "Hibernaculum":

> it allows freedom to fall
> back from the thrust to the absolute into the world
>
> so manifold with things and beings: the hollyhock,
> what a marvel, complete in itself: the bee,
> how particular, how nothingness lets him buzz
>
> around:[13]

The *Genjō Kōan*, from the *Shōbōgenzō* of Dogen, contains the lines,
"To study the self is to forget the self. To forget the self is to be
enlightened by all things." A. R. Ammons's approach to science and
poetry is one which might be similarly understood: "To study the
world is to forget the world. To forget the world is to enter into the
richness of its life." We move from the orientation of a single edge
to apprehend the boundaries and connections of bark, skin, and fur,
air and earth.

In emphasizing the liberation of "nothingness," Ammons opposes
his vision of the world to what Whitehead called "the static morphological universe": the world's order is dynamic, with process rather
than things providing the primary reality. Accordingly, Ammons
often organizes his poetry on the model of a swirl. Like a landscape's, a poem's wholeness is centered nowhere but consists in its
circuit of energy. The mind and earth, throughout *Sphere*, clarify the
cyclic nature of each other's order. One of Ammons's emblems for
such dynamic balance is the Coriolis effect: the vast circular move-
ments of atmosphere and ocean brought about by the earth's rotation. In Section 13 of *Sphere* we see how

> elemental air in a spin, counterclockwise
> for us, lets its needlepoint funnel down and gives us
> a rugged variety of the formless formed: and the great
> slow stir of the Sargasso cycles the weed in, a holding,
> motion's holding.[14]

And in Sections 22 and 23 he points to where

> beans have
> twined (counterclockwise, again) up the stakes. . . .[15]

The smaller process mirrors the larger, not concentric in any fixed
way but participating in the circuit of fluid wholeness. To observe
the beautiful adjustments of the earth's stability, from the revolutions of air and water on a spinning planet to the coevolution of

animals and plants in a given terrain, is to celebrate the integrity of
"motion's holding."

The human mind—and that poetry which discloses it—reflects the
natural cycles in its own encompassing movement. There is an inherent instability in any human formulation of order that demands the
counterbalance of reaction. Wordsworth's ambivalence led him to
walk, pacing off the wholeness of a diverse life. In a mind, as in the
atmosphere, the swirl swirls against itself. The mind's weather, like
the earth's, arises from imbalance. A planet turns through light and
dark; like Ammons's estuary it is sometimes high and dry and sometimes freezing. In *Sphere*, Section 132, Ammons writes,

> I am like the earth about

twenty-three degrees off, which gives me summer and winter
moods, sheds hopes and sprouts them again:[16]

Ammons's simile recalls the moment in *Paradise Lost* when, after
the fall and before the expulsion from the Garden, Adam and Eve
realize that the harmony of nature as they have known it is disappearing. The animals of their peaceable kingdom suddenly grow
wary or threatening, and the earth's axis tilts, shattering the temper-
ate air with blasts of cold. The loss of immediate harmony and
security is one Adam and Eve feel keenly: with the tilting of their
world, their own lives first feel weather.

> . . . high winds . . .
> . . . .
>   . . . shook sore
> Their inward State of Mind, calm Region once
> And full of Peace, now tost and turbulent.[17]

But in losing their "static morphological" peace, Adam and Eve gain
a new possibility, the dignity of participating in the adventure of
dynamic order. Human history, as viewed by Adam and the Arch-
angel Michael from the mountain of temporality, is a narrative of
wandering and struggle, and each new reconciliation only brings
one night of rest. But there is also the larger swirl of Providence,
within which an individual gains the dignity to affirm his own life.

The 23-degree slant of Ammons's axis is a fortunate tilt in that it
buffets him into a weather matching the earth's. It makes possible
for him, as for Wordsworth, a "correspondent breeze," a vital relation with the world, though sometimes vexed. Fritjof Capra has
written, "In modern physics, the universe is . . . experienced as a
dynamic, inseparable whole which always includes the observer in

an essential way. In this experience, the traditional concepts of space and time, of isolated objects, and of cause and effect, lose their meaning."[18] A person assimilated—through the revelations of science—into such a world comes to understand himself, too, as "a dynamic, inseparable whole." The world's process, as Whitehead also has shown, is simultaneously unifying and, in its advancing edge of newness, liberating. Substances decay and particular configurations collapse, but the swirl of energy continues. As Ammons writes in one of the most luminous passages of *Sphere*, "inspiration spends through":

> step out, nothingness welcomes us: inspiration spends through:
> by the snowroad the boulder floats afire: fir-bark,
> skittering under a startled squirrel, falls in flames
>
> rattling and flecks the burning snow: the moundhill wintered
> lean lifts a shackling of cindery trees into the element
> unending: the stream, drawing radiance, collects and casts
>
> the light, kindled glancing:[19]

Like Heraclitus and Dillard, Ammons perceives in natural forms the measures of eternal fire entering and leaving our world: flames swirl in the wind of their own combustion.

In addition to his interest in intertidal ecology, Ammons is particularly interested in the science of genetics. The double helix of DNA expresses simultaneously the fragility and fecundity of life's estuarine edge and the cosmic spiral of "motion's holding." The genetic metaphor is of special value to Ammons because of his poetry's delight in sexuality and his conviction of the crucial value of tenderness. From the first section of *Sphere*, with its allusion to "the / haploid hungering after the diploid condition,"[20] he celebrates human sexuality as a way of entering a world of sensual process. Through sex he understands *eros*, the drive through pleasure to culmination, holding the world new. In "Essay on Poetics," he writes,

> organisms, I can tell you, build up under the thrust to
>
> joy and nothing else can lift them out of the miry circumstance:
> and poems are pure joy, however divisionally they sway with
>   grief:
> the way to joy is integration's delivery of the complete lode:[21]

Sexuality is the avenue of joy; it is like what Whitehead calls "the lure for feeling," leading an individual to surrender to the enfolding swirl of process. At one point in *Sphere* Ammons writes, "matter is a mere seed / afloat in radiance."[22] Because the human sexual seed is afloat in the radiance of joy, the person becomes a seed as well, opening as it penetrates the earth. And earth, too, turning in the sun's light, and in the mind's, becomes a seed.

Such a vision of sexual affinities throughout the range of creation accords with the tone of gentle sympathy in Ammons's observation of natural phenomena. Like Whitehead he feels a "tender concern for all growing things," in the understanding that only in nature's "community of patience" may the values of joy and self-surrender be nurtured. Sexual union reveals the world's wholeness as an amplified circuit of energy, rather than as the sum of discrete parts. Responsiveness, not domination, perpetually unifies the swirl of life:

> (I have come lately to honor gentleness so:
> it's because
> of my engagement with
> tiny sets and systems of energy, mechanisms, constructs,
> that I'm unnerved with the slight and needful
>   of consideration: part of consideration's
> slightness: it approaches and stands off peripherally
> quiet and patient should a gesture
> be all that's right
> but of course it will on invitation tend:
> it never blunts or overwhelms with aid
> or transforms in order to be received):[23]

Ammons's verse, in its "fulsome" testimony to "formlessness," typifies gentleness. Water and air flow by the objects in their paths: they touch things as they turn to go around. A shining line climbs the slope of broken shells and mud, as land and ocean find each other in the shuttle of the tide.

The double helix also expresses the spiraling combinations of new life along the edge. All edges are dangerous in their vital novelty, like the gamble of creatures in an estuary or like the grasping into pattern of an open-ended poem. As Ammons writes in "Essay on Poetics,"

> . . . real change occurs along the chromosomes, a risky business
> apparently based on accidence, chance, unforeseeable distortion:
> the proportion of harmful to potentially favorable mutations is
>
> something like 50,000 to 1: how marvelous that the possibility of
> favorable change is a flimsy margin in overwhelming, statistically,
> destruction and ruin: that is the way nature pours it on:[24]

The fragility of change along the edge is balanced, though, by another quality of genetic transformation: successful mutations can replicate themselves throughout the range of species and environment. Hugh Kenner writes, in relating the enduring meaning of poetry to the ceaseless decay of language, "And in this verbal kaleidoscope, what remains? . . . A patterned energy. . . ."[25] Poetry reflects the genetic patterning of life, the proliferating swirl whose edge is the tangle of change and assimilation. As Ammons says in "Essay on Poetics," following lengthy quotations from books on *The Sea* and on *The Science of Botany:*

>   . . . poems are verbal
> symbols for these organizations: they imprint upon the mind
> examples of integration in which the energy flows with
>   maximum
>
> effect and economy between the high levels of oneness and the
> numerous subordinations and divisions of diversity: it is simply
> good to have the mind exposed to and reflected by such
>   examples.
>
> It firms the mind, organizes its energy, and lets the controlled
> flows occur: that is simple good in itself: I can't stress that
> enough: it is not good for something else—although of course
>
> it is good for infinite things else:[26]

The patterned energy of the world imprints itself in the poem, which in turn imprints its integrations in the mind. The print, however, is not a static thing in either case, but rather a model reproducing itself with an infinite array of slight variations. This principle of unification through intertangling proliferation is evident on many levels in Ammons's poetry, one of the most obvious in "Essay" being his use of substantial scientific citations. The insights of science become seeds afloat in the poem's radiance, genes replicating and adapting themselves in the tissues of the poet's and the reader's minds.

Ammons is very precise and persistent in following up the relation between the transmission of DNA's "patterned energy" and the human assimilation of poetry. In *Sphere,* Section 15, he addresses tradition in terms of an evolving species—the verbal and spiritual counterpart of biological *Homo sapiens:*

> good saying are genes, the images, poems, stories
> chromosomes and the interminglings of these furnish beginnings

within continuities, continuities within trials, mischances, fortunate forwardings: gene pool, word hoard:[27]

And in *Tape for the Turn of the Year*, he brings out the application of such an analogy to the individual of the species:

> run my poem through
> your life & it will
> exist in you
> like a protein
> molecule[28]

If the molecules of a poem intertwine in the lives of enough individuals over a significant enough period of time, the values and emotions of the race regroup around what was at first an edge.

A recent volume on genetic theory speaks to Ammons's metaphor in provocative ways. Richard Dawkins, in *The Selfish Gene*, shows that the concept of "survival of the fittest" is meaningful in terms only of the individual gene, not of the organism or the species. Particular creatures, in the austere perspective of Dawkins's science, are only important as genetic vehicles, and that importance ceases as soon as the reproductive phase of life is over. The concept of species has been emphasized less by biologists as they have grown aware of how hazy are the demarcations between such groups: "populations," the more environmentally specific term, replaces it as a way of defining a gene pool. Dawkins's thrust throughout most of the discussion is to demolish humanistic generalizations, bringing human behavior and culture back to a strict genetic rationale. In view of "the selfish gene's" primary function in determining the course of evolution, such concepts as altruism, in particular, make little sense to him. At the end of his book, though, he acknowledges the fact that human beings do in fact transmit cultural values as well as genes. And in his coinage of the word "memes," he identifies a factor very much like what Ammons sees in the protein molecule of his poetry:

> The new soup is the soup of human culture. We need a name for the new replicator, a noun which conveys the idea of a unit of cultural transmission, or a unit of *imitation*. "Mimeme" comes from a suitable Greek root, but I want a monosyllable that sounds a bit like "gene." I hope my classicist friends will forgive me if I abbreviate mimeme to *meme*. If it is any consolation, it could alternately be thought of as being related to "memory," or to the French word *même*. . . . Examples of memes are tunes, ideas, catch-phrases, clothes fashions, ways of making pots or

building arches. Just as genes propagate themselves in the gene pool by leaping from body to body via sperm or eggs, so memes propagate themselves in the meme pool by leaping from brain to brain via a process which, in the broad sense, can be called imitation.[29]

Memes are a particularly useful way to introduce genetic theory into the cultural realm, since they address culture's central task of reconciling the present with the past. Both the gene and the meme are units of replication, laying claim to an enormous past. All genes are direct descendants of the first DNA molecules, while memes distill and interpret the history of the human race. On the other hand, both units seek to project their own present configuration intact into the future. Spatially, this double impulse of "selfishness" might be expressed as the apparently paradoxical demand to be at once the center of life and its leading edge. But a genetic perspective also makes it possible to see how an organism, experience, or poem may in fact *achieve* such a dual status. As Ammons writes at one point in his "Essay on Poetics," "strings of nucleation please me more than representative details." The string, or sequence, of nucleation is its temporal expression: it is the coalescence of presentnesses into a pattern of relation. And the nucleation of a poem—or in Whitehead's more comprehensive term, of any "prehension"—is *always* pressing in its immediacy. In genetics and poetry alike the seed both includes the encoded genetic material within itself and, in the future seeds latent within its spiraling germ, is included in that process. What seems at first a paradox becomes an interfolding pattern that connects: an edge that circles to contain its own meandering life.

In the course of this chapter I have tried to acknowledge the swirling radiance of scientific and poetic process within which Snyder's and Ammons's nucleations perpetuate themselves. I want in closing, though, to focus on the way a single seed can contain the spiral of process. As in Wordsworth and Bashō, there is in these two contemporary poets a rhythm of expansiveness and distillation. Ammons shows, in concluding his poem "Expressions of Sea Level," how each particle holds the world and each moment carries within it the tide of time:

> that is the
>   expression of sea level.
> the talk of giants,
> of ocean, moon, sun, of everything,
> spoken in a dampened grain of sand.[30]

One way to address the conflicts between nature and culture which this book considers is in relation to the difficulty of expressing experience simultaneously in terms of space and of time. It is noteworthy that Eliot, and the other artists of his time who challenged established senses of tradition, also moved away from a traditional temporal patterning of reality. As Joseph Frank has written, ". . . modern literature, as exemplified by such writers as T. S. Eliot, Ezra Pound, Marcel Proust, and James Joyce, is moving in the direction of spatial form. . . . All these writers ideally intend the reader to apprehend their work spatially, in a moment of time, rather than as a sequence."[31] And for a writer such as Jeffers, who carries Eliot's cultural despair into the wilderness and renews his sense of reality in the face of rock and sea, the immediacy of space becomes a focus for natural attentiveness as well as for literary form. The problem, though, is how to understand the spatial revelation within the spiral of a life. I think that here, too, science helps to effect a reconciliation in terms that echo a saying of Thoreau's: "Time is but the stream I go a-fishing in. I drink at it; but while I drink I see the sandy bottom and detect how shallow it is."[32] To look at the river as closely as one does when drinking from it is to see the bottom. But it is also true that to study the bottom is to see the river—in the testimonies of siltation, of the sorting of gravel by weight, of the parallel sweep of eel grass under the current. The last two centuries' revolutions in geology, biology, and physics make it possible to read the story of the world at every point on the turning globe. The igneous "monadnock" mountains of New England testify to millions of years of erosion all around them; granite outcrops record the foray of glaciers south and north; remnants of stone walls deep in the woods are a way the hill farmers remain after their fields have disappeared. To walk attentively through any landscape is to drink at the river of time. This is the "spatio-temporal perspective" on the world which Whitehead advocates. Sympathy, compassion, and adventure arise from the marriage of science and poetry—"concrete fact with a high light thrown on what is relevant to its preciousness."

Gary Snyder's poem "For Nothing," from *Turtle Island*, illuminates this deeper identity of space and time, science and poetry. It focuses on a single image and on its germinal unfolding of wholeness:

> Earth a flower
> a phlox on the steep
> slopes of light
> hanging over the vast

solid spaces
small rotten crystals;
salts.

Earth a flower
by a gulf where a raven
flaps by once
a glimmer, a color
forgotten as all
falls away.

a flower
for nothing;
an offer;
no taker;

Snow-trickle, feldspar, dirt.[33]

There are certain images that arrest the mind: in their integrity and self-containment they possess a stillness that allows human reflection on the whirling world of process. The heap of stones at the beginning of "Michael" was one such image of containment. The blue-green ball of earth, marbled with clouds and showing against deep blackness, is another. One of the astronauts who first saw earth from space wept at its beauty. And the photograph of earth which has been so widely distributed retains a fascination and an emotional appeal that no amount of exposure can reduce to a cliche. "For Nothing," my favorite of all Snyder's poems, evokes this image's implications, capturing at once its representation of an entire universe of process and its possible contribution to a more vivid and accurate response to the earth.

When Snyder writes of "a phlox on the steep / slopes of light," he recalls John Muir's "range of light," the Sierra Nevada. A mountain wildflower, its delicacy all the more precious because surrounded by the vastness of dramatic geological forms, draws responses of tenderness, restraint, and quietness from a hiker who comes on it. The pink and white of alpine phlox makes you careful where you put your feet; it mutes the talk and laughter of a group but enhances the spirit of friendship and adventure shared. A flower's smallness, shown up against such a slope, is matched by its transience. Blooming in the brief period between the melting of snow and the snowmelt's evaporation into thin, dry air, phlox finds its completeness in a moment. Phlox—flame, but only the briefest flicker—vanishing back so quickly into the gulf from which its small order arose. Such brief, fragile beauty evokes a response of longing; even as we see it,

we know it is passing away. The gift of Snyder's poem is an ability
to feel the beauty of this earth-flower, too, so often beneath our
caring even as it is beneath our feet.

Like Bashō's haiku, "For Nothing" gains in reverberation through
its avoidance of closed syntax. By letting the image speak un-
bounded by a single sentence, Snyder approaches the open-ended
simplicity of nature. Even his title carries such divergent possibilities, in much the same way as does Frost's simultaneously self-
deprecating and defiant title "The Most of It." "For Nothing" may
be related to a sense of the *futility* of earth's beauty: "an offer; / no
taker." So much of human history and culture has disregarded
earth's delicate harmony, its short achievement of order beside "a
gulf" of time and space. As technology abstracts many aspects of
human experience from the surrounding natural order, and as
wastes and armaments threaten the ecosphere, earth seems already
to become "a color / forgotten as all / falls away." "For Nothing"
also speaks, though, to the *liberating* quality of such beauty for a
humanity ensnared in its own heedlessness: earth, like a wildflower,
is beautiful for no purpose beyond itself. It is a world offering only
relationship, not any decisive resolution. In this connection, one
might see the title "For Nothing" in yet another way—as a dedica-
tion. "Nothingness," as in Ammons's *Sphere*, can be an escape from
hierarchical order into the freedom of immediacy and particularity.

Part of the liberation in "For Nothing" comes in the fact that,
along with definitive syntax, the personal pronoun is left behind.
There is a certain detached, "impersonal" quality about the poem
that possesses tremendous potential for human meaning. To see the
earth without the shadows of our projects falling across the slope of
light, we have to step back. Science's astronomical perspective on
our planet helps to accomplish such a beneficial distancing. To see
earth as a planet blooming briefly in its reflected light is to gain a
new emotional response to it, just as, for Wordsworth, to read a
human story in an isolated pile of stones was the access to widened
sympathy. In a seminar focusing on "For Nothing," a student with a
background in natural sciences said of the last line—"Snow-trickle,
feldspar, dirt"—that it describes the genesis of soil. The flower van-
ishes, but the inert world in its turn also decays, with its "rotten
crystals" growing into new life. Water and rock prepare for the
turning of the seed. Poetry, informed by science, learns to consider
every object in the world as a universe complete in itself. And in the
spiraling unity of the everywhere-centered earth, a poem too can
circle its arms in motion's holding. Ammons, in his poem "One:

Many," celebrates attentiveness to the world as an escape from abstractions and a return to the manifold processes of earth:

>   when I considered alone
> a record
> of the waves on the running blue creek,
>   I was released into a power beyond my easy failures,
> released to think
> how so much freedom
>   can keep the broad look of serenity
>   and nearly statable balance.[34]

CHAPTER
9

The Wilderness at
Poetry's Edge

REGROUNDING culture in the natural world involves a descent.
Decay, the central word for Section I, derives after all from *cadere*, to
fall. The decay of old systems both allows and necessitates fresh
attention to the soil's process of regeneration. And poets like
Snyder, Berry, and Pack fall through the dislocations of history as
they take root in their chosen terrains. Section II further explores the
process through which American poetry has found a coherence in
gravitation. Tradition becomes a landscape of human meaning, continually paced off on the ancient, renewing earth. This poetic landscape, too, is enriched by a process of decay, as physical impression
and artistic expression absorb one another.

Decay is also characterized, however, by its expansiveness.
Tightly packed organic compounds loosen their carbon bonds and
separate into their constituent elements. The earth itself, through
the constant organization and disorganization of physical forms,
takes part in vast cycles of energy. The first two chapters of this final
section show how close attention to nature's expansive particularity
also broadens the field of human responsiveness. "For Nothing"
exemplifies the balance, within poetry's sphere, of centripetal and
centrifugal impulses. The expansiveness gained by poetry's incorpo-
ration of scientific insight propels the human perspective beyond
earth's gravity. But from the vantage of space, earth itself becomes a
radiant particular of decay—a crystal, a seed. Poetry and science,
nature and culture, all are included within such an oscillation. In the
mutual surrender of process and particular there is a model for
human assent. Reconciliation takes the form of alternation: observa-

tion and imagination, left foot and right, a person finds the wholeness of a world flickering through time and space.

Physics generalizes the alternations in nature as waves of differing
frequency. In addition to the analogy between waves and the
momentary cycles of human experience, it is possible to see Western
civilization, too, in terms of its own longer waves. Writers have
often perceived a cultural descent in the twentieth century, a curving of the line beneath a horizontal axis. Freud assessed culture's
prospects this way in *Civilization and Its Discontents*:

> Men have gained control over the forces of nature to such an
> extent that with their help they would have no difficulty in
> exterminating one another to the last man. They know this, and
> hence comes a large part of their current unrest, their unhappi-
> ness and their mood of anxiety. And now it is to be expected
> that the other of the two "Heavenly Powers," eternal Eros, will
> make an effort to assert himself in the struggle with his equally
> immortal adversary. But who can foresee with what success and
> with what result?[1]

I would like to connect Freud's terms with those of a letter Jeffers
wrote in 1937:

> . . . power is with the radicals—the destroyers—in thought and
> literature, ever since the movement that preceded the French
> Revolution. The memorable names are mostly the names of
> men who broke down some set of conventions or "ideals"—
> Voltaire, Rousseau, Byron—Nietzsche etc.—away down to D.
> H. Lawrence. Conventions of monarchy, warlike patriotism,
> Christian dogma, purity, down to reticence even. Many of
> these radicals were builders of ideals too, or aspired to be; but
> what they built was temporary and without much influence;
> what they threw down stays down. Much of their power de-
> rives from this catalysis; as an animal's power from breaking
> down starch and protein. Men like Dante or Thomas Aquinas
> were more like the plants that preceded the animals and built
> up the complex molecules that are food for them. (The plants
> live by power from the sun, the animals by power from the
> plants.) Perhaps this shift of power, from the builders to the
> destroyers, is another sign that our culture-age has culminated
> and turned down again, in a creative sense? —That now its
> "ideals" and ideas need to be broken up and lie fallow awhile,
> in preparation for a later age?[2]

Freud's analysis is implicit to the rationale of contemporary nature poetry: alienation from an inherently destructive culture is,

by that token, an impulse of health and self-preservation. Excessive human control over nature endangers human survival. Although Freud was thinking of the imminent threats from totalitarianism, his terms are at least equally descriptive of our own day, with its enormous dangers from environmental degradation and the nuclear arms race. It is also important to note that he associates cultural alienation with Eros, the force of love. In bursting out of traditional confinements, poets express the life-force, the pleasure principle. They assert the value of wilderness in the face of the wasteland's deadening conventions.

Where Freud—like Eliot—sees civilization's "discontents" as longing for a restored natural order, Jeffers treats the negative dimension of modern culture as itself a *manifestation* of natural balance. An ecologist would identify Jeffers's earlier writers as *producers*, his Romantics and moderns as *consumers*. But a scientist could fill out the metaphor by indicating the food cycle's third main component—the bacterial *reducers*. In all eras, of course, the process of cultural decay and reconstruction is an ongoing one; but the character of prevailing awareness also shifts. In the period from Eliot and Jeffers to the present, poets have often emphasized "breaking down" a rigid civilization's "starch and protein." For today's poets of nature that process is turning toward a reinaugurated phase of production. Having achieved decomposition's particularity, they attempt once more to see the world whole.

I have spoken of poets' attentiveness to nature as the focus for a wider change in our culture's vision of nature. But how may the expansiveness and attentiveness of poetry be assimilated into a tradition, and into the present life of a people, without once more domesticating it in a restrictive order? Efforts at cultural continuity inevitably take on an ironic relationship with modern masterpieces of alienation. As Lionel Trilling has written in his essay on "The Teaching of Modern Literature, ". . . with the works of art of our own present age, university study tends to accelerate the process by which the radical and subversive work becomes the classic work, and university study does this in the degree that it is vivacious and responsive and what is called non-academic."[3] If there were in fact only *human* contributions to culture, there could be *no* reconciliation of these opposed impulses of discontinuity and continuity. The earth, though, distracts humanity from its introversion; it awakens culture to its context and counterbalance. Today's poetry of nature is the vehicle by which the cultural tradition at once surrenders and restores itself.

As the previous chapter has explored, poetry is in ecological terms the *edge* between mankind and nonhuman nature, providing an access for culture into a world beyond its preconceptions. A similar sense of poetry's mediating role informs Robinson Jeffers's attempt at a vision of "inhumanism." Jeffers's hope was to locate his poems beyond the narrow circle of human understanding, to speak past his own humanity. Expansive subject matter serves a similar function in the poetry of Snyder and Ammons; though their voices remain personally self-conscious, revelations of nature's intricacy burst continuously through the frameworks of their understanding, as well as through conventional Western attitudes. Rather than domesticating nature, the poets are themselves assimilated into its ever-emerging and overwhelming particularity. The richness of natural process shatters human expectations, recentering mental circles and broadening their necessary circumference. Poetry's landscape is an ecotone where human and natural orders meet.

For Freud, culture could be largely explained in terms of "the single task of finding an expedient accommodation" between the claims of the individual and those of the group.[4] Contemporary poetry of nature may also be understood in terms of a cultural accommodation, but the realms in need of balance are those of self-conscious humanity and nonhuman nature. The poets considered in this discussion have clearly been affected by such developments as the emergence of strong conservation organizations, the growth of a wilderness ethic, and the passage of legislation governing standards of environmental quality. But my appreciation of America's poetry of nature also reflects a belief that it advances such a cultural shift in a fundamental way. As Eliot writes in his essay on "The Social Function of Poetry," ". . . in the long run, [poetry] makes a difference to the speech, to the sensibility, to the lives of all the members of a society, to all the members of the community, to the whole people, whether they read and enjoy poetry or not."[5]

An obvious example of poetry's influence is that environmental activists look to the poets in formulating their own language of commitment. Friends of the Earth's newsletter, *Not Man Apart*, draws its title from one of Jeffers's poems and frequently acknowledges the vision of Gary Snyder and other current writers. Even more important, however, is the way in which all the poets whose work I discuss here *embody* a world of mutual suffusion between human personality and closely observed and experienced terrain. Poetry has, in all ages, extended the circle of human understanding, as its traditional reliance on metaphor—"carrying beyond"—has shown. Contemporary poetry has developed an appreciation of nature itself as a continually discovered metaphor. This is not the traditional sense of natural metaphor—the physical expression of a human truth otherwise difficult to communicate. Rather, it is a recognition of natural reality as meaningful *beyond* specifically human experience, yet ultimately fulfilling and including such apprehension. A poem can achieve such a transformative exchange both because of its ability to include details of nature in its own verbal fabric and because of the fact that, more self-consciously than any other linguistic expression, it becomes a place as well as a proposition. The paradox of poetry's reconciliation of man and nature is thus that a poem can be at once the landscape into which a reader enters and a landmark to which he can return.

Poetry's ironic status as a place may be compared with that of contemporary wilderness areas. In both cases human reason draws and defends a boundary beyond which its own dominance will not be allowed. A wilderness area established by legislation is thus, like poetry, an attempt at finding an edge: an area outside the control of civilization in which a freer meeting of man and nature may occur. My thoughts in this regard have been stimulated by forays to Bristol Cliffs, a small wilderness area near my home in the Green Mountains. I want to round off the book with an account of Bristol Cliffs— as a way of reconnecting with the dichotomy in Chapter 1 between wilderness and culture and as a final grounding of the discussion in the landscape of experience.

When I walk in from the farm-road, the ground swells and breaks in a dripping tangle of ferns. Broad flat fronds of the sensitive fern hang heavy with dew, drooping like the canopy of a rain forest over interspersed communities of broad beech fern and New York fern. The Latin names of the three associated ferns also extend and intertwine—*Onoclea sensibilis, Thelypteris hexagonoptera, Thelypteris noveboracensis*—as sinuously as the green life of the hollow. Vermont, with its cool, shady forests and its abundant water, is richest of all the states in fern-life; over fifty varieties grow here, and in this part of the state there are hillsides like whole ecosystems of fern, each niche waving at the world with a frond of its own design.

The three species bedded around my dew-dark boots mark off a wide band in the spectrum of fernliness. The sensitive fern, whose name refers only to its rapid demise with the onset of frost, has sturdy, undifferentiated pinnules of dark green tinged with brown. New York ferns, barely half as high at fifteen inches, are a contrasting study in delicacy: each leaflet, or pinnule, is cut into mirrored files of rounded subleaflets, and the larger frond, or leaf, is doubly tapered into a slender diamond of translucent green. Located between the other two species, in terms equally of size, color, and intricacy, comes the broad beech fern. Its fronds, of bright primary green, look like paper cutouts, their scalloped pinnules setting off the lacework of New York fern or breaking through the sensitive fern's shelf to lounge across and take the air.

With its yard-high post of green metal and its wooden placard stained a dusty red, the sign makes a visual bridge between the ferns and the stand of leggy maples among which they flourish. Centered on the rough board, as if matted, is a steel plate printed with a message. The top half, large white letters on black, proclaims "National Forest Wilderness." Spaced below are black letters on white: "Closed to motor vehicles and motorized equipment." Lower still, and in yet smaller letters, it says, "Area back of this sign is managed and protected under Public Law (16 U.S.C. 551; 16 U.S.C. 1131–1136)." The design is completed by a parenthetical comment at the bottom "(Violations punishable)," by a code number in the left corner, "(27–6a)," and by the shield of the Forest Service in the lower right corner. The badge-shaped logo contains the capitals U and S flanking a stylized pine tree; curving around the top of the official emblem is "Forest Service" and circling underneath is "Department of Agriculture."

The sign rises authoritatively in the midst of dense, undifferentiated woods. No path leads up to it, and there is no road or town much closer to the sign on one side than on the other. The larger area from which the Bristol Cliffs Wilderness Area takes its name is in fact a patchwork of private lands and national forest. Bounded on the western side by the cliffs overlooking the Champlain Valley, and defined on the north and east by the New Haven River, this rising terrain forms a secondary ridge, just topping 2,000 feet, beside the central chain of the Green Mountains. The 4,495-acre parcel of Bristol Cliffs designated wilderness is not even distinguished from the surrounding territory by virtue of being virgin forest. The area was largely logged off in the nineteenth century and has now grown into a dense mixed forest of maple, birch, beech, poplar, oak, pine, hemlock, and spruce. Stone walls climb the eastern slope, reminders of an era when hill farms flourished briefly; the walls sometimes follow the boundary of wilderness but often cut indiscriminately across the posted lines. Nor does there seem to be any significant difference in the use or immediate prospects of the land on either side of the border: the grade is too steep and the terrain too irregular for logging with modern machinery to be profitable. Next to the sign on the nonwilderness side is a tall young maple yoked to the placard with a hammock of spiderweb. Split by the invisible edge is an enormous, much older maple, with dark bracket fungus spiraling up and around it in a meditation on the compass.

If, in the case of Bristol Cliffs, wilderness is not distinguished from nonwilderness in terms of terrain, accessibility, history, or current use, the question is what the sign does mean. What are we to make of this governmentally certified boundary running through fern thickets and over mossy backs of boulders frost-resurrected deep in the woods? A similar question might be asked about contemporary poetry, where attentiveness to nature expands to include details of human history and science. What distinguishes this landscape as an edge? In Bristol Cliffs the black-on-white portion of the sign is the easier part to understand. This blocked-off piece of wilderness will be kept free of roads and snowmobiles; we can also learn, by consulting the appropriately numbered statutes, that any camping here must be of the "undeveloped" sort and that the trees will be left to pursue their own ideas about sound timber management. The metal plate bears a public notice inversely analogous to a building permit: it certifies this area as one—in the language of the 1964 Wilderness Bill—"where the earth and its community of life are untrammeled by man."[6]

What is the positive value, in this tract of land without a centerpiece, of "the earth and its community of life"? The negative injunctions at the bottom of the Forest Service sign are clearly a sort of codicil: they *assume* a primary importance in wilderness which justifies certain restraints on human freedom. But to investigate this value in itself is to return to the top half of the sign at Bristol Cliffs. White on black, a reversal of standard typography appropriate to the reversal of national attitudes it represents, the sign announces "wilderness" as a primary fact. The value of Bristol Cliffs's undramatic terrain cannot, however, be focused on any monumental feature; nor may the experience of it be attached to an extended backpack trip. It can only be understood as a mode of attentiveness.

There is, as Hopkins writes, the dearest freshness deep down things, but when hikers find trails we also find the strongest need to follow them, pursuing the goals of peak, valley, campsite, lake. To be in the woods without a purpose or a path is to sink in, to open to the sweet regroupings of fragments and forms. Rachel, my four-year-old, is the perfect companion for a trip into this shaggy, unnoticed little wilderness area. She covers so little ground, and that in

fits and falls, that one is perpetually aware of the density of life on
the forest floor—toads tan and spotted among last year's leaves,
punky trees dissolving where they fell. Rachel will bend over an
inviting rotten log and pull it apart, looking for grubs with the
abandon of a small bear. "Building soil!" she shouts, for the benefit
of unseen tree wardens. Walking along without a level path, we
become involved in the land's logic of wet and dry. Returning after a
week, we see that the wilderness keeps moving too: spittlebugs and
heal-all pass; mosquitoes, with their tadpole retinue, come on. There
is a circuit of life in the woods, as trees crash into the ground to rise
again. Bristol Cliffs is only a small patch of wilderness, a lyric poem
rather than an epic. But like a lyric it possesses the value of sensual
immediacy; it centers the larger swirl of culture and wilderness on a
local habitation and a name.

Aldo Leopold, in his celebrated essay "On the Need for a Land
Ethic," writes of Western civilization's need to transcend its "Abra-
hamic" conception of land. We need to move beyond a sense of the
earth as property to be disposed of as its owners see fit, to a feeling
of respect for the land's own dignity and rights. His choice of terminology connects in an interesting way with Matthew Arnold's "Hebraism." England, in Arnold's view, was a dominantly Hebraic, or
moralistic, nation, in need of Hellenism's sense of openness and
play: "The governing idea of Hellenism is *spontaneity of consciousness;*
that of Hebraism, *strictness of conscience.*" Contemporary poetry of
nature fulfills both of these cultural values. The poets, in their pains-
taking, self-conscious approach to poetic form and rhythm, are like
Everson's waterbirds, sending up "the strict articulations of their
throats." But as they bear their poetry into the particularity of terrain beyond established orders and intentions, they also gain the
birds' openness to nature's intricate immediacy.

A wilderness area as transparent as Bristol Cliffs approaches the
terms of poetry's reconciliation very closely. The sign and its surrounding legislation have a restrictive force. But because of the
kinds of interference with natural process ruled out by that strictness, there are within the bounded area greatly enhanced possibilities for people to encounter what Ammons has called the fulsome-
ness of nature. Both human culture and individual consciousness
possess a certain imperialistic tendency—a sweep to dominance—
which is thwarted and redeemed by the paradoxical strictness of art
and of wilderness. In each case, human choice restricts itself so that,
acknowledging bounds, it may be enlarged.

A place like Bristol Cliffs shows how wilderness can emerge from culture's decay. As stone walls melt back into these woods, they provide a beneficial orientation: both a way to ground human history and culture in the land and, in their crumbling retreat, a liberation into the present. Today's poets of nature allow for a similar accommodation and emergence. Poetic form secures a plot where the fruitful decay of order and intentions may occur; an unsuspected landscape rises through the traces of a poem's plan. Wordsworth has helped me, throughout this volume, to frame the terms of current poetry's great value. It is appropriate, then, to close with this passage from Book V of *The Prelude,* describing the Boy of Winander. The owls' sudden stillness shatters the Boy's game of call and echo. But in thwarting his conscious framework for relationship, nature conveys to him the gift of a larger world.

> Then sometimes, in that silence while he hung
> Listening, a gentle shock of mild surprise
> Has carried far into his heart the voice
> Of mountain torrents; or the visible scene
> Would enter unawares into his mind,
> With all its solemn imagery, its rocks,
> Its woods, and that uncertain heaven, received
> Into the bosom of the steady lake.[7]

Startled, the Boy's mind becomes one with the image of the steady lake which it receives. Through their attentiveness, expansiveness, and strategies for reaching beyond what they have learned to say, America's poets of nature, too, surprise us into imagining the earth.

Notes

INTRODUCTION

1. Samuel Taylor Coleridge, *On the Constitution of Church and State.* Quoted in Raymond Williams, *Culture and Society* (New York: Harper and Row, 1966), p. 11.

2. From *Science and the Modern World*, by Alfred North Whitehead, p. 186. © 1925 by the Macmillan Publishing Co.; and © 1953 by Evelyn Whitehead. Excerpts reprinted by permission of the Macmillan Publishing Co. This and subsequent references are to the 1967 Free Press edition.

3. Ibid, pp. 72, 198.

CHAPTER 1

1. From *The Selected Poetry of Robinson Jeffers*, p. 581. ©1927–28, 1938 by Robinson Jeffers; © 1924 by Peter G. Boyle; © 1925 by Horace Liveright; © 1935 by the Modern Library; and © 1933, 1937 by Random House. Excerpts reprinted by permission of Random House. This and subsequent references are to the 1938 edition.

2. William Wordsworth, *Selected Poems and Prefaces,* ed. Jack Stillinger (Boston: Houghton Mifflin, 1965), p. 167.

3. Ibid., pp. 166, 167.

4. Jeffers, *Selected Poetry*, p. 260.

5. Wordsworth, *Selected Poems and Prefaces,* p. 161.

6. Ibid., p. 158.

7. Jeffers, *Selected Poetry*, p. 564.

8. Rupert Brooke, *The Collected Poems* (London: Sidgwick and Jackson, 1942), p. 146.

9. Jeffers, *Selected Poetry*, p. 262.

10. Ibid., pp. 198–99.

11. William H. Nolte initially opposes Jeffers's "Stoicism" to Eliot's vision of history but later also connects the two writers' convictions that modern "civilization denotes decay; it is a hardening of the arteries of culture." *Rock and Hawk: Robinson Jeffers and the Romantic Agony* (Athens: University of Georgia Press, 1978), pp. 72, 192.

12. Whitman's "Song of the Open Road," invigorating the present with the promise of a future, is the implicit contrast to Wordsworth's cartographic memory. But Robinson Jeffers, whose long breaths in "The Coast-Road" connect him so obviously with Whitman, exemplifies the difficulty a twentieth-century poet finds in expressing Whitman's optimism. With his back to the continent's edge, Jeffers needs to find a more circular understanding of poetry's advance. Wordsworth's poetic map provides Jeffers with directions other than west.

13. From *Collected Poems, 1909–1962*, by T. S. Eliot, p. 56. © 1936 by Harcourt Brace Jovanovich; © 1963–64 by T. S. Eliot. Excerpts reprinted by permission of Harcourt Brace Jovanovich. This and subsequent references are to the 1963 edition.

14. Ibid., p. 57.

15. Jeffers, *Selected Poetry*, p. 168.

16. Ibid., p. 576.

17. Ibid., p. 166.

18. Eliot, *Collected Poems, 1909–1962*, p. 69.

19. Ibid., p. 62.

20. Jeffers, *Selected Poetry*, pp. 87, 88.

21. Wordsworth, *Selected Poems and Prefaces*, p. 191.

22. Jeffers, *Selected Poetry*, p. 594.

23. Eliot, *Collected Poems, 1909–1962*, p. 69.

24. Jeffers, *Selected Poetry*, pp. 78–79.

25. Wordsworth, *Selected Poems and Prefaces*, p. 166.

CHAPTER 2

1. Leo Marx, *The Machine in the Garden* (New York: Oxford University Press, 1964), p. 69.

2. Ibid., p. 70.

3. This sense of *Moby-Dick* derives from an unpublished essay by Eric Kolvig.

4. T. S. Eliot, *The Sacred Wood: Essays on Poetry and Criticism* (London: Methuen, 1960), p. 49.

5. From *The Real Work: Interviews and Talks, 1964–1979*, by Gary Snyder, ed. Scott McLean, pp. 173–74. © 1980 by Gary Snyder. Excerpts reprinted by permission of New Directions Publishing Corp. Robert Kern has also explored Snyder's connection with modernist writers, Williams and Stevens

in particular. "Clearing the Ground: Gary Snyder and the Modernist Imperative," *Criticism* 19:158–77, 1977.

6. Matthew Arnold, *Culture and Anarchy* (Cambridge: Cambridge University Press, 1960), pp. 162, 48.

7. Ibid., p. 48.

8. Raymond Williams, *Culture and Society* (New York: Harper and Row, 1966), p. 125.

9. Arnold, *Culture and Anarchy*, p. 52.

10. Eliot, *The Sacred Wood*, p. 52.

11. Snyder, *The Real Work*, pp. 56, 57.

12. Ibid., pp. 71, 62.

13. Ibid., p. 62.

14. Eliot, *The Sacred Wood*, p. 59.

15. Snyder, *The Real Work*, p. 65.

16. C. G. Jung, *Memories, Dreams, and Reflections* (New York: Vintage, 1969), pp. 235–346.

17. Snyder, *The Real Work*, p. 116.

18. Ibid., p. 58.

19. A. L. Kroeber and Clyde Kluckhohn, *Culture: A Critical Review of Concepts and Definitions* (New York: Vintage, 1963), p. 61.

20. Snyder, *The Real Work*, pp. 63, 64.

21. Ibid., p. 132.

22. Kroeber and Kluckhohn, *Culture: A Critical Review*, p. 84.

23. Eliot, *The Sacred Wood*, pp. 53, 54.

24. From *Turtle Island*, by Gary Snyder, p. 107. © 1973, 1974 by Gary Snyder. Excerpts reprinted by permission of New Directions Publishing Corp. This and subsequent references are to the 1974 edition.

25. Robert Bly, *News of the Universe* (San Francisco: Sierra Club, 1980), p. 4.

26. John Fowles and Frank Horvat, *The Tree* (London: Aurum Press, 1979), p. 37.

27. From *The Cantos of Ezra Pound*, p. 803. © 1972 by the Estate of Ezra Pound. Excerpts reprinted by permission of New Directions Publishing Corp. This and subsequent references are to the 1975 edition.

28. Whitehead, *Science and the Modern World*, p. 199.

29. Ibid., p. 72.

30. Geoffrey Hartman, "Wordsworth and Goethe in Literary History," *New Literary History* 6:393–413, 1975.

31. Gilbert White, *The Natural History of Selborne* (Middlesex: Penguin, 1977), p. 55.

32. Ibid., p. 125.

33. Williams, *Culture and Society*, pp. 254, 337.

34. Kroeber and Kluckhohn, *Culture: A Critical Review*, p. 62.

35. Cited in Charles Darwin, *The Illustrated Origin of Species*, abridged and with an introduction by Richard Leakey (New York: Hill and Wang, 1979), p. 33.

CHAPTER 3

1. From *Myths and Texts,* by Gary Snyder, p. 23. © 1978 by Gary Snyder. Excerpts reprinted by permission of New Directions Publishing Corp.

2. Ibid., p. viii.

3. Gary Snyder, *Earth House Hold* (New York: New Directions, 1968), p. 119.

4. Ibid., p. 120.

5. William Faulkner, *Go Down, Moses and Other Stories* (New York: Random House, 1942), p. 164.

6. Ibid., p. 178.

7. Ibid., p. 165.

8. Snyder, *The Real Work,* p. 161.

9. Ibid., p. 112.

10. Gary Snyder, *Riprap & Cold Mountain Poems* (San Francisco: Four Seasons Foundation, 1977), p. 6.

11. Snyder, *The Real Work,* p. 33.

12. Gary Snyder, *The Back Country* (New York: New Directions, 1968), p. 16.

13. Snyder, *The Real Work,* p. 32.

14. Snyder, *Turtle Island,* p. 7.

15. From *Regarding Wave,* by Gary Snyder, p. 45. © 1969 by Gary Snyder. "Sours of the Hills" first appeared in *Harper's Magazine* in August 1969. Excerpts reprinted by permission of New Directions Publishing Corp. This and subsequent references are to the 1970 edition.

16. From *Farming: A Hand Book,* by Wendell Berry, p. 3. © 1970 by Wendell Berry. Excerpts reprinted by permission of Harcourt Brace Jovanovich. This and subsequent references are to the 1971 edition.

17. Snyder, *The Real Work,* p. 123.

18. Berry, *Farming: A Hand Book,* p. 21.

19. Wendell Berry, *Recollected Essays, 1965–1978* (San Francisco: North Point Press, 1981), p. 44.

20. Wendell Berry, *A Continuous Harmony* (New York: Harcourt Brace Jovanovich, 1975), p. 4.

21. Ibid., p. 33.

22. Ryokan, *One Robe, One Bowl: The Zen Poetry of Ryokan,* translated and introduced by John Stevens (New York: Weatherhill, 1977), p. 39.

23. Berry, *Farming: A Hand Book,* p. 19.

24. Ibid.

25. Berry, *Recollected Essays,* p. 104.

26. Ibid., p. 82.

27. From *A Part,* by Wendell Berry, p. 83. © 1980 by Wendell Berry. Excerpts reprinted by permission of North Point Press. This and subsequent references are to the 1981 edition.

28. Wordsworth, *Selected Poems and Prefaces,* p. 112.

29. John Milton, *Paradise Lost,* ed. Scott Elledge (New York: W. W. Norton,

1975), p. 240. My attention was called to this significant pun by colleagues in the staff of EL201, "Interpretation of Literature," at Middlebury College.

30. Berry, *Recollected Essays*, p. 91.

31. From *Clearing*, by Wendell Berry, p. 50. © 1974 by Wendell Berry. Excerpts reprinted by permission of Harcourt Brace Jovanovich. This and subsequent references are to the 1977 edition.

32. Wendell Berry, *The Unsettling of America* (New York: Avon, 1928), p. 124.

33. Berry, *A Continuous Harmony*, p. 161.

34. Berry, *Recollected Essays*, p. 63.

35. Berry, *The Unsettling of America*, p. 123.

36. Berry, *Farming: A Hand Book*, p. 41.

37. Robert Pack, *Waking to My Name: New and Selected Poems* (Baltimore: Johns Hopkins University Press, 1980), pp. 93–94.

38. Ibid., p. 12.

39. John Donne, *Poetical Works*, ed. Sir Herbert Grierson (London: Oxford University Press, 1933), p. 11.

40. Robert Pack, *Faces in a Single Tree.* (Boston: David R. Godine, 1984), pp. 29, 30.

41. Pack, *Waking to My Name*, p. 9.

42. Ibid., p. 87.

43. Ibid., p. 89.

44. Ibid.

45. Ibid., p. 43.

HITCHING A RIDE

1. Wordsworth, *Selected Poems and Prefaces*, p. 15.

2. Ibid., p. 17.

3. Ibid., p. 16.

4. Ibid., p. 14.

5. Ibid., p. 150.

6. Ibid., p. 115.

7. Ibid., p. 18.

8. Ibid., p. 287.

9. Ibid., p. 288.

10. Ibid., pp. 122, 120.

11. From *The Complete Poems of Wallace Stevens*, p. 524. © 1923, 1931, 1936–37, 1942–52, 1954 by Wallace Stevens. Excerpts reprinted by permission of Alfred A. Knopf. This and subsequent references are to the 1969 edition.

12. From *The Poetry of Robert Frost*, ed. Edward Connery Lathem, pp. 377–78. © 1947, 1969 by Holt, Rinehart and Winston; and © 1975 by Lesley Frost Ballantine. Excerpts reprinted by permission of Holt, Rinehart and Winston, Publishers. This and subsequent references are to the 1968 edition.

13. Ibid., pp. 259, 260.

14. Berry, *Clearing*, p. 25.

CHAPTER 4

1. M. H. Abrams, *Natural Supernaturalism: Tradition and Revolution in Romantic Literature* (New York: W. W. Norton, 1971), p. 285.

2. Wordsworth, *Selected Poems and Prefaces*, p. 193. My references throughout are to the fourteen-book *Prelude*.

3. Ibid., p. 195.

4. Milton, *Paradise Lost*, p. 281.

5. Wordsworth, *Selected Poems and Prefaces*, p. 239.

6. Ibid., p. 199. My reading of the *Prelude* is directly influenced by Geoffrey Hartman's chapter "Via Naturaliter Negativa," in *Wordsworth's Poetry, 1787–1814* (New Haven, Conn.: Yale University Press, 1971).

7. Wordsworth, *Selected Poems and Prefaces*, p. 352.

8. Henry David Thoreau, *Walden and Other Writings* (New York: Modern Library, 1950), p. 597.

9. Wordsworth, *Selected Poems and Prefaces*, p. 207.

10. Ibid., p. 147.

11. Ibid., p. 215.

12. From *The Selected Poems, 1951–1977*, by A. R. Ammons, pp. 23, 24. © 1955, 1964–66, 1970–72, 1974–75, 1977 by A. R. Ammons. Excerpts reprinted by permission of W. W. Norton and Co. This and subsequent references are to the 1977 edition.

13. Wordsworth, *Selected Poems and Prefaces*, p. 115.

14. Ibid., p. 234.

15. Ibid., p. 240.

16. Ibid.

17. Ibid., p. 241.

18. Ibid., p. 242.

19. Ibid., p. 251.

20. Ibid., p. 250.

21. Ibid., p. 273.

22. Thoreau, *Walden and Other Writings*, p. 608.

23. From Bashō, *A Haiku Journey: Bashō's Narrow Road to a Far Province,* trans. and ed. Dorothy Britton, p. 29. © 1974. Excerpts reprinted by permission of Kodansha International Ltd. This and subsequent references are to the 1980 edition. Not knowing Japanese, I am at the mercy of translations. In terms of its plainer language and unrhymed haiku, I prefer the version of Nobuyaki Yuasa, *The Narrow Road to the Deep North* (Middlesex: Penguin, 1966). But, finally, Dorothy Britton's rendering strikes me as possessing greater compression and resonance. Her own justification for the unusual expedient of rhyme is that it is "a device unsuited to the Japanese language, but in English it helps to suggest the formal elegance achieved in the original by those elements impossible to translate" (*A Haiku Journey*, p. 9).

24. Wordsworth, *Selected Poems and Prefaces*, p. 448.

25. Bashō, p. 41.

26. Wordsworth, p. 368.

27. R. H. Blyth, *Haiku* (Tokyo: Hokuseido Press, 1949), vol. 1, p. vii.

28. Wordsworth, *Selected Poems and Prefaces*, p. 345.

29. Ibid., p. 347.

30. R. H. Blyth, *A History of Haiku* (Tokyo: Hokuseido Press, 1963), vol. 1, p. 1.

31. Blyth, *Haiku*, vol. 1, p. 316.

32. Wordsworth, *Selected Poems and Prefaces*, p. 448.

33. Bashō, p. 85.

34. Wordsworth, *Selected Poems and Prefaces*, p. 242.

35. Ibid., p. 230.

36. Shunryu Suzuki, *Zen Mind, Beginner's Mind* (New York: Weatherhill, 1970), p. 77.

37. Hartman, *Wordsworth's Poetry*, p. xv.

38. Wordsworth, *Selected Poems and Prefaces*, p. 347.

39. Blyth, *A History of Haiku*, vol. 1, p. 25.

40. Wordsworth, *Selected Poems and Prefaces*, p. 366.

41. Ibid., pp. 212, 213.

CHAPTER 5

1. Wordsworth, *Selected Poems and Prefaces*, p. 343.

2. Arthur Schopenhauer, *The World as Will and Idea*, tr. R. B. Haldane and J. Kemp (London: Trübner and Co., 1883), vol. 1, p. 128.

3. From *Life in the Forest*, by Denise Levertov, pp. 103, 104. © 1978 by Denise Levertov. Excerpts reprinted by permission of New Directions Publishing Corp.

4. From *The Freeing of the Dust*, by Denise Levertov, pp. 33, 34. © 1975 by Denise Levertov. Excerpts reprinted by permission of New Directions Publishing Corp.

5. Wordsworth, *Selected Poems and Prefaces*, p. 325.

6. Ibid., p. 319.

7. Ibid., p. 39.

8. Levertov, *The Freeing of the Dust*, p. 35.

9. Ibid., p. 39.

10. From *Relearning the Alphabet*, by Denise Levertov, p. 52. © 1968 by Denise Levertov Goodman. Excerpts reprinted by permission of New Directions Publishing Corp. This and subsequent references are to the 1972 edition.

11. Denise Levertov, *With Eyes at the Back of Our Heads* (New York: New Directions, 1959), p. 10.

12. William Everson, *The Veritable Years* (Santa Barbara, Calif.: Black Sparrow Press, 1978), pp. 83–85.

13. Dante Alighieri, *Paradiso*, trans. John Sinclair (New York: Oxford University Press, 1961), p. 52.

14. Brother Antoninus, *Robinson Jeffers: Fragments of an Older Fury* (Berkeley, Calif.: Oyez, 1968), pp. 14–15.

15. Walt Whitman, *Leaves of Grass and Selected Prose*, ed. Sculley Bradley (San Francisco: Kinchar Press, 1949), p. 211. My colleague Bruce Peterson pointed out to me that Whitman's verse imitates the bird's call it describes.

16. Denise Levertov, *O Taste and See* (New York: New Directions, 1964), p. 35.

17. From *Man-Fate*, by William Everson, pp. 21, 22. © 1974 by William Everson. Excerpts reprinted by permission of New Directions Publishing Corp.

18. From *Poems, 1960–1967*, by Denise Levertov, pp. 110, 111. © 1964 by Denise Levertov Goodman. Excerpts reprinted by permission of New Directions Publishing Corp. This and subsequent references are to the 1983 edition.

CHAPTER 6

1. From *Sphere: The Form of a Motion*, by A. R. Ammons, p. 73. © 1974 by A. R. Ammons. Excerpts reprinted by permission of W. W. Norton and Co.

2. Berry, *A Continuous Harmony*, p. 4.

3. Harold Bloom, *The Ringers in the Tower: Studies in Romantic Tradition* (Chicago: University of Chicago Press, 1971), p. 270.

4. Wordsworth, *Selected Poems and Prefaces*, p. 146.

5. Ibid., p. 147.

6. From *Process and Reality*, by Alfred North Whitehead, p. 64. © 1929 by the Macmillan Publishing Co.; and ©1957 by Evelyn Whitehead. Excerpts reprinted by permission of the Macmillan Publishing Co. This and subsequent references are to the 1969 Free Press paperback edition.

7. Ibid., p. 270.

8. Ralph Waldo Emerson, *Selections from Ralph Waldo Emerson*, ed. Stephen E. Whicher (Boston: Houghton Mifflin, 1960), p. 174.

9. Ammons, *Selected Poems, 1951–1977*, p. 51.

10. Ibid., pp. 43–46.

11. Whitman, *Leaves of Grass and Selected Prose*, p. 77.

12. David Kalstone, "Ammons' Radiant Toys," *Diacritics* 3(4):18, 1973.

13. Whitehead, *Science and the Modern World*, p. 119.

14. From *Tape for the Turn of the Year*, by A. R. Ammons, p. 112. © 1965 by Cornell University. Excerpts reprinted by permission of W. W. Norton and Co. This and subsequent references are to the 1972 edition.

15. Ibid., p. 116.

16. Ammons, *Selected Poems, 1951–1977*, p. 24.

17. Whitehead, *Process and Reality*, p. 105.

18. Ammons, *Tape for the Turn of the Year*, p. 145.
19. Ibid., p. 11.
20. Whitehead, *Process and Reality*, p. 411.
21. Ammons, *Sphere*, p. 75.
22. Ammons, *Selected Poems, 1951–1977*, pp. 27–29.

WINTER WITHOUT SNOW

1. Aldo Leopold, *A Sand County Almanac* (New York: Oxford University Press, 1970), p. 4.
2. Henry David Thoreau, *Walden and Other Writings* (New York: Modern Library, 1935), p. 259.
3. Emerson, *Selections*, p. 36.
4. From *Pilgrim at Tinker Creek*, by Annie Dillard, p. 257. © 1974 by Annie Dillard. Excerpts reprinted by permission of the author and her agent Blanche C. Gregory. This and subsequent references are to the 1975 Bantam Books edition.
5. Emerson, *Selections*, p. 43.
6. Ibid., p. 46.
7. Whitehead, *Process and Reality*, p. 241.

CHAPTER 7

1. Hyatt Waggoner, *The Heel of Elohim: Science and Values in Modern American Poetry* (Norman: University of Oklahoma Press, 1950), pp. 117, 201.
2. Whitehead, *Science and the Modern World*, p. 55.
3. Ibid., p. 156.
4. William Leiss, *The Domination of Nature* (New York: G. Braziller, 1972), p. 139.
5. Quoted in Richard Dawkins, *The Selfish Gene* (New York: Oxford University Press, 1976), p. 1.
6. Whitehead, *Process and Reality*, p. 138.
7. Whitehead, *Science and the Modern World*, p. 87.
8. Wordsworth, *Selected Poems and Prefaces*, pp. 455, 456.
9. Ibid., p. 446.
10. Whitehead, *Science and the Modern World*, p. 83.
11. Michael Polanyi, *Personal Knowledge* (New York: Harper and Row, 1964), pp. 17, 3.
12. Whitehead, *Science and the Modern World*, p. 13.
13. Ibid., p. 13.
14. Ibid., p. 15.
15. Ibid., p. vii.
16. Ibid., p. 202.
17. Whitehead, *Process and Reality*, p. 260.

18. Whitehead, *Science and the Modern World*, p. 103.

19. Ibid., p. 19.

20. Whitehead, *Process and Reality*, p. 205.

21. Ibid., p. 220.

22. Ibid., p. 97.

23. Ibid., p. 287.

24. Whitehead, *Science and the Modern World*, p. 152.

25. Ibid., p. 192.

26. Whitehead, *Process and Reality*, p. 127.

27. Ibid., p. 91.

28. Whitehead, *Science and the Modern World*, p. 192.

29. Ibid., p. 91.

30. Whitehead, *Process and Reality*, p. 179.

31. Quoted in Paul Brooks, *Speaking for Nature: How Literary Naturalists from Henry Thoreau to Rachel Carson Shaped America* (Boston: Houghton Mifflin, 1980), p. 283.

32. Whitehead, *Process and Reality*, p. 187.

33. Ibid., p. 312.

34. Ammons, *Sphere*, p. 33.

35. Richard Wollheim, *Sigmund Freud* (New York: Viking Press, 1971), p. 162.

36. Whitehead, *Science and the Modern World*, p. 201.

37. Ibid., p. 199.

38. Whitehead, *Process and Reality*, p. 401.

39. Dillard, *Pilgrim at Tinker Creek*, unnumbered page facing table of contents.

40. Ibid., pp. 95–96.

41. Whitehead, *Process and Reality*, p. 412.

42. Dillard, *Pilgrim at Tinker Creek*, p. 182.

43. Ibid.

44. Ibid., p. 105.

45. Whitehead, *Process and Reality*, p. 102.

46. From *The Snow Leopard*, by Peter Matthiessen, p. 18. © 1978 by Peter Matthiessen. Excerpts reprinted by permission of Viking Penguin.

47. Ibid., p. 35.

48. Ibid., p. 157.

49. Ibid., p. 108.

50. Ibid., p. 99.

51. Whitehead, *Process and Reality*, p. 10.

52. Whitehead, *Science and the Modern World*, p. 3.

53. Matthiessen, *The Snow Leopard*, pp. 237–39.

54. Quoted in Lincoln Barnett, *The Universe and Dr. Einstein* (New York: New American Library, 1948), unnumbered page facing title page.

55. Whitehead, *Process and Reality*, p. 192.

56. Ibid., p. 413.

CHAPTER 8

1. Jeffers, *Selected Poetry*, p. 574.
2. Snyder, *The Real Work*, p. 4.
3. Snyder, *Turtle Island*, pp. 82–85.
4. Snyder, *The Real Work*, p. 89.
5. Darwin, *The Illustrated Origin of Species*, p. 222.
6. Snyder, *The Real Work*, p. 130.
7. Eugene P. Odum, *Fundamentals of Ecology*, 3d ed. (Philadelphia: W. B. Saunders Co., 1971), p. 37.
8. Ibid., p. 45.
9. Ammons, *Sphere*, p. 42.
10. From *Selected Longer Poems*, by A. R. Ammons, p. 52. © 1972, 1975, 1980 by A. R. Ammons. Excerpts reprinted by permission of W. W. Norton and Co. This and subsequent references are to the 1980 edition.
11. Ibid., p. 45.
12. Ammons, *Sphere*, p. 15.
13. Ammons, *Selected Longer Poems*, p. 96.
14. Ammons, *Sphere*, p. 16.
15. Ibid., p. 20.
16. Ibid., p. 69.
17. Milton, *Paradise Lost*, p. 210.
18. Fritjof Capra, *The Tao of Physics* (New York: Bantam, 1977), p. 70.
19. Ammons, *Sphere*, p. 25.
20. Ibid., p. 11.
21. Ammons, *Selected Longer Poems*, pp. 47, 48.
22. Ammons, *Sphere*, p. 39.
23. Ammons, *Selected Longer Poems*, pp. 40–41.
24. Ibid., p. 51.
25. Hugh Kenner, *The Pound Era* (Berkeley: University of California Press, 1971), p. 144.
26. Ammons, *Selected Longer Poems*, pp. 49, 50.
27. Ammons, *Sphere*, p. 17.
28. Ammons, *Tape for the Turn of the Year*, p. 64.
29. Dawkins, *The Selfish Gene*, p. 206.
30. Ammons, *The Selected Poems, 1951–1977*, p. 37.
31. Joseph Frank, *The Widening Gyre: Crisis and Mastery in Modern Literature* (New Brunswick, N.J.: Rutgers University Press, 1963), p. 8.
32. Thoreau, *Walden and Other Writings*, p. 88.
33. Snyder, *Turtle Island*, p. 34.
34. Ammons, *The Selected Poems, 1951–1977*, p. 39.

CHAPTER 9

1. Sigmund Freud, *Civilization and Its Discontents*, trans. James Strachey (New York: W. W. Norton, 1962), p. 92.

2. Ann N. Ridgeway, ed., *The Selected Letters of Robinson Jeffers, 1897–1962* (Baltimore: Johns Hopkins University Press, 1968), p. 246 (letter to Frederic Ives Carpenter, July 14, 1937).

3. Lionel Trilling, *Beyond Culture: Essays in Literature and Learning* (New York: Viking Press, 1965), p. 11.

4. Freud, *Civilization and Its Discontents*, p. 43.

5. T. S. Eliot, *On Poetry and Poets* (New York: Noonday Press, 1961), p. 11.

6. John McPhee, *Encounter with the Archdruid* (New York: Farrar, Straus and Giroux, 1971), p. 7, takes note of a similar "oddly formal landmark" in Washington State: "It was a sign that said, 'You Are Now Entering the Glacier Peak Wilderness Area.' In other words, 'Take one more step and, by decree, you will enter a preserved and separate world, you will pass from civilization into wilderness.' Wilderness was now that definable, that demonstrable, and could be entered in the sense that one enters a room."

7. Wordsworth, *Selected Poems and Prefaces*, p. 250.

Index

Kierkegaard, Soren, 58
Kluckhohn, Clyde. *See* Kroeber, A. L., and Clyde Kluckhohn
Kroeber, A. L., and Clyde Kluckhohn, 32, 34, 38

Lawrence, David Herbert, 179, 208
Leavis, F. R., 38
Leiss, William, 163
Leopold, Aldo, 152, 214
Levertov, Denise, 2, 115, 118–26 *passim*, 193; "Artist to Intellectual (Poet to Explainer)," 119–24 *passim*, 176, 178; "Claritas," 131; "The Coming Fall," 133–35, 140; "Goodbye to Tolerance," 125; "In Thai Binh (Peace) Province," 124–25; "Matins," 125; "Not Yet," 125–26; "With Eyes at the Back of Our Heads," 126
Lévi-Strauss, Claude, 33
Locke, John, 138

MacHarg, Ian, 14
Magic, 20–21, 33, 43, 50
Mann, Thomas, 12, 30
Marvell, Andrew, 54
Marx, Leo, 24–25
Matthiessen, Peter, 3; *The Snow Leopard*, 162, 174–84 *passim*
Mayr, Ernst, 39
Memes, 201–2
Milton, John, 2, 60, 69, 95; *Paradise Lost*, 59, 84, 94, 105, 184, 197
Moby Dick, 24–25
Muir, John, 54, 204

Native American cultures. *See* Culture: Native American
Newton, Isaac, 29
Nietzsche, Friedrich, 117, 208
Not Man Apart. See Friends of the Earth

Odum, Eugene, 34, 191; *Fundamentals of Ecology*, 191
Odyssey, The, 54, 105
Owen, Wilfred, 13

Pack, Robert, 2, 39, 61–74, 82–83, 85, 133, 144, 168, 207; "Jeremiah," 70–72; "Looking at a Mountain Range While Listening to a Mozart Piano Concerto," 69; "Pruning Fruit Trees," 72–74; "Rondo of the Familiar," 63–65; "The Stone Wall Circling the Garden," 61–63; "Trying to Separate," 67–68
Parmenides, 66
Plato, 115
Poetry: prophetic authority of, 1; as landscape of memory, 10, 108, 137; Romantic, 11, 36, 137, 164, 209; contribution to culture's decay and renewal, 30–31, 34, 47, 63, 82, 184; grounded in particular regions, 40, 61, 83; and walking, 93–108 *passim*, 111, 114, 137, 140, 178, 208; Wordsworth's definition of, 107; compared with wilderness, 210–15
Polanyi, Michael, 166
Pope, Alexander, 14
Pound, Ezra, 35, 53, 187, 203
Proust, Marcel, 203

Reconciliation through poetry: of human and natural worlds, 1–3, 10, 14, 20, 50, 58, 81–82, 88–89, 98, 107, 132, 149, 211; of past and present, 10, 50, 98, 108–12 *passim*; of estranged human beings with one another, 18–19, 88; of Western and Eastern culture, 30–31, 181; of "absolutist" and "relativist" views of culture, 33; of "two cultures" ("lyrical science"), 174–84 *passim*, 186–87, 197–98, 203, 207–8
Rexroth, Kenneth, 54, 83
Robespierre, François de, 123
Roethke, Theodore, 83
Rosenberg, Isaac, 13
Rousseau, Jean Jacques, 208
Ryokan, 55

Saigyo, 107
Schopenhauer, Arthur, 117
Science: relation with poetry, 4, 165; Whitehead on science's "misplaced concreteness," 163–67 *passim*; as a form of faith, 167–69; "lyrical science." *See* Reconciliation through poetry
Shakespeare, William, 69; *Hamlet*, 165; *King Lear*, 48–49, 53; *The Tempest*, 24

A Note on the Author

JOHN ELDER is a faculty member in the English Department at Middlebury College, in Vermont. He was educated at Pomona College (B.A., 1969) and Yale University (Ph.D., 1973), and has published in *New England Review, Massachusetts Review,* and *Orion.* This is his first book.

dong